A Hunter–Gatherer Landscape

Southwest Germany in the Late Paleolithic and Mesolithic

INTERDISCIPLINARY CONTRIBUTIONS TO ARCHAEOLOGY

Series Editor: Michael A. Jochim, *University of California, Santa Barbara*
Founding Editor: Roy S. Dickens, Jr., *Late of University of North Carolina, Chapel Hill*

Current Volumes in This Series:

THE ARCHAEOLOGY OF WEALTH
Consumer Behavior in English America
James G. Gibb

CASE STUDIES IN ENVIRONMENTAL ARCHAEOLOGY
Edited by Elizabeth J. Reitz, Lee A. Newsom, and Sylvia J. Scudder

DARWINIAN ARCHAEOLOGIES
Edited by Herbert Donald Graham Maschner

HUMANS AT THE END OF THE ICE AGE
The Archaeology of the Pleistocene–Holocene Transition
Edited by Lawrence Guy Straus, Berit Valentin Eriksen, Jon M. Erlandson, and
David R. Yesner

A HUNTER–GATHERER LANDSCAPE
Southwest Germany in the Late Paleolithic and Mesolithic
Michael A. Jochim

HUNTERS BETWEEN EAST AND WEST
The Paleolithic of Moravia
Jiří Svoboda, Vojen Ložek, and Emanuel Vlček

MISSISSIPPIAN POLITICAL ECONOMY
Jon Muller

PROJECTILE TECHNOLOGY
Edited by Heidi Knecht

STATISTICS FOR ARCHAEOLOGISTS
A Commonsense Approach
Robert D. Drennan

STONE TOOLS
Theoretical Insights into Human Prehistory
Edited by George H. Odell

VILLAGERS OF THE MAROS
A Portrait of an Early Bronze Age Society
John M. O'Shea

A Chronological Listing of Volumes in this series appears at the back of this volume.

A Continuation Order Plan is available for this series. A continuation order will bring
delivery of each new volume immediately upon publication. Volumes are billed only upon
actual shipment. For further information please contact the publisher.

A Hunter–Gatherer Landscape

Southwest Germany in the Late Paleolithic and Mesolithic

MICHAEL A. JOCHIM

University of California
Santa Barbara, California

PLENUM PRESS • NEW YORK AND LONDON

Library of Congress Cataloging-in-Publication Data

Jochim, Michael A.
    A hunter-gatherer landscape : southwest Germany in the late
Paleolithic and Mesolithic / Michael A. Jochim.
        p.   cm. -- (Interdisciplinary contributions to archaeology)
    Includes bibliographical references and index.
    ISBN 0-306-45740-7 (hardcover). -- ISBN 0-306-45741-5 (pbk.)
    1. Paleolithic period--Germany. 2. Mesolithic period--Germany.
3. Hunting and gathering societies--Germany. 4. Excavations
(Archaeology)--Germany. 5. Germany--Antiquities.   I. Title.
II. Series.
GN772.22.G4J63   1998
936.3--dc21   98-22734
                                                                   CIP

ISBN 0-306-45740-7 (Hardbound)
ISBN 0-306-45741-5 (Paperback)

© 1998 Plenum Press, New York
A Division of Plenum Publishing Corporation
233 Spring Street, New York, N.Y. 10013

http://www.plenum.com

10 9 8 7 6 5 4 3 2 1

Printed in the United States of America

Foreword

As an archaeologist with primary research and training experience in North American arid lands, I have always found the European Stone Age remote and impenetrable. My initial introduction, during a survey course on world prehistory, established that (for me, at least) it consisted of more cultures, dates, and named tool types than any undergraduate ought to have to remember. I did not know much, but I knew there were better things I could be doing on a Saturday night. In any event, after that I never seriously entertained any notion of pursuing research on Stone Age Europe—that course was enough for me. That's a pity, too, because Paleolithic Europe—especially in the late Pleistocene and early Holocene—was the scene of revolutionary human adaptive change. Ironically, all of it was amenable to investigation using precisely the same models and analytical tools I ended up spending the better part of two decades applying in the Great Basin of western North America.

Back then, of course, few were thinking about the late Paleolithic or Mesolithic in such terms. Typology, classification, and chronology were the order of the day, as the text for my undergraduate course reflected. Jochim evidently bridled less than I at the task of mastering these chronotaxonomic mysteries, yet he was keenly aware of their limitations—in particular, their silence on how individual assemblages might be connected as part of larger regional subsistence-settlement systems. As he points out, ground-breaking work was being done on this problem in North America at the time, initially by my colleague the late Howard D. Winters, followed shortly by another close colleague of mine, David Hurst Thomas. Winters, for instance, was likely the first to argue that compositionally distinct archaeological assemblages might represent the various functional poses of a single regional system, and not different cultural or ethnic entities as was commonly assumed by old-school taxonomists. Thomas, on the other hand, essentially bypassed assemblages altogether and worked with the relative density and dispersion of individual artifact categories across different environmental zones. Unfortunately, little of what they did was directly relevant to the regional analysis of the European—more specifically, southern German—Mesolithic assemblages that intrigued Jochim. Both Winters and Thomas developed their research around models that drew heavily on North American ethnography, which were of little use to Jochim who lacked reasonable analogs for the Mesolithic. Accordingly, he set about devising what was perhaps the first general model of hunter–gatherer subsistence and settlement behavior.

The reader who has never read Jochim's *Hunter–Gatherer Subsistence and Settlement: A Predictive Model* is strongly advised to do so. Its basic proposition, now largely taken for granted, was startlingly radical at the time. Jochim maintained that one could predictively model subsistence, settlement, and population size for hunter–gatherers entirely on the basis of the characteristics of their resources (e.g., mobility, size, etc.). Hunter–gatherer specialists, of course, had been acting for some time as though they could do this. Steward's culture-ecological model of the Great Basin, for example, had argued that ethnographic Shoshonean subsistence, settlement, population, and even social organization were altogether understandable given Shoshonean resources and technology. He clearly intended this to be read as meaning (at least in some sense) that these were the behaviors one would expect—which is to say, *predict*—given only information about Great Basin resources and Shoshonean technology. What Steward and others did not provide were the quantitative predictive algorithms that would allow one to check their predictive abilities independently. Until Jochim, it was enough, upon completing such an analysis, simply to assert that this or that ethnographic pattern *could* have been predicted given knowledge of the technoenvironmental context, i.e., without peeking, so to speak, at the ethnographic data beforehand.

Jochim decided to see if that were so. The analysis that followed was ambitious and—because he chose not to follow the lead of evolutionary ecology— dauntingly complex. It required that specific subsistence resources, say boar and moose, be characterized with respect to a common set of quantitative variables that captured the goals and constraints that were presumed to determine hunter–gatherer subsistence, which, in turn, were said to determine settlement location and population size. Resources emerged not as distinct taxa but as strings of costs and benefits (e.g., weight, density, aggregation, and mobility). These costs and benefits were then manipulated by precise algorithms to ascertain optimal resource mixtures, settlement locations, and population sizes for the Mesolithic in the Upper Danube of southwestern Germany. These expectations, in turn, were compared with the archaeological evidence then available. The correspondence was close enough to suggest that the model captured at least some of the variables that had shaped Mesolithic subsistence and settlement.

The match, unfortunately, was far from perfect—too weak, as it turned out, to justify all of the simplifying assumptions one had to make for sake of expedience along the way. Perhaps more than anything else, this and similar predictive exercises, including my own, revealed how shockingly crude and simplistic one had to be in order even to attempt quantitative prediction of the archaeological record from heuristic behavioral models. Just modeling subsistence and settlement behavior proved so difficult, for instance, that we ignored almost altogether the taphonomic and formation processes that directly shaped their archaeological expression.

To make a long story short, this form of predictive model turned out not to be the wave of the archaeological future. Nevertheless, clumsy as they were, these models—especially the one Jochim developed for the Mesolithic of southwestern Germany—radically transformed archaeological thinking about human behavior, hunter–gatherer behavior in particular. They established the contemporary analytical framework cast in terms of costs, benefits, currencies, strategies, and decision rules. And they had one additional advantage: because their predictions were precise, they could be—in fact, had to be—tested on the ground. They forced archaeologists preoccupied with heuristic theories of behavior to survey and excavate and, in so doing, to find better ways of connecting abstract theoretical concepts with real archaeological data. The present volume, which documents the results of Jochim's field test of his predictive model, is an outstanding example of this new synthesis of behavioral theory and archaeological data.

So what are the differences between this approach and that of Jochim's earlier predictive account? Most important, the archaeology is in the foreground, not the background. In contrast to *Hunter–Gatherer Subsistence and Settlement: A Predictive Model*, which contained not one site map or artifact drawing, the present volume spends a good deal of time discussing and illustrating the sites and dealing with sampling strategy, stratigraphic interpretation, and archaeological assemblages. As a result, the reader emerges with a clear notion of what the Mesolithic archaeological record in southern Germany actually looks like. Further, to make sense of this archaeological record at all, Jochim was required to contend with problems of taphonomy and site formation, and in many instances was simply unable to acquire the kind of data he really wanted. Houses, for instance, could have answered a host of important questions about Mesolithic settlement pattern and social organization—but Jochim just could not find any. He had to settle for alternative sources of evidence bearing on those issues. There is an important message here, echoed in the old football adage to the effect that one should "take what the opposition is willing to give you." If a team will let you run the ball, then you should run the ball, even if you would really rather pass. Whether or not that is true in football, it surely is true in archaeology: good archaeology is finding a way to make sense of the archaeological record that you actually encounter, not the one you wanted or expected to encounter. That, ultimately, was the problem with our predictive models: they did not—could not—anticipate real field situations. Models and research designs are great (essential, in fact) but I have never had one that I did not have to overhaul more or less completely in order to make it actually work in the field. *A Hunter–Gatherer Landscape* is refreshingly candid in detailing the problems Jochim encountered in dealing with the Mesolithic archaeological record and the tactics he employed in coping with them.

At the same time, *A Hunter–Gatherer Landscape* is not just about the Mesolithic archaeological record in southern Germany. It is not a compilation of site reports and artifact descriptions. From the start it is problem oriented and framed to examine how, and explain why, human behavior changed from the late Pleistocene to Middle Holocene. As Jochim notes, climate/environment change is central to understanding these things. How could it not be? During the period in question, southern Germany changed from glacial desert to verdant tundra to closed woodland, profoundly reshuffling the number and kind of plant and animal resources available to humans. Jochim uses a combination of simple adaptive principles, derived from his original model (e.g., reliability), and from evolutionary ecology, to predict in a general way the likely consequences of these changes on human behavior (e.g., expansion of diet breadth in the presence of reduced prey availability), and then evaluates the record against these expectations. Models and theory do not dominate this analysis. Nonetheless, they provide its materialist orientation and frame of reference, directing Jochim to the kinds of data most revealing of the patterns in which he is interested. Firmly grounded in this basic framework, Jochim expands his view to consider the complicating effects of social and historical context. The interpretation that results is coherent in its pursuit of the basic outlines of Mesolithic adaptation and adaptive change, yet attentive to other forces and trajectories that profoundly affected their expression.

A Hunter–Gatherer Landscape is an important work, a theoretically informed synthesis of existing knowledge and new information that will dominate thinking about the European Mesolithic for years to come. Michael Jochim is to be credited for attempting the task and succeeding so well.

ROBERT L. BETTINGER
University of California
Davis, California

Preface

Southwestern Germany today is a cultural landscape, a rich land that has been owned and tilled, inherited and fought over for millennia. It is a land that has been continually molded by history and constantly reminds us in a clear voice of its past. Incursions and settlement by Germanic tribes and by Roman, medieval, and modern armies are reflected in place names and documents, old frontiers marked by roads and rivers. Every location has its own history of intellectual innovation and growth, of expansion and emigration, of hardship, warfare, and famine.

Ten thousand years ago this was also a cultural landscape, but the voice of this era is a whisper. Before there were neat farms and walled cities this was a region cherished and contested by generations of hunter–gatherers whose impact on the land leaves barely a trace today. This book is an attempt to visit this landscape and hear the whisper of this distant past. The individual voices are irrevocably lost, but the aggregate voice can still be heard.

The archaeological tools for evoking this voice have changed and expanded in recent years. After a brief introduction (Chapter 1), I review a number of theoretical and methodological developments in the study of prehistoric hunter–gatherers, particularly as they relate to my own previous approaches to the German Mesolithic (Chapter 2). Chapter 3 discusses the region and periods of interest, focusing on aspects of the natural landscape. In subsequent chapters I present an overview of the archaeological record of three periods: Late Palaeolithic (Chapter 4), Early Mesolithic (Chapter 5), and Late Mesolithic (Chapter 6). These chapters not only summarize the archaeological data available but also provide a context for a discussion of my excavations in the area that occurred from 1980 through 1991. These excavations, which began with a phase of subsurface survey (Chapter 7), focused on three open-air, lakeside sites:

Henauhof Nordwest (Chapters 8 and 9), Henauhof West (Chapter 10), and Henauhof Nordwest 2 (Chapter 11). Such open-air sites with preservation of bones and other normally perishable materials are rare for the central European Palaeolithic and Mesolithic and complement a record dominated by caves and lithic scatters. Chapter 12 steps back again from these excavations to view them on a regional scale, as part of the larger archaeological record. In Chapters 13 to 15 the focus remains at the regional scale, but is on behavior rather than sites and artifacts. For each period I try to suggest the general organization of settlement, subsistence, and social relations, based on the archaeological materials but heavily influenced by my own rather materialist theoretical orientation. Finally, Chapter 16 changes scale once again to view southwestern Germany within the broader context of developments in western Europe, emphasizing the importance of this scale of analysis for understanding local cultural developments.

There are many questions about this past that will never be answered. What did it mean, for example, to sit by a fire and draw the figure of a wild aurochs with red pigment on a slab of stone some 8000 years ago, or to carefully bury deep in a cave the skulls of women together with seashells imported from over 600 kilometers away? This book is a case study in reconstructing the lives of hunter–gatherers from the distant past, but it is also a cautionary tale about how limited our abilities are, how soft the whisper really is.

Acknowledgments

This work benefited from numerous individuals and organizations, to whom I want to express sincere thanks. To start with the bottom line, financial support was provided by the National Science Foundation; the National Geographic Society; University Research Expeditions Program, the University of California, Santa Barbara; and the Lions Club of Bad Buchau, Germany. Their generosity and confidence are much appreciated.

The archaeological community in Germany has provided enormous hospitality and support. I am particularly indebted to Hansjürgen Müller-Beck, Joachim Hahn, Claus-Joachim Kind, Helmut Schlichtherle, Erwin Keefer, Wolfgang Taute, Dieter Planck, Jörg Biel, Hartmann Reim, Ingo Campen, Anne Scheer, and Connie Lauxmann. Without their practical help and inspiration, this work could never have been done.

The residents of Oggelshausen and Bad Buchau, Germany, were extremely tolerant of our intrusions and generous in their assistance. Above all I want to express my gratitude to our friends Alois and Toni Dangel, who always provided a warm reception and came to our assistance time and time again. I will never forget a long, memorable day of backfilling by a crew of volunteers hastily organized by Alois to help us meet a deadline. It is also impossible to thank adequately the Josef Laub family, who graciously allowed us to return to their fields year after year, disturbing their cattle and interfering with their harvests.

A host of graduate students provided crucial assistance and expertise in the fieldwork and lab analyses, as well as being wonderful colleagues and willing coparticipants in various Bierfests. My thanks go to Susan Gregg, Andrew Stewart, Teresa Rudolph, Doug Bamforth, Sean O'Halloran, Ken Kvamme, Joann Kvamme, Jean Hudson, Alison Rautmann, Dorothy Krass, Marc Kodack, Kathy Mills, William Olmstead, Darcy Berry, Steven Kruft, Roger Colten, Dave

Hise, Michael Rosner, Denise Fitch, Gwen Bell, Bill Hyder, Pat Lambert, Alice
Berggreen, Matt Syrett, Ethan Bertrando, Nelson Siefkin, Susan Siefkin, JoEllen
Burckholder, and Bill Hudspeth. Dirk Brandts was instrumental in preparing
some of the figures.

    Other colleagues here and abroad had a profound influence on my think-
ing about this research, and I want to express my gratitude particularly to Berit
Eriksen, Paul Mellars, Lynn Fisher, Bob Bettinger, Jelmer Eerkens, and Susan
Harris.

    Finally, my wife Marcy and my children Michael and Katie willingly ac-
companied me to southern Germany and greeted each adventure with enthusi-
asm. I thank them for their support, and for reminding me that there is a
modern world out there as well.

Contents

Chapter 1 • Introduction 1

1.1. The Archaeology of Hunter–Gatherers.................. 1
1.2. The Mesolithic 3
1.3. Southwestern Germany.............................. 6
1.4. A Previous Interpretation 9

Chapter 2 • The Changing Theoretical Landscape.............. 13

2.1. Introduction 13
2.2. Evolutionary Ecology 13
    2.2.1. Decision Goals.............................. 14
    2.2.2. Currencies of Choice......................... 20
2.3. The Social Context 23
2.4. Beyond Ecology 26
2.5. Summary.. 28

Chapter 3 • The Natural Landscape 31

3.1. Introduction 31
3.2. The Area 31
3.3. Temporal Patterns................................. 33
3.4. Spatial Patterns 37

Chapter 4 • Sites on the Landscape: The Late Palaeolithic **43**

4.1. Introduction   43
4.2. Rhine Lowlands   44
4.3. Rhine Valley   49
4.4. Neckar Drainage   50
4.5. Black Forest   51
4.6. Alpine Foothills   52
4.7. Swabian Alb   53
4.8. Oberschwaben   55
4.9. Lake Constance   56

Chapter 5 • Sites on the Landscape: The Early Mesolithic **57**

5.1. Introduction   57
5.2. Rhine Lowlands   58
5.3. Rhine Valley   62
5.4. Neckar Drainage   63
5.5. Black Forest   69
5.6. Alpine Foothills   69
5.7. Swabian Alb   70
5.8. Oberschwaben   80
5.9. Lake Constance   83

Chapter 6 • Sites on the Landscape: The Late Mesolithic **87**

6.1. Introduction   87
6.2. Rhine Lowlands   88
6.3. Rhine Valley   92
6.4. Neckar Drainage   92
6.5. Black Forest   93
6.6. Alpine Foothills   93
6.7. Swabian Alb   93
6.8. Oberschwaben   96
6.9. Lake Constance   98

Chapter 7 • Sites on the Landscape: Survey **99**

7.1. Introduction   99
7.2. Site Fe-3   100

7.3. Site Fe-8 103
7.4. Site Fe-18 105
7.5. Site Fe-5s. 107
7.6. Site Fe-5 108

Chapter 8 • Sites on the Landscape: Henauhof Nordwest 111

8.1. Excavation Techniques. 111
8.2. Stratum 6 113
    8.2.1. Lithic Assemblage 114
    8.2.2. Faunal Assemblage 114
    8.2.3. Other Finds 116
8.3. Stratum 5 117
    8.3.1. Lithic Assemblage 119
    8.3.2. Faunal Assemblage 119
    8.3.3. Other Finds. 123
8.4. Stratum 4 124
    8.4.1. Lithic Assemblage 127
    8.4.2. Faunal Assemblage 130
    8.4.3. Features. 132
    8.4.4. Other Finds. 133
    8.4.5. Summary 135
    8.4.6. Stratum G 135
8.5. Stratum 3 137
    8.5.1. Lithic Assemblage 138
    8.5.2. Faunal Assemblage 140
    8.5.3. Features. 142
    8.5.4. Other Finds 143
    8.5.5. Summary 148
8.6. Stratum C 148
    8.6.1. Lithic Assemblage 149
    8.6.2. Faunal Assemblage 149
    8.6.3. Other Finds. 150
    8.6.4. Summary 151
8.7. Stratum 1 and Stratum P. 151
    8.7.1. Lithic Finds 151
    8.7.2. Faunal Materials 152
8.8. Stratum B and the Iron Age Feature 152
    8.8.1. Feature 153
    8.8.2. Artifacts. 153

Chapter 9 • Change through Time at Henauhof Nordwest **155**

9.1. Introduction 155
9.2. Preservation 155
9.3. Assemblage Formation 156
9.4. Sample Size 157
9.5. Behavioral Variation 158
    9.5.1. Lithic Raw Material Procurement and Technology 158
    9.5.2. Activities 162
9.6. Summary 167

Chapter 10 • Sites on the Landscape: Henauhof West **169**

10.1. Introduction 169
10.2. Late Palaeolithic 171
10.3. Late Mesolithic 175

Chapter 11 • Sites on the Landscape: Henauhof Nordwest 2 ..... **177**

11.1. Introduction 177
11.2. Late Mesolithic 177
11.3. Other Finds 181
    11.3.1. Palaeolithic 181
    11.3.2. Early Mesolithic 181
    11.3.3. Bronze Age 181

Chapter 12 • Henauhof and the Federsee in the Regional Landscape 183

12.1. Introduction 183
12.2. Problems of Comparison 184
12.3. General Comparison 185
12.4. Seasonality at Henauhof Nordwest 188
    12.4.1. Stratum 4 189
    12.4.2. Stratum 3 190
12.5. Implications 191

Chapter 13 • The Late Palaeolithic Landscape **193**

13.1. Resource Productivity, Efficiency, and Risk 193
13.2. Settlement Patterns 195

13.3. Synthesis.. 198

Chapter 14 • The Early Mesolithic Landscape................. 201

14.1. Resource Productivity, Efficiency, and Risk.................. 201
14.2. Settlement... 202
14.3. Synthesis.. 206

Chapter 15 • The Late Mesolithic Landscape 209

15.1. Resource Efficiency, Productivity, and Risk................. 209
15.2. Settlement... 210
15.3. Synthesis.. 212

Chapter 16 • Southwest Germany in the West European Landscape 215

16.1. Introduction 215
16.2. Environmental and Cultural Changes 216
16.3. The Importance of Environmental History................. 217
16.4. The Importance of Social Relations 219
16.5. Conclusions 223

References **225**

Index **235**

Chapter 1

Introduction

1.1. THE ARCHAEOLOGY OF HUNTER–GATHERERS

Prehistoric hunting and gathering peoples pose unique problems to archaeologists. Many modern groups such as the Pygmies, Australian Aborigines, and !Kung San share characteristics of low population density, high mobility, and scant material culture. For such people we have to try to reconstruct past lifeways from the remains of a few individuals who move around a lot and leave little behind as they go. If ever archaeology is to be characterized as the study of just "stones and bones"—no temples, no elaborate tombs, rarely even house floors—it is the archaeology of hunters and gatherers. Added to this material poverty are other problems: the exposed nature of most campsites favors destruction even of bones; the frequent reoccupation of attractive camping spots results in a mixing of materials from different occupations; and the slow change through time in styles of material objects discourages the construction of a detailed chronology, forcing us often to lump together sites separated by hundreds of years as "contemporary."

Obviously, these problems, although real, are overdrawn. Many modern hunter–gatherers, particularly those on the northwest coast of North America, lived at high population densities in relatively permanent villages and amassed an impressive material record. Archaeologists have recognized the possibility of similar departures from the simple stereotypes among past groups as well (Price and Brown, 1985). Particular kinds of site locations that offer exceptional conditions of preservation (caves, bogs, river floodplains, shell mounds) can help supplement the record of stones with not only bones but also with wood and other normally perishable materials. Improvements in dating techniques

1

(accelerator radiocarbon dating, thermoluminescence, tree-ring dating, obsidian hydration) allow us to build refined chronologies independent of stylistic changes in artifacts.

Nevertheless, the problems remain formidable. Hunter–gatherers generally distribute their activities over a large landscape. Rarely will any single site contain evidence of more than just a small sample of their behavior. Sites with unusual conditions of preservation may dominate the archaeological record because of their richness, but they are not likely to be "typical" or representative of more than a fraction of the activities carried out. Archaeologists have to maintain a broad focus that encompasses numerous sites distributed over a region, and they have to do this without knowing beforehand how large such a region should be. They must examine the spatial patterns of artifacts and sites and try to compare sites of vastly different quality, from surface scatters of stones on plowed fields to deeply stratified caves with abundant bones and other organic materials.

In response to such challenges, archaeologists have been extremely innovative, and many methodological advances in the discipline have originated out of the frustrations of hunter–gatherer archaeology: microscopic use-wear analysis of stone tools, quantitative methods of spatial cluster analysis, detailed study of animal body parts and age–sex ratios, and refitting of stone chipping debris, to name a few.

There have been theoretical advances as well. Perhaps because the interaction between hunter–gatherers and the natural environment is so direct and obvious, ecological approaches to understanding these people have dominated research for the past generation. Broad, cross-cultural correlations between subsistence, settlement and social organization, and gross environmental zones encouraged the delineation of "culture areas" and the inference that these patterns reflected the different adaptive problems of surviving in each habitat type. The material poverty of the hunter–gatherer archaeological record encourages this view, since utilitarian tools and food remains are much more likely to be preserved than is evidence of social relations or ideology. This focus continues, but has become more sophisticated by recognizing variation within culture areas and natural habitats, by focusing on individual behavior rather than that of entire groups, and by borrowing and adapting mathematical models of decision-making and behavior from evolutionary ecology (Bettinger, 1991; Mithen, 1990; Smith and Winterhalder, 1992). In addition, significant advances have been made in our understanding of the relationship between behavior and the patterns in material remains, largely through ethnoarchaeological studies of living groups (Binford, 1978; Kroll and Price, 1991; Yellen, 1977).

At the same time, a call to expand our perspective beyond ecology and the material conditions of life has been sounded throughout the discipline and is beginning to influence hunter–gatherer studies. New questions about gender relations, power structures, and the symbolic constructs of meaning in prehistoric societies pose challenges to our interpretive approaches (Gero and Conkey, 1991; Hodder, 1986; Tilley, 1990).

This book tells the story of one hunter–gatherer landscape in prehistory, and how methodological and theoretical advances have contributed to its narrative. It is an unfinished story, like all archaeological tales. As new data are gathered and new perspectives are used, the story is changing and will continue to change. There is an objective reality to the past, but our views of this reality are always partial and always clouded. This account is an example of how much we have come to know and how incomplete is our knowledge.

1.2. THE MESOLITHIC

The Mesolithic of Western Europe exemplifies both the problems and the potential of hunter–gatherer archaeology. Its position as the "Middle Stone Age" between the Palaeolithic, with its spectacular decorated caves and portable art objects, and the Neolithic, offering substantial sites with permanent houses and elaborately decorated ceramic vessels and figurines, encouraged a long period of neglect by archaeologists. Contributing to this neglect was the unimpressive nature of the Mesolithic archaeological record. The majority of known sites are simply surface scatters of stone tools and debris, and the tools themselves are often tiny, with minimal shaping. With few stratified sites to allow monitoring of changes through time, and with a scarcity of preserved bones preventing reconstruction of subsistence activities, there was simply little to attract archaeologists and little they could say about the period if so inclined.

These deficiencies are unfortunate in light of the important role that the Mesolithic occupies in European prehistory. Mesolithic groups are the last hunter–gatherers of Europe. Their lifeways represent the culmination of major adjustments by European populations to the dramatic environmental changes that transformed the continent at the end of the last ice age. Tundras were replaced by forests and large animal herds disappeared, and with them a way of life that had successfully endured for thousands of years. The Mesolithic thus presents an opportunity to study the impact of environmental change on human societies. The end of the Mesolithic is similarly dramatic, marked by the first appearance of agricultural economies and settled village life. A detailed knowledge of later Mesolithic societies would contribute greatly to an understanding of this economic transformation and the role of such factors as immigration and subsistence stress. Finally, the Mesolithic itself represents thriving populations of hunter–gatherers in temperate woodland environments. Such habitats are among the most culturally altered of modern landscapes and are areas for which we have the least ethnographic and ethnohistoric information on their use by foraging populations. The Mesolithic, like the Archaic of the eastern woodlands of North America, offers a chance to explore the behavior of such groups and to compare it to hunter–gatherer lifeways in other habitats.

Anyone familiar with the archaeological record of the Mesolithic realizes that reconstructions of this period are dominated by data from northern Europe. This bias has several causes. Most important are the exceptional preservational conditions provided by the numerous bogs of the deglaciated North European Plain. A large number of Mesolithic sites have been found sealed in the peat of these bogs and consequently contain bones, antler, and wooden artifacts that greatly enhance our abilities to reconstruct past behavior. Moreover, many parts of northern Europe lack substantial archaeological records of occupation before the Mesolithic, primarily because so much of this region was scoured by glaciers during the last ice age, destroying or deeply burying remnants of earlier peoples. As a result, archaeologists interested in earlier prehistory in such regions have been forced to look at the Mesolithic, at least more so than those working in areas with rich Palaeolithic materials. Finally, archaeology in many parts of northern Europe has had a long history of popular and governmental support, which has encouraged prolific and productive research.

A consequence of this research bias is that general reconstructions of the Mesolithic are heavily skewed toward the north European data. Nevertheless, some broad generalizations about the Mesolithic are possible and do seem applicable across much of the continent. Subsistence economies were dominated by three prey species: red deer, roe deer, and boar. Other large mammals, such as aurochs, moose, and ibex, were also frequently important, but this varied more in time and space. Although big game hunting dominated the economy in most areas, it was consistently supplemented by small furbearing mammals (probably trapped), fish, birds, and plant foods, so that the economies appear quite diverse. Exceptions to these generalizations are provided by certain northern coastal regions, where marine fish, mammals, and shellfish dominate the economy, and parts of southern Europe, where rabbits, snails, and plant foods occasionally outweigh large mammals in importance.

Associated with the hunting focus, the dominant stone tool technology was the manufacture of microliths from blade segments and microblades. These are generally interpreted as hunting equipment used as inserts for composite arrows and knives, some of which have been found still attached to wood or bone shafts in northern peat bogs. Many sites are small and have a relatively low density of artifacts, suggesting high mobility and small groups. Again, this agrees with the interpretation of a hunting-based economy, one that would have required frequent residential shifts to maintain access to the generally dispersed game. Sites are characterized as often located near lakes and rivers, corresponding to the supplementary importance of fish and waterfowl. Largely because of the general lack of evidence for many of the ethnographically known correlates of social complexity—sedentary residences, extensive food storage, differentiated graves, intensive exchange, and craft specialization—Mesolithic society is usually assumed to be essentially egalitarian. In sum, this picture is one of classically simple hunting folk, supplementing their diet of venison and pork with fish, fowl, and assorted nuts and berries. They moved frequently in small family groups and, lacking the need, the opportunity, or the will, never developed a very complex social or material life.

This simple picture is admittedly drawn in very broad strokes, yet is faithful in a way to the archaeological evidence. Nevertheless, there are currently raging some intense debates and speculations about some of its components. Moreover, recent work, especially away from northern Europe, is revealing intriguing regional variations that have been previously ignored or unknown. The question of the role of plant foods in the diet, for example, has engendered much discussion. The crux of the problem is whether the general paucity of direct evidence for plant use reflects actual behavior or simply archaeological invisibility. Zvelebil (1994) has recently gathered together much of the evidence, direct and indirect, in an attempt to evaluate this question, prompted largely by Clarke's (1976) arguments that the temperate forest hunter–gatherers *should* have been making great use of plant foods. A related question deals with the function of microliths, with a number of investigators questioning their use exclusively as hunting and butchering gear and raising the possibility that they may have served multiple functions, including the gathering or processing of plants (Finlayson, 1990). The importance of marine resources for coastal populations has been investigated with mixed results, for while bone isotope studies suggest virtual reliance on such foods by some groups (Tauber, 1981), other evidence indicates that even some coastal sites may have a preponderance of freshwater, not marine, fish (Enghoff, 1986).

Beyond such questions of diet and technology, questions have also been raised about the supposedly egalitarian nature of Mesolithic society. Perhaps because complexity among hunter–gatherers has become such a visible research topic generally, it has also come into vogue in Mesolithic studies. This new focus, together with recent excavations of cemeteries and settlements in northern Europe especially, has led to characterizations of groups in Denmark and Sweden as more affluent and differentiated than the general stereotype portrays (Clark and Neeley, 1987; Price, 1985).

Regional variations within the Mesolithic have also become more prominent, and these variations raise questions of their own. Despite the overall technical uniformity, for example, northern Europe stands out by its possession of stone axes and so-called "mace-heads," or perforated stones. The former are usually interpreted as implements used for tree-felling and woodworking; the latter as digging-stick weights for root-gathering. Both trees and roots, however, were widespread throughout the continent and it is difficult to see why such potentially useful tools would not have rapidly diffused across Europe. Cemeteries are also largely a north European manifestation, especially in coastal areas, leading to speculations about differences in degree of mobility and patterns of land use across the continent. One region that departs even more from the simple, mobile stereotype is the Iron Gates region of the Danube between Yugoslavia and Romania, where villages of permanent houses, sculptures, and shrines appear (Radovanovic, 1996). These regional differences cry out for further investigation.

1.3. SOUTHWESTERN GERMANY

Southwestern Germany has long been recognized as a landscape of past hunter–gatherers. As early as 1866, masses of reindeer bones and associated stone tools were exposed when railroad construction cut into deposits by a spring that forms the source of the Schussen River. This site of Schussenquelle has since been recognized as an important Upper Palaeolithic Magdalenian summer/early fall camp, dating to 13,000–12,000 b.p., when most of the region was covered with steppe-tundra. Other early discoveries of Palaeolithic materials, including numerous pieces of portable art, were made in a series of caves to the north along the Danube and its tributaries, which have etched their way through the limestone plateau of the Swabian Alb.

Early research into the Mesolithic, that period of ca. 10,000–6500 years ago when the Alpine ice sheets had fully retreated and forests had expanded into the region, was pursued largely by two men, Hans Reinerth and Eduard Peters, beginning in the 1920s and continuing until the 1950s. Peters conducted extensive explorations and excavations of a number of caves and was the first in this area to practice systematic screening of deposits to retrieve small artifacts. Several of these sites, such as Falkensteinhöhle, were quite rich in bone and stone artifacts, faunal remains, jewelry, and hearths, and brought international attention to the Mesolithic of this region (Clark, 1952). Unfortunately, most of the materials were lost during World War II and only fragmentary collections, preliminary reports, and a summary/reconstruction of finds written after the war survive (Peters, 1935, 1941, 1946).

Reinerth focused his attention on open-air sites in the morainic landscape of Oberschwaben to the south of the Danube. He introduced systematic field-walking along the shores of lakes and former lakes (now bogs), locating, mapping, and describing numerous sites at Lake Constance, the Federsee, and smaller bodies of water (Reinerth, 1929, 1953). He also carried out extensive excavations into the peat bogs where preservation of organic remains was excellent. Although his excavations concentrated on Bronze Age and Neolithic sites, he also investigated buried Mesolithic deposits, including the problematic site of Tannstock on the Federsee. His reconstruction of this site depicted two periods of occupation, each characterized by a series of reed huts occasionally joined to form compounds. The occurrence of pottery found mixed with the other artifacts, as well as the supposed placement of hearths adjacent to flammable walls has made interpretation of this site difficult. He built a life-size replica of this settlement for display, but this was destroyed by fire. Publications of his work are sketchy and much of the material has been relatively inaccessible at his private museum on Lake Constance, which draws thousands of visitors a year to the adjacent reconstructed Bronze Age pile dwellings. He was quite prominent in the cultural affairs of the Third Reich and drew much attention and many visitors (including Reichsmarschal Goering) to the Federsee. The results of this work, a concentration of over 100 known Mesolithic sites around the former lake, together with a number of gravel and wood ridges in the peat, which have been interpreted as both natural beach ridges and man-made tracks, prompted one zealous historian to recognize the world's first Mesolithic "state" of a series of villages interconnected by complex roads around the lake (Paret, 1951).

A new era of systematic Mesolithic research was inaugurated in the 1960s by Wolfgang Taute of the University of Tübingen. He carried out new excavations at several of Peters's cave sites, as well as discovering and excavating new caves, including the multilevel site of Jägerhaushöhle. His emphasis was on establishing the chronological sequence of typological changes in artifacts during the Mesolithic and on linking these securely to radiocarbon dates and pollen studies documenting the vegetational changes through time. The result of this work was the recognition of two main stages: the early Mesolithic "Beuronien" and the Late Mesolithic, distinguished by technological and typological differences in the stone tools. The Beuronien was divided into three substages (A, B, C) based upon the presence of different shapes of microlithic points (Taute, 1972/73). In addition, he arranged for specialized studies of sediments, botanical remains, and faunal material in order to investigate aspects of the environment and subsistence economy (Taute, 1978).

Subsequent research has largely built upon Taute's framework. Alongside intensive investigations of Upper Palaeolithic cave sites, Joachim Hahn of the University of Tübingen has excavated a new Mesolithic rockshelter and analyzed and synthesized existing collections from other sites in the Alb (Hahn, 1983, 1984; Hahn and Scheer, 1983). Claus-Joachim Kind of the State Office of Historic Preservation of Baden-Württemberg (Landesdenkmalamt) excavated another new rockshelter and carried out detailed spatial analyses of its material (Kind, 1987). Both have also investigated important new open-air sites in the peat of the Federsee and the alluvium of the Neckar Valley north of the Alb (Hahn and Kind, 1991, 1992; Kind, 1990, 1996). Since 1980 I have been conducting subsurface surveys and excavations of sites also sealed in the Federsee peat, and recently began a surface survey in the areas away from the lake. In addition, numerous surface finds by private collectors throughout southwestern Germany have been recorded and partially analyzed (Eberhardt, Keefer, Kind, Rensch, and Ziegler, 1987; Schmitt, 1984). Summaries of some of this new work appeared a decade ago (Hahn, 1983; Müller-Beck, 1983), but the most recent has yet to be integrated into a regional framework.

In summary, this region has an extraordinarily rich and varied archaeological record for the Mesolithic. Numerically, open-air scatters of stone artifacts predominate, but in terms of quality of information the sites with preserved organic remains are more prominent. These sites now include, in addition to caves and rockshelters, a number of lakeside and river-edge sites with different conditions of deposition and possibly different functional roles. Extremely active state and university archaeologists as well as interested and informed private individuals have created an archaeological record for this period unparalleled in most of Europe.

The natural components of the Mesolithic landscape have not been ignored. To the contrary, a tremendous amount of palaeoenvironmental research has been conducted here, both in association with archaeological research and independently. Early regional pollen studies by Bertsch (1931, 1961) and Firbas (1949) established the broad outlines of vegetational succession since the last ice age. Frenzel (1983) elaborated this information and linked this sequence to that of other parts of Europe. Subsequent sedimentological and palynological research at the Federsee resulted in a wealth of information at finer temporal and spatial scales (Zimmermann, 1961). Since 1979, Helmut Schlichtherle of the Landesdenkmalamt has supervised extensive interdisciplinary research focused on the Neolithic and Bronze Age of Oberschwaben from Lake Constance north to the Federsee. Important components of this research program have been studies of pollen, macrobotanical remains, sediments, and faunal materials, some of which extend back into earlier Mesolithic times (Billamboz and Schlichtherle, 1982; Liese-Kleiber, 1988). As a result, our knowledge of changes in lake levels, shoreline positions, and vegetational communities has grown immensely. Important analyses of botanical and faunal assemblages from a number of caves and rockshelters have provided more detail for areas north of the Danube (Taute, 1978; von Koenigswald, 1972). A long history of natural scientific interest, together with the realization of the importance of interdisciplinary research in archaeology, have produced an environmental record of unusual detail and value.

Despite their richness, the limitations of these records must be recognized. As mentioned, many earlier archaeological finds have been lost and were only partially reported. Until recently, excavations were almost solely limited to the interior of caves, ignoring both the cave terraces and other sorts of sites. Regional probabilistic surveys have not been conducted until recently, so that the representativeness of the known sites is doubtful. Because of the uneven distribution of lakes and bogs, pollen studies have largely concentrated on the morainic region south of the Danube; our knowledge of areas farther north is much more crude. Faunal studies vary widely in approach, so that bone fragment number, weights, minimum number of individual animals and body parts are differentially reported, making comparisons difficult. Thus, this region's extremely good record (in relative terms) is far from perfect, and will be found inadequate as different questions about the past are posed. This is, of course, true of all archaeological records, and is part of the challenge and the frustration.

1.4. A PREVIOUS INTERPRETATION

I first approached the archaeology of southwestern Germany as a graduate student eager to apply anthropological training to a concrete record of prehistoric hunter–gatherers. My education had stressed viewing prehistoric groups through the prism of ethnographies, starting with my first graduate seminar about the Palaeolithic, which Ed Wilmsen introduced by an examination of the !Kung of the Kalahari. This was a welcome relief from the numbing textbook discussions of lithic typology. Over the course of my graduate career, I was particularly impressed by the work of Howard Winters in reconstructing the seasonal settlement patterns of the Riverton Culture along the Wabash River (Winters, 1969) and by David Hurst Thomas's simulations and archaeological tests of Shoshone seasonal rounds in the Reese River Valley of Nevada (Thomas, 1973). Both (albeit in very different ways) demonstrated the possibility of finding regional patterning in hunter–gatherer sites and of making sense of these patterns in terms of living people. My intention was to examine the German Mesolithic data with these same goals, to take sites described and analyzed in isolation and fit them together into a coherent regional pattern. Southwestern Germany, with its established chronology and wealth of sites with subsistence remains, appeared to be an ideal study area.

Almost immediately I realized the truth of what I had been taught in seminars: data do not speak by themselves. There was no way for me to fit these sites together without a theoretical framework that would tell me which site characteristics were important and which similarities and differences among sites ought to be emphasized. Unlike Thomas, I had no ethnographic descriptions to use as a model to test against this archaeological record. I realized that what I needed was a theoretical model, or set of expectations, of how hunter–gatherers *ought* to behave in the south German forests of 8000 years ago.

I had some reasons for taking this view. My reading of the ethnographic record of modern hunter–gatherers convinced me that important aspects of their behavior were highly patterned. Within any one habitat type, whether Australian desert or Canadian forest, familiarity with a few groups allowed fairly confident prediction about the general patterns of subsistence and settlement of other groups in that area. The animals hunted and those ignored, the seasons of aggregation and the seasons of dispersal, the size of groups and the timing of movements all appeared to be reasonably redundant among groups within a similar environment. Certain patterns of behavior seemed to suit certain habitats; particular ways of behaving appeared sensible and even predictable in particular environments.

Because these behaviors were the result of conscious decisions and traditions of these people, I began to examine the bases of these decisions, the reasons given by the people themselves for choices of what to eat, where to camp, and when to move. My reasoning was that there might be a limited set of rather universal goals guiding such decisions, goals that, when realized in various habitats, created the cross-cultural patterns of similarities and differences I had observed. If such should be the case, then those same goals could be applied within the context of the southwest German Mesolithic environment to predict general patterns of Mesolithic hunter–gatherer behavior.

My dissertation research, then, took this approach (Jochim, 1976). It developed a general model of hunter–gatherer decision-making based on cross-cultural regularities in the ethnographic record, applied it to the reconstructed environment of the Upper Danube Valley of southwestern Germany, and used the predicted patterns of subsistence and settlement to develop an interpretation of the role of various Mesolithic sites in the seasonal round.

According to this model, subsistence would have focused sequentially upon big game in fall, smaller game in winter, and fish and plants in spring and summer. Campsites would have followed this sequence by shifting between the valley of the Danube and its tributaries from fall through spring to the lakes of Oberschwaben in summer. The largest gatherings would have occurred in summer; the smallest in spring.

The reactions to this model and its application were rather surprising. Perhaps because regional syntheses of Mesolithic settlement patterns were rare, this interpretation of the southwest German Mesolithic was seized upon and used as an example in several texts and general overviews (Champion, Gamble, Shennan, and Whittle, 1984; Milisauskas, 1978; Barker, 1985). The model itself was seen as a useful device for generating expected subsistence and settlement patterns and so was applied in some form not only to the Mesolithic in Holland and Sweden (Price, 1973; Larsson, 1978) but also to prehistoric hunter–gatherers in Washington (Croes and Hackenberger, 1988) and the High Plains (Greiser, 1985) in the United States, among other places. Almost simultaneously, it came under criticism from a variety of scholars for different reasons, both theoretical and substantive. The changing views of this model and its application reflect in many ways the developments in hunter–gatherer theory and Mesolithic archaeology over the years. These developments suggest that a reevaluation of both theory and interpretation is in order. The focus will be on the period of ca. 11,800 to 6,500 b.p., the late glacial and early postglacial, coinciding with the Late Palaeolithic and the Mesolithic. It is a period when hunter–gatherers had to cope with a landscape of changing forests in southwestern Germany.

### Chapter 2

The Changing Theoretical Landscape

2.1. INTRODUCTION

The study of hunter–gatherers has seen an enormous amount of activity over the past generation, both in terms of field research and theoretical developments. Several excellent syntheses of some of this work have recently appeared (Bettinger, 1991; Smith and Winterhalder, 1992), but much of it still remains as separate and isolated studies. My goal here is not to attempt to bring it all together into some coherent framework, but rather to discuss what I see as certain dominant themes and problematic issues that must be addressed by archaeologists interested in prehistoric hunter–gatherers. Many of these issues played a role in my original modeling efforts or their subsequent criticisms.

2.2. EVOLUTIONARY ECOLOGY

The dominant approach to understanding hunter–gatherer behavior is still one that stresses the relationships between behavior and the natural environment. The rationale underlying all of this work is evolutionary: behavior is assumed to be adaptive in the Darwinian sense and to be related ultimately to genetic fitness. One stream of recent research focuses on the ultimate level of causation and seeks to explore the evolution of psychological mechanisms underlying behavior (Barkow, Cosmides, and Tooby, 1992) or to demonstrate direct links between particular behaviors and reproductive benefits (Hawkes,

1990). Another theoretical current examines the mechanisms of cultural transmission and therefore the processes by which behaviors are learned and transformed through time (Boyd and Richerson, 1985). Most recent research, however, has worked at a more proximate level, investigating the relationships between various behaviors and certain factors *assumed* to be, in turn, ultimately related to fitness. It is upon this research that I will focus.

2.2.1. Decision Goals

In my original review of the conscious motives underlying decisions by hunter–gatherers about what to eat, when to move, and where to camp, two goals emerged as most significant: efficiency or ease, and risk-minimization or reliability. These two goals were incorporated into the model as the major factors guiding decisions. These same two goals dominate most ecological and evolutionary research and models in anthropology. Both have been viewed as proximate factors that can ultimately be related to reproductive fitness.

Efficiency in food procurement or camp location can free time for other activities (such as fighting or exchange) that may increase reproductive success, or can produce surpluses that may be used or manipulated to an individual's reproductive advantage (by securing mates, attracting followers, and so on). At the same time, because efficiency is a ratio of output to input that can be measured over various time periods, it is possible that food procurement could be highly efficient over a long time interval, but quite variable over shorter periods. As this situation could be life-threatening, risk-minimization as a goal recognizes the need that *some* food be obtained within each shorter, behaviorally significant period, perhaps a day.

2.2.1.1. Efficiency

Most hunter–gatherer models use some sort of efficiency measure. Optimal foraging models, borrowed from biological ecology, maximize net acquisition efficiency (Winterhalder and Smith, 1981). The linear programming economic models of Reidhead (1980) and Keene (1981) seek least-cost solutions to foraging problems. Mithen's (1990) recent decision models build in a goal of increasing foraging efficiency. A major contribution of all of these models is the attempt to measure efficiency with quantitative precision by specifying the costs and benefits of pursuing each resource.

My original model did not do this, but rather devised a qualitative measure that incorporated prey weight, aggregation size, nonfood benefits, and mobility. The latter two characteristics were arbitrary numbers designed to represent the relative magnitude of their effect on procurement efficiency. Criticisms of the model have attacked this measure for various reasons:

1. Prey aggregation size may have been too high for the Mesolithic forests because the figures were drawn too heavily from modern examples in different habitats (Mithen, 1990).
2. The concept of prey mobility was poorly defined, incorporating too many variables (speed of movement, distance, and frequency of moves) into one arbitrary measure (Mithen, 1990).
3. Equal weight was assigned to different attributes (prey weight, aggregation) with no justification that they contribute equally to efficiency (Smith, 1991).
4. The importance of an attribute, such as prey weight, was considered to be equal for all resources, again with no justification (Mithen, 1990).
5. Efficiency was assumed to be linearly related to prey weight, which is not necessarily true (Smith, 1991).
6. Efficiency was also assumed to be negatively correlated with prey mobility, although the reverse may be true when tracks are used to find prey (Winterhalder, 1981).
7. Efficiency was assumed to be determined solely by prey attributes, ignoring the effects of technology, hunting tactics, storage, transportation, and information-gathering (Binford, 1978; Mithen, 1990; Smith, 1991).
8. The impact of hunting pressure on prey costs was ignored (Bettinger, 1980).
9. Variation in efficiency was ignored by relying on mean values for prey attributes (Bettinger, 1980).
10. Plants were omitted from the calculations because of the model's reliance on prey mobility as a key attribute (Bettinger, 1980).
11. Nutrients were ignored because the model was essentially emic, based on consciously recognized factors in hunters' decisions (Keene, 1981).

Many of these criticisms focus on the fact that this model relied upon an *indirect* measure of foraging efficiency. Recent work with optimal foraging theory, by contrast, relies on direct measures of costs and benefits in terms of time and energy in situations where modern foragers and their technology and tactics can be observed. Certainly, this direct approach is desirable, but it simply cannot be used with prehistoric hunter–gatherers. Even direct observation of living hunters cannot tell us about the costs of resources that are *not* used, which is a significant problem when trying to explain this lack of use in terms of the inefficiency of pursuing these resources.

Because archaeologists cannot directly observe and measure the efficiency of pursuing various resources by prehistoric foragers, we must rely upon some surrogate measure if efficiency is to be included as a factor in explaining past subsistence practices. Three options are available for developing this surrogate. First, we can draw analogies with living groups, among whom direct measurements can be made. This requires, however, assumptions about the comparability of prey, habitat, technology, and social constraints, any or all of which may, in fact, differ. Second, we can conduct experiments in procuring various resources in different ways, measuring the efficiency of each trial. Here again, the comparability of the artificial experimental situation to the past is dubious or unknown. Third, we can continue to devise indirect measures of efficiency, informed by both theoretical considerations and the ethnographic and experimental studies.

Given the problems with each of these options, perhaps we simply should not seek quantitative precision. Any particular numbers, any particular weighting of variables, are only crude estimates, given all of the unknowns in the past context. It seems to me to be more useful if we seek *general relationships* and *rankings* among resources in terms of their efficiency. Such rankings are likely to be more robust under a variety of assumptions. This approach may not allow us to apply the precise mathematics of models like those of optimal foraging theory or linear programming, but it may follow the principles of such models and also allow us more confidence in our conclusions.

If we attempt to develop an indirect measure of efficiency that reflects only general rankings of resources, we are faced with the practical problem of how to do so. Hames and Vickers (1982) used prey size as such a measure in a study in Amazonia, with larger animals considered to be more efficiently procured meat sources. This approach, as embedded in my original model, however, is precisely that criticized by Smith and Winterhalder (1992). A counterexample from Winterhalder's own work among the Cree is provided by fish, which may be much more efficient energy sources than moose at certain periods. Keene (1981) constructed an indirect measure that incorporates prey characteristics (including size, density, mobility, and aggregation size) as well as assumptions about technology. Mithen (1990) also devised an indirect measure using a number of variables, including prey size, aggregation size, density, pursuit cost, and processing cost, but the latter three of these variables were, in turn, calculated as functions of prey size.

It is clear from the ethnographic record that prey size can be strongly correlated with procurement efficiency: big game hunting can be tremendously efficient. But there are enough exceptions to demonstrate that other factors can be more important at times. The high efficiency of fishing in certain seasons among the Cree and many other groups and of some forms of plant-gathering by the Ache and others suggests the importance of prey aggregations and of technology (nets, surrounds) that enhances such aggregations. The *package size*, whether of individual resources or clusters, and whether naturally occurring or culturally created, may be a more generally important variable than prey size. Another factor promoting efficiency is technology that lowers search and pursuit costs, such as traps and dogs, which can account for cases of high efficiency in procuring small mammals such as hare.

Nonetheless, it is unlikely that any single measure can be constructed to take all of these factors into account, weight them realistically, and reliably reflect their role in prehistoric situations. There are so many questions that we would need to answer first: what were the prey densities, aggregations, and so on? Did the foragers use traps, surrounds, or dogs, and if so, what was their cost and effectiveness? Did they use nets, and if so, what was the mesh size, where were they set, and so forth? Of course, we could make plausible estimates of all such factors and throw them together into one equation, but how reliable would the end result of so many estimates be?

Quantitative models can be enormously useful in demonstrating the effects of certain variables. *If* efficiency were measured in a particular way, and *if* efficiency were the sole goal of foraging, then the subsistence economy can be shown to have a particular form. The simpler such models are, the easier it is to see the results of varying the initial assumptions. At the same time, the simpler the models are, the less likely they are to be realistic.

I am convinced of the importance of efficiency as one determinant of foraging patterns cross-culturally. I am also convinced that as archaeologists we should be concerned with understanding the general structure of available resources in terms of efficiency, and with using very simple models to guide our thinking.

In this endeavor, perhaps we should not, however, assume that we can rank all resources along a single dimension of efficiency according to a particular measure. The nature of efficiency varies *qualitatively* among resources depending on both their yields (edible/inedible, calories/nutrients, food/nonfood) and their costs (according to technology and tactics of procurement). Mithen (1990) recognized this by focusing his modeling efforts only on large game that were all presumably hunted in a similar manner of encounter and stalking, ignoring small mammals, birds, fish, and plants, all of which may have been trapped, netted, or harvested in different ways. Winterhalder (1981) suggests this when he points out the changing relationship between fishing and big game hunting, depending on season and technology. Hill, Kaplan, Hawkes, and Hurtado (1987) conclude this in their study of the complex relationship between hunting and plant-gathering among the Ache. I had this in mind when I omitted plant foods from my original model.

We should examine efficiency for different sets of similar resources and evaluate how these sets may have related to each other and been integrated into the subsistence economy. An important method of integration is through the division of labor by age and sex (Jochim, 1988). There may, in fact, be several economies practiced simultaneously, each the result of its own set of decisions and goals.

2.2.1.2. Reliability

The other major theme of ecological studies in anthropology that has emerged as an important consideration in understanding hunter–gatherer behavior is risk and reliability (Cashdan, 1990; Halstead and O'Shea, 1989). I originally modeled reliability of resources as a criterion equal in importance to efficiency and constructed a measure incorporating resource yield, density, and mobility. Work using optimal foraging theory initially ignored risk, but more recently has included it in two ways. First, it has been suggested, based on simulations by Stephens and Charnov (1982), that resource variations have little effect on solutions for the optimal diet, and therefore can often be ignored. Second, models that include resource-sharing among individuals have been used to suggest that even small-scale sharing among a few people can compensate for individual variations in success in food-getting (Winterhalder, 1986). Mithen (1990) devises methods of simulating from prey attributes the probabilities of encounters and kills in hunting different prey and includes these in his model. He also sets up two different models of hunting decisions, one aimed at improving efficiency, and the other with the added stipulation that a certain amount of food be guaranteed within a particular time period.

Ethnographies contain dramatic evidence of variation in procurement success among resources and habitats, among seasons and years, and among individuals and groups. All environments and economies contain some variation and risk. It is also clear from the ethnographic literature that reliability is a conscious goal in many decisions about food choice, habitat use, and camp location. In order to understand the behavior of past hunter–gatherers, we must take subsistence risk into consideration. It is no easy task, however, to construct simple models that allow us to do so. One reason for this is that the responses by hunter–gatherers to subsistence risk can take so many forms, including not only the sorts of choices mentioned earlier, but also food storage, sharing, and exchange (Kaplan, Hill, and Hurtado, 1990; Wiessner, 1982; Winterhalder, 1990). Our models of these responses would have to be very complex, embedding individual short-term subsistence decisions within a broader temporal, spatial, and social context. We would also need to develop means of estimating environmental and resource variations in the past, a formidable task given our poor chronological resolution in most cases (Jochim, 1991).

Again, I believe that the most reliable and useful approach for archaeologists to take is to seek not quantitative precision but general understanding of the structure of subsistence variability and risk in particular past situations, and to consider different simple models of means of coping with this risk. Individual resource variability can certainly be plausibly simulated (Mithen, 1990), but we might also simply establish rankings among different sets of resources in terms of their variability. We could attempt to understand the general structure of variations in resources through time and space and its implications for patterns of site reoccupations and redundancy of association among particular sites, activities, and seasons—to create a subsistence landscape reflecting the structure of variability (Jochim, 1991).

It might also be possible to develop simple models of food choice or camp location based on risk alone, separate from considerations of efficiency. Such "pure" risk models, while obviously unrealistic, might more easily help highlight the role of this factor in subsistence decisions than do complex models incorporating both efficiency and risk. It may often be the case, for example, that resource rankings by short-term reliability are practically the reverse of rankings by efficiency. In Mithen's (1990) model of five big game species, this is certainly the case. As a result, reconciling and integrating both goals into a single subsistence economy might pose problems. I have suggested elsewhere (Jochim, 1988) that the division of labor is one means by which this may be accomplished in some situations, with women and the elderly and very young often providing the more reliable components of the diet, while men procure the more efficient big game.

Not only may risks vary among habitats and resources, and solutions vary among individuals and groups, but the entire attitude of foragers to risk may vary. Rather than assuming that risk is always something to minimize, we must recognize that some individuals act in a risk-prone manner (Kaplan and Hill, 1985). In certain situations, high-risk endeavors such as big game hunting may be actively pursued, often because it is high-risk and thereby provides prestige. In order to persist over the long term, such behavior must, however, occur in a context in which some subsistence reliability is provided, perhaps through the division of labor. Mithen (1990) argues that certain environments, with an abundance of generally reliable resources, facilitate this behavior more than poorer habitats.

I have discussed decision goals (and modeling criteria) primarily emphasizing food choice, but the same issues emerge in recent work on a variety of other aspects of behavior as well. Use of the landscape, for example, has been viewed from the perspective of efficient patch choice (Winterhalder, 1981). Binford's (1980, 1982) studies of settlement location, reoccupation, and organization along the dimensions of residential and logistic mobility are grounded ultimately in concepts of efficiency of land use. Similarly, his studies of prey butchering and the economic utility of prey body parts have an underlying basis of efficient use and transport (Binford, 1978). Both aspects of his research have had enormous impact on archaeological studies, encouraging a focus on the *organization* of behavior in a regional framework. The investigation of technology has similarly been stimulated by a concern for efficiency of organization in conditions of time stress (Torrence, 1989), by an examination of the relationship between mobility or raw material availability and efficiency of manufacture, use, and transport (Bamforth, 1991; Parry and Kelly, 1987), and by the study of the relationship between efficiency of maintenance and reliability of use in different situations (Bleed, 1986). Exchange has been viewed as both an efficient subsistence option (Spielmann, 1986) and a means of buffering risk (Wiessner, 1982). In all of these areas of behavior it may be possible to establish the general structure of activities as they relate to the two factors of efficiency and reliability. Furthermore, these activities must be placed in a regional context, constructing landscapes of efficiency and reliability.

2.2.2. Currencies of Choice

2.2.2.1. Energy and Matter

In traditional ecology, behavior has been viewed as transactions in three currencies: energy, matter, and information. In the broadest sense, these three (particularly the first two) have dominated discussions of hunter–gatherer behavior as well. Ecological anthropology has long had a "calorific obsession" and optimal foraging models of hunter–gatherers have continued this by focusing on net energy acquisition rates associated with different resources, patches, and group sizes (Winterhalder and Smith, 1981). More recently, optimal foraging approaches have been broadened to include food nutrients (matter), in part due to the recognition that caloric efficiency is not sufficient to explain the special role meat plays in many hunter–gatherer diets. The two nutrient categories that have received most attention are protein and fat (Belovsky, 1987, 1988; Jochim, 1976, 1981; Speth and Spielmann, 1983). Keene (1981) included various vitamins and minerals in his linear programming model as well.

The evolutionary rationale of including these factors in foraging models is clear. Successful adaptation requires the regular procurement of a minimum amount of essential nutrients. What has not been adequately explored is how these food components, unrecognized by the foragers themselves, are regularly obtained when the conscious decision criteria guiding food choices are quite different. We need more research into the biological and psychological mechanisms underlying food preferences to allow us to address this issue. The strong links between fat content of foods and both taste and satiety may help explain the relationship between subjective preferences and objective nutritional needs (Jochim, 1981). In fact, fat content was one of the important decision criteria that emerged from my review of the ethnographic literature on hunter–gatherer food choice (Jochim, 1976). Another such link may be sweetness of taste (consciously recognized) with certain vitamin contents (nutritionally necessary).

On the other hand, perhaps our models of hunter–gatherer behavior do not need to be overly concerned with the fine details of nutrition. Natural foods are generally more nutritionally diverse than our refined foods. In all but the most extreme environments, it may be difficult *not* to obtain a relatively balanced diet by foraging. I have previously noted that there may be a general association between fat and protein contents in wild foods, such that foods with high fat contents (and therefore perhaps consciously recognized as tasty and filling) tend to have high protein contents (and are therefore likely to fill needs for both essential amino acids, fatty acids, and fat-soluble vitamins). In addition, another common motive for food choices by ethnographic hunter–gatherers is dietary variety (Jochim, 1976), which, by promoting diversity of wild foods eaten, must surely contribute to nutritional balance. Furthermore, to the extent that gender roles are defined in part by the types of foods gathered (Jochim, 1988), the division of labor also helps ensure dietary (and probably nutritional) diversity.

As a result, I do not believe that it is very worthwhile trying to incorporate detailed nutritional needs into complex models of hunter–gatherer foraging. The more variables we include, the more difficult it is to understand the output and the degree of fit with actual behavior. Moreover, there is considerable variation in nutritional needs among people, making estimates of requirements difficult for past hunter–gatherers. Rather, we can consider nutritional adequacy to be normally embedded within food choices based on other criteria, and then examine the results of simple models, based on limited currencies, to see if they would cause nutritional imbalances.

Another category of "matter" in ecological transactions is raw materials of various sorts. Included are the nonfood constituents of food resources: hides, sinew, teeth, antler, and shells. The presence of such materials may add to the attractiveness of certain resources and have been included in models of food choices (Jochim, 1976; Keene, 1981; Mithen, 1990). In each case the results have been rather unsatisfactory because the nonfood value cannot be measured in the same currency as the food value. Each model has sidestepped this problem by multiplying the food value by some arbitrary number meant to reflect the additional utility. This means that useful hides are viewed as increasing the caloric content of deer, for example.

Again, the problem may be that of trying to construct one all-encompassing model. Perhaps we need to realize not only that resources may be divided into incomparable groups (stalked big game, trapped small game, and so on) but also that their constituents may be incomparable. Our models may need to separate food and nonfood requirements. Resources could be separately ranked in terms of hides, useful bone and antler, and other materials, just as they may need to be separately ranked according to efficiency and reliability of procurement. Fulfillment of these nonfood needs, like that of nutritional requirements, could be assumed to be embedded within the food choices. Subsequent evaluation of predicted resource use could determine if these needs appear to be met.

Other material needs are unrelated to foods. Stone raw material, wood, fibers, medicines, and mineral pigments may all be considered vital and their procurement may consume considerable time and energy. Little work, however, has been done with most of these, simply because it is so difficult to generalize about the nature and magnitude of requirement for such materials. Some attention has been given to stone raw material, including the relationship between the mode, location, and intensity of reduction and degree of curation, the quality of the material and the costs of its transport, all within an optimizing, cost-benefit approach (Bamforth, 1991; Torrence, 1989). A problem with such studies is again one of currency: raw material quality is difficult to assess in relation to energy costs and other factors (Jochim, 1989). Raw material acquisition is conceptually a separate domain from that of food choice and they cannot really be modeled together because of the incomparability of utility measures. Ironically, stone collection often seems to be embedded within foraging trips among living hunter–gatherers (Binford, 1976).

2.2.2.2. Information

Information is, perhaps, the most interesting currency, if only because it has been relatively neglected in most ecological studies, with a few notable exceptions. Information about resources and other groups can be vital determinants of successful adaptation. The majority of hunter–gatherer models have assumed perfect, complete knowledge by the decision-maker. This assumption is unrealistic, and the ethnographic literature abounds with accounts of how foragers go about obtaining as much information as possible. In an intriguing set of computer simulations, Moore (1981) demonstrated how imperfect knowledge of the location of resources and other groups can have dramatic effects on the settlement patterns and foraging efficiency of hunter–gatherers. I have suggested that foragers tend to operate with imperfect knowledge, and even to simplify decision-making further by using a limited set of criteria considered sequentially rather than simultaneously (Jochim, 1983). Consequently, food choices with a conscious motive of efficiency might differ considerably from predictions based on a complex mathematical model of energetic efficiency. Mithen (1990) has developed the most sophisticated approach to including the gathering and sharing of information about resources in mathematical models, allowing for short- and long-term experience to guide future decisions.

The gathering and sharing of environmental information is a topic, however, that needs much more research, for there appears to be considerable variation among individuals and groups in types of information emphasized and means by which it is transmitted. Nelson (1973) has emphasized the differences between the Eskimo and Athapaskan groups he studied in terms of curiosity about the natural world, sharing of information about location of prey, and consensus about the proper ways of hunting. The elaborate mythology of desert Aborigines of Australia, which seems to incorporate much critical geographic information about resource locations (Berndt, 1972), does not find a parallel among most other known groups of hunter–gatherers. By contrast, oral traditions among groups of northwest Alaska appear to emphasize proper responses to environmental challenges, rather than resource geography (Minc, 1986). Mithen (1990) has suggested that Palaeolithic cave art in Europe incorporated information about prey behavior and characteristics that may have been taught within a ceremonial context.

At this point we have little theoretical framework for examining these diverse sorts of information and generalizing about their impact on behavior or the cross-cultural patterns of transmission. It may be, however, that codified *geographic* knowledge, like that in Australian myths, is aimed largely at reducing the risks associated with *searching* for food, and is most valuable: (1) in environments in which there exist fixed areas of stable importance; (2) as the number or density of such areas increases (so that there is more information to keep track of); and (3) as the productivity of each area decreases (so that many areas must be used). On the other hand, codified knowledge about proper *behavior*, as incorporated into the stories of Alaskan groups, appears more likely to reduce the risks of *pursuing* prey, and would be most valuable in situations in which: (1) there are great differences in the success rates of different hunting procedures (so that failure is more likely with deviations from the "proper" way); and (2) there is a large penalty for the total failure of obtaining a particular prey (because one pursuit takes a long time, or there are few backup resources). If such patterns are correct, it may be possible to develop ideas about codified knowledge tied to the geography of risk.

2.3. THE SOCIAL CONTEXT

A persistent weakness of most ecological models of foragers is their omission of social factors that can provide important motives for and constraints on behavior. These omissions are the result of a number of simplifying assumptions:

1. Subsistence and settlement decisions are predicated largely on ecological factors.
2. All individuals have the same goals and reach the same decisions.
3. All individuals have the same information and abilities.

4. Local groups are egalitarian.
5. Local groups are economically autonomous.

As a result of these assumptions, it is possible to construct general models of *group* behavior, with the group made up of identical individuals responding solely to environmental factors.

Recent dissatisfaction with the unrealistic nature of these models has led to a reevaluation of these assumptions. Some of the most exciting research on hunter–gatherer behavior has focused on deviations from the conditions of these underlying premises and the implications of such deviations for ecological explanations of behavior.

For example, strongly nonegalitarian groups have always been recognized, most notably along the northwest coast of North America, where individual differences in status are pronounced. As a result, dichotomous typologies of hunter–gatherers have been developed, contrasting "complex" groups in which prestige-seeking, aggrandizing, or accumulating behavior by individuals is prominent, with "simple" groups characterized by more sharing and social mechanisms to maintain equality (Gould, 1976; Hayden, 1990; Keeley, 1988). Because even the most egalitarian groups, however, may demonstrate differences among individuals in status, roles, and nutrition (Walker and Hewlett, 1990), recent work has focused on the factors underlying the cross-culturally different expression of these differences. Some of this work has been explicitly evolutionary, linking prestige-seeking directly to reproductive benefits of increased access to mates and better nutrition for offspring (e.g., Hawkes, 1990).

Other research has examined more proximate ecological factors that facilitate or constrain social differentiation. The importance of resource abundance and reliability in permitting individual striving for prestige has been emphasized by Gould (1976), Hayden (1990) and Mithen (1990). Prestige is normally obtained through gifts and feasting, which create obligations. Habitats that are too poor and variable encourage more egalitarian sharing, higher mobility and residential flexibility, and less accumulation of food and material goods to give away. One of the primary means of acquiring prestige is through consistently successful big game hunting, by which large amounts of meat can be given to others. Mithen (1990) has suggested that this is most likely to be the case where big game are sufficiently abundant that hunting skill outweighs luck in promoting success, and where sufficient, more reliable backup foods are present to allow some individuals to concentrate on improving hunting efficiency.

In addition, Hayden (1990) emphasizes the role of specific resource characteristics and harvesting technology. Production of a surplus to be given away is easier if certain resources (like salmon or grains) are present that can be harvested with increasing intensity through technological developments (like nets, weirs, or domestication). Moreover, he suggests that feasts often feature foods with nutrients that are otherwise scarce, such as fat and protein in plant-dominated diets or carbohydrates in high-latitude, meat-dominated economies. Such patterns would certainly deviate from simple optimal foraging models of diet choice.

Prestige has also been linked to exchange, in this case used to provide access to exotic or scarce resources that are highly valued and displayed (Hayden, 1990). The simple models of autonomous local groups ignore regional patterns of exchange, whether explained in terms of prestige, efficient procurement of foods (Spielmann, 1986), or risk-buffering (Wiessner, 1982), and as a result, ignore any effects of this exchange on the local subsistence economy. These local effects can be significant, for example, the production of a large surplus of meat by Pygmy groups for exchange with village farmers in return for crops. Along the northwest coast, preparations for potlatches include huge amounts of labor devoted to amassing food and gifts for distribution (Piddocke, 1969). Any concept of "optimal" behavior must include the practice and consequences of regional exchange.

Another factor too often ignored is the existence of individual differences in behavior due to age, sex, family size, or skill. Ethnographic studies of hunter–gatherers document considerable variation in individual hunting success, for example (Hawkes, 1990), with implications for differences in diet and influence. Mithen (1990) has included such individual differences in his simulations of foraging economies, but their effects on the archaeological record are not clear, except for laying the groundwork for social inequalities.

Division of labor by sex is another social factor requiring more attention. I have discussed briefly the possibility that two different foraging models may be necessary to portray this adequately (Jochim, 1988). In addition, the effects of the division of labor on subsistence decisions and change should be examined. Simple optimal foraging models predict, for example, that diets will broaden in situations of economic stress (such as a decline in big game abundance). The implications of this broadening, however, for the activities of each sex may vary. In a stereotypic situation where men hunt and women gather, what would men do if hunting returns declined appreciably and backup foods that could be added to the diet were mainly plants? Would men cross the barrier of sex roles and gather plant foods? Or would they confine their activities to hunting, either accepting lower returns or intensifying their efforts to maintain higher yields? If men did begin gathering, would a dichotomy develop between "women's plants" and "men's plants?"

Apparently, responses to such situations are variable cross-culturally. Among the G/Wi of the Kalahari, "in periods when hunting is poor, the men may gather full time" (Tanaka, 1980:70). Similarly, among the Mardudjara of Australia, men will easily participate in plant-gathering, normally the province of women (Tonkinson, 1978:34–5). In these two highly variable environments, the men easily cross the boundaries between sex roles as part of the overall flexibility of behavior necessary to cope with the variability of resources.

Men among the Cree of Canada, on the other hand, responded to hunting declines in a different manner: "the group became dependent on small mammals, small birds and fish, which was usually the woman's productive speciality; the men scoured the countryside with a gun, living off small game, searching further and further afield, at first for big game, and sometimes later seeking help" (Tanner, 1979:56). Here the sex roles remained more distinct, and although the men did venture somewhat into the women's realm, they also intensified their efforts within their big game sphere.

Among groups in the richest, most stable environments, the sex roles may be the most rigidly defined. Tlingit men along the northwest coast, for example, "are loath to pick berries or gather herbs—to do, in fact, anything which is considered women's work" (Oberg, 1973:80). Among the Tiwi of north Australia, "it is not considered 'wrong' for [men] to hunt these small game animals, as it is considered 'wrong' for them to collect vegetables or for women to go turtle hunting or goose killing" (Goodale, 1971:154). Given the variations in rigidity of sex roles, it seems likely that dietary responses to economic stress could also vary widely; these variations are not predictable from simple models of diet breadth that ignore the organization and ideology of subsistence.

2.4. BEYOND ECOLOGY

Ecological approaches in ethnology and, especially, archaeology, have been criticized as being overly deterministic and reductionist. In emphasizing environmental variables and optimal adaptations, it is, admittedly, easy to assume or imply some sort of environmental determination of human behavior. As the foregoing discussion makes clear, however, much of the focus in recent ecological work with hunter–gatherers has been on active decision-making in the environmental context. That is, human agency is given paramount importance. This stance allows for the existence of different behavioral optima and also recognizes that any model of predicted optimal behavior should be considered as a baseline of expectations, not a description of real behavior. Optimal models allow us to visualize how people would behave *if* the conditions of the models were the only factors affecting their behavior. The benefit of using many different models then becomes clear: we can vary our assumptions radically and have multiple baselines, vastly different perspectives on the behavior of interest. Ecological models, then, are an analytical tool, not a mirror of reality, and they do not deny a role for individual agency, as long as it is examined within its environmental context.

The criticism of reductionism is somewhat more serious. Certainly, most ecological approaches do have a very narrow focus on subsistence, demography, and settlement, for which direct relationships to the natural environment are most clear. An encouraging trend in ecological research has been the recognition that other aspects of behavior are also patterned cross-culturally in relation to variations in the environment, including technology, exchange, and social complexity. As mentioned earlier, it may also be possible to determine significant environmental patterning of such characteristics as the rigidity of the sexual division of labor and the codification of environmental and ecological knowledge in myths and folklore.

Despite these broadening trends in the subjects of ecological inquiry, this entire approach is reductionist. By adopting an ecological perspective the investigator assumes that the most important elements in the explanation of behavior lie in the realm of the interactions with the environment. As a result, two cultural domains tend to be ignored: (1) certain areas of behavior, such as gender relations or symbolism, for which environmental influences are not obvious; and (2) nonenvironmental influences on behavior, such as history, social interaction, or psychological drives.

These topics are important, not simply because they enable us to "flesh out the past" and humanize past groups, but also because they may have major impact on those topics we think we *can* talk about more easily—subsistence, technology, and settlement. Unfortunately, little theory about such topics exists to provide a coherent framework for their examination or to generate hypotheses that we can test. Discussions tend to be inductive, looking for patterning and offering interpretations. These interpretations are based on assumptions, which are often unstated, but form a stereotype of past hunter–gatherers:

1. Nuclear families are an (the) important economic and residential unit.
2. Relations between the sexes are essentially equal or favor men.
3. Ideology deals largely with relations with the natural and supernatural realms, not the social realm.
4. History is irrelevant; adjustments to changing environments carry no ideological or organizational baggage.
5. Perceptions of and relations with the landscape are largely economic.
6. Social relations are flexible and can easily respond to changing economic imperatives.
7. Any differences in social status have an economic, and ultimately ecological, foundation.

These assumptions are not tested, but they may be very wrong. At the very least we need to make our assumptions explicit. Better would be for us to challenge them, to generate alternatives and examine how well they do in making sense of the past. We could tell stories with different premises. I am not abandoning a commitment to testing our interpretations, but I am urging us to broaden the basis of developing interpretations in the first place.

Recently, some archaeologists have begun to expand their vision by asking radically new questions of the archaeological record. Examples from European prehistory include Conkey's (1991) work with Upper Palaeolithic art, Handsman's (1991) discussion of the Mesolithic site of Lepenski Vir, and Hodder's (1990) and Tringham's (1991) examinations of the Neolithic. All of these are characterized by a focus on ideology, meaning, and social relations. Although I welcome the attempts to broaden the concerns of archaeology, I am troubled by three features of this and other recent work. First, there is a tendency for making sweeping interpretations that go far beyond the patterns in the data and little demonstrated concern for how these interpretations could be tested. In essence, I receive the impression that *any* story about the past is as good as any other. If that is the case, then we really do not need to do any more fieldwork: the artifacts will simply get in the way of our stories. Second, some of this work is characterized by a frightening vagueness of terms, the meanings of which are not clear, much less their visibility in the archaeological record. Third, social and ideological interpretations are being offered every bit as self-righteously as ecological and economic ones have been, as though they were true. There is little sense of the need to play with alternative approaches, little humility in the face of our ignorance.

2.5. SUMMARY

The growing sophistication of hunter–gatherer theory makes archaeological research a complex and formidable endeavor, but an exciting one as well. In the preceding discussion I have tried to make my own perspective clear. An ecological approach to hunter–gatherer behavior is valuable, not only because of the logical coherence such an approach provides but also because there is real patterning between behavior and environment in the ethnographic record. In using this approach, however, I am very much in favor of developing numerous, simple models rather than one complex one. I am also leery of attempting too much quantitative precision, except for heuristic purposes to explore the ramifications of particular variables. I imagine that general rankings of resources and locations, according to different goals and criteria, will provide us with useful and rather robust tools for analysis. With such an approach we can profitably examine, not only subsistence, technology, and settlement but also exchange, social differentiation, the division of labor, and even some aspects of the codification of knowledge. In addition, the context of social differences and interaction, the history of the organization of behavior, and the ideological basis of social interaction must be given more attention, at least by exploring differing assumptions about their nature. All of these considerations must be translated into archaeological terms in light of recent developments in our understanding of site formation processes. Moreover, they must be adapted to an archaeological record of hunter–gatherers that typically contains fragmentary and biased remains from long, undifferentiated temporal blocks distributed across a large region.

Chapter 3

The Natural Landscape

3.1. INTRODUCTION

The landscape history of southwestern Germany is one of the best studied in Europe. Early geomorphological work by Penck and Brückner (1909) along the Riss, Würm, and other small streams draining the Alps was seminal in the development of our understanding of glacial history, while pollen studies by Bertsch (1961) and Firbas (1949) in this area established the basic vegetational history for much of central Europe. This research emphasis has continued to the present, producing a rich record unparalleled in most of the continent. Rather than attempt to summarize this vast record of detailed studies, I hope to use it selectively to evaluate this region as a human environment, a hunter–gatherer habitat, in light of the issues discussed in the Chapter 2.

3.2. THE AREA

Ultimately, the area of interest here is largely an arbitrary one: it encompasses a number of regions of archaeological investigations and site concentrations. Measuring approximately 230 by 200 kilometers, it is bounded in part by some impressive natural features: the foothills of the Alps in the southeast and Lake Constance and the Rhine on the south and west (Fig. 1). All of these features would have presented formidable barriers to easy movement. The north and east, on the other hand, are arbitrarily bounded by the extent of known site concentrations.

With an area of 46,000 square kilometers, the region is large enough to include significant environmental diversity. Average early summer (May to Ju-

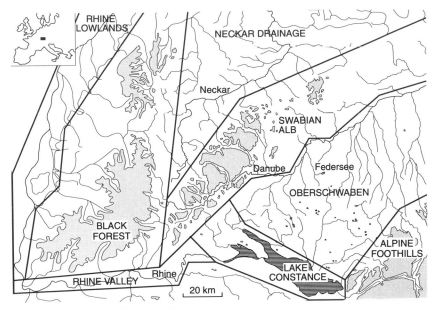

Figure 1. The southwest German study area.

ly) temperatures range from less than 10 degrees C to over 16 degrees C and average yearly rainfall from less than 650 millimeters to greater than 2500 millimeters. Some portions of the region have fewer than 80 days per year in which the temperature drops below freezing, while others have more than 160 such days per year. In some areas there is snow on the ground for less than a month each year; others have snow cover for more than five months. The lowest elevation is 110 meters above sea level in the northwest and the highest is 2645 meters in the southeast.

The major geographic subregions, which are quite distinct in terms of geology and relief, climate, vegetation, and modern land use, are as follows:

1. *The Rhine lowlands*: a broad flat "graben" approximately 30–35 kilometers wide, made up of alluvial deposits, large patches of loess soils, and formerly extensive marshes. This is the lowest (under 200 meters), warmest, and driest of the subregions and today is devoted largely to intensive agriculture and vineyards.

2. *The Rhine valley*: a narrow portion of the Rhine upstream from the lowlands, bounded by the Black Forest on the north and the Swiss Jura on the south. The river gradient is somewhat steeper, with numerous shoals and rock outcrops. Summer temperatures are high, but winters are colder than in the lowlands, and overall precipitation

is higher. Intensive agriculture characterizes the modern land use in lower elevations, with higher areas largely forested.

3. *The Neckar drainage*: a rolling, hilly landscape, ranging from 200 to 700 meters in elevation, drained by the Neckar and its numerous tributaries. While the Neckar Valley itself is quite warm and dry in the north, temperatures fall and precipitation rises with increasing elevation both upstream and in the hills. Modern land use is similar to that of the Rhine lowlands, although there are large meadowlands in the higher elevations and extensive forest patches.

4. *The Black Forest*: a large granite and sandstone region of steep topography and incised valleys, with elevations up to 1493 meters. This is a cool and wet region dominated by forests and grazing today.

5. *The Alpine foothills*: similar to the Black Forest in climate and land use, but with peaks ranging well above 2000 meters.

6. *The Swabian Alb*: a high limestone plateau running southwest to northeast across the area, forming the divide between the Neckar and Danube watersheds. Elevations range from approximately 1000 meters in the west to 600 meters in the east, with relatively flat plateaux cut by the narrow valleys of tributary streams. Although rainfall is moderate (higher in the west), the karst topography creates conditions of rather dry soils and little surface water. Modern use of the landscape is a mix of grazing and grain agriculture, with large and small forest tracts.

7. *Oberschwaben*: the morainic clay and gravel lowlands largely south of the Danube, with numerous low hills, streams, lakes, and bogs. Elevations range between 500 and 800 meters, and both temperature and rainfall are relatively moderate, with the southeast being generally cooler and wetter. Agriculture predominates in the north today, gradually replaced by grazing to the southeast.

8. *The Lake Constance Basin*: a large lake (roughly 10 by 60 kilometers) and its surrounding lowlands that form a warm and dry enclave (especially in the west) in the cooler and more moist morainic lowlands. Today, tropical and subtropical plants grow well on the island of Mainau in the western part of the lake. Modern land use is dominated by grain agriculture and vineyards to the west, with greater emphasis on meadows and grazing to the east, with increasing precipitation.

3.3. TEMPORAL PATTERNS

Figure 2 presents a chronological chart dating from 11,000 b.p. to 6000 b.p.

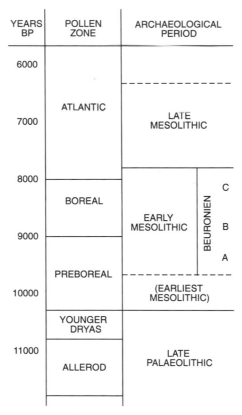

Figure 2. Chronological chart of archaeological and palynological periods.

During the peak of the last ice age, approximately 18,000 years ago, a significant portion of this area lay under glaciers. The Alpine ice sheet extended north well into Oberschwaben and smaller glaciers covered peaks in the southern Black Forest. Despite warm summers, the unglaciated regions were a forbidding landscape of long, dry winters, scant vegetation, and high winds (Frenzel, 1983). A lack of archaeological sites in the area for this period reflects the harsh climate and low productivity, as well, perhaps, as the poor conditions for preservation of archaeological materials.

Over the next few thousand years temperatures began to rise rather rapidly, reaching modern levels possibly as early as 13,300 b.p. and continuing to a postglacial maximum approximately 8000 years ago. During this early postglacial, however, seasonal contrasts in temperature appear to have been greater than today. This warming process was episodic, with one clear cool phase, the Younger Dryas (10,800–10,300 b.p.) period of the pollen sequence, which followed the warm Alleröd period (ca. 11,800–10,800 b.p.). As temperatures rose the ice sheets retreated, exposing the Lake Constance Basin well before 13,000 b.p. In its wake the Alpine glacier left fresh clay and gravel deposits, outwash sands, high water tables, and numerous depressions that became lake basins. The high volume of meltwater caused erosional downcutting in the upper courses of glacier-fed rivers, creating dry terraces along their courses. Fed by Alpine melting, the Rhine near Basel, for example, scoured its bed more than 20 meters lower during the last glacial. By contrast, with low runoff largely from scant precipitation in the Black Forest and Alb, the Danube and Neckar deposited sediments along their lower courses until approximately 9400 b.p., when increased moisture led to greater erosion in the lowland portions of these rivers and their tributaries, exposing dry terraces along their length. This downcutting generally continued until around 5100 b.p., when rising water tables and human land clearance and surface erosion led to the accumulation of fine sediments throughout the Danube and Neckar watercourses. This deposition was not uniform across the region, however. The total depth of accumulated postglacial sediments in the Blaubeuren Valley in the central Swabian Alb is 8–10 meters (Wagner, 1979), while in the Brenz Valley farther east and in the Neckar Valley by Rottenburg it is only about 2 meters.

The lake basins of Oberschwaben began infilling early in the postglacial but proceeded at different rates. The best studied of these is the Federsee, where peat growth began in the shallowest southwestern part of the basin during the late glacial. But with frequent changes in water level, the shoreline displacement was episodic and variable (Liese-Kleiber, 1988). As a consequence, during the late glacial and postglacial periods, Oberschwaben was dotted with lakes, bogs, and marshes in various stages of development. The lower, flatter portions of the floodplains of the Danube, Rhine, and some of their tributaries also contained extensive marshy areas.

The vegetational history of this region during this time period is essentially one of reforestation and succession. At the last glacial maximum the area was an open steppe tundra with scant vegetation and extremely low animal biomass (Frenzel, 1983). With the onset of climatic amelioration there was an influx of pioneer herbaceous plants together with some birch and juniper. Beginning around 13,000 b.p pollen cores show a tremendous increase in pollen production so that by 11,800 b.p., the beginning of the Alleröd period, the entire region was covered by forests dominated by pine, with varying amounts of birch and willow, up to the tree line, which was approximately 900–1000 meters in the Black Forest. Forest density decreased with elevation and the amount of herbs and grass in the understory correspondingly increased. The subsequent cooling during the Younger Dryas forced the tree line down to around 800 meters in the Black Forest and may have resulted in some decreased forest density below this.

During the course of the ensuing postglacial period, encompassing the palynologically determined periods of the Preboreal, Boreal, and Early Atlantic, differential migration of species and forest succession were the dominant processes influencing vegetation. Hazel and trees of the mixed-oak forests, including oak, elm, lime, maple, and ash, gradually spread throughout the area and dominate the pollen record. Pine and birch pollen decrease correspondingly and grass and herb pollen are extremely low, indicating the absence of any extensive clearings. Pollen and charcoal studies near Lake Constance suggest that frequent, small surface fires characterized the early postglacial, causing local vegetational disturbances but creating no large open areas (Clark, Merkt, and Müller, 1989).

One striking result of these changes was a progressive increase in vegetational diversity. The number of plant species well represented in the pollen record increases dramatically, with the effect that the diversity of potential foods for both animals and humans increased, as did the potential sources of raw materials such as wood, bark, and fibers. Clarke (1976) emphasizes the high productivity of foods in these temperate deciduous forests in the form of nuts, roots, and berries. Another result was a dramatic increase in density of vegetation, which presumably would have hampered both visibility and travel. In addition, the increasing proportion of deciduous trees at the expense of pine meant that the seasonal contrasts in shade and vegetational cover would have increased as well.

Animal communities changed in accordance with vegetation. During the late glacial warming, but before reforestation had occurred, mammoth, woolly rhinoceros, reindeer, horse, arctic hare, and ptarmigan appear to have been abundant, but the mammoth and rhinoceros became locally extinct relatively early, around 13,000 b.p. (Weniger, 1982). As forests moved in the character of the fauna changed. Among large mammals, reindeer and horse declined in abundance, to be replaced by aurochs, red deer, and elk and, somewhat later, roe deer and wild boar as well. The average size of red deer was relatively small in these closed forests until the onset of extensive clearance during the Neolithic. By contrast, both roe deer and boar were relatively large, reflecting the good forage conditions available to these species more adapted to closed forests. Smaller woodland mammals such as beaver, marten, fox and squirrel also became numerous, and rodent and snail assemblages show clear changes to temperate forest communities. The succession of birds and fish is less well known, but the postglacial landscape certainly contained a diverse array of game birds and waterfowl and the rivers and lakes had a variety of different species of fish and shellfish.

Again, these changes indicate a gradual increase in diversity of species, resulting in a greater variety of potential sources of food and raw materials. At the same time, the size of individual animals and of aggregations—the package size—decreased, as smaller and more solitary animals replaced the more gregarious reindeer and horse. Together with the increasing difficulty in travel and the decreasing visibility in the closed forests, these changes must have had profound effects on hunting techniques, costs, and efficiency.

In terms of rates of environmental change, the late glacial and earliest postglacial, corresponding to the Late Palaeolithic and Early Mesolithic, appear to have been the most dynamic, with the most rapid transformations and most temporally variable environments. By around 7500 b.p. temperatures were more stable and succeeding vegetational changes were comparatively slight.

3.4. SPATIAL PATTERNS

Given the geological and topographic diversity of this area, there were always environmental differences among subregions at different scales. The Rhine lowlands, Neckar Valley, and western Lake Constance were always the warmest and received the least rain and snow. The Alpine foothills and Black Forest, by contrast, were always the coolest and wettest regions with longer winters and more rain and snow cover. The Danube, Neckar, and most of the small lakes of Oberschwaben had high water in spring, while the upper Rhine and Lake Constance showed highest water levels in summer with the later Alpine thaw. Surface water was always scarce on the Alb and abundant in Oberschwaben and the river valleys.

Because of the low vegetational diversity of the late glacial period, however, the effects of these geographic differences on vegetational communities were not great. The entire region was largely covered by pine-birch forest. Subregional differences expressed themselves in terms of the ratio of birch to pine (higher, for example, on richer soils and at higher elevations), the density of the forest cover (lower at higher elevations), and the admixture of willow and shrubs (especially near water). As new species of trees moved into the area, each having its own requirements and tolerances, the subregional and microenvironmental differences became more pronounced. Large-scale contrasts would have developed between high elevation, pine-birch–dominated areas and lower areas covered with deciduous forest, but in addition, smaller-scale differences in plant communities would have emerged according to soils, drainage, exposure, and elevation. The greater vegetational diversity would have given rise to greater spatial heterogeneity or patchiness.

As a more diverse and spatially structured vegetational patterning developed in the later postglacial, it is likely that animal distributions and movements became more patterned and predictable. Seasonal contrasts in snow cover and available browse between different patches would have created different seasonal mosaics of animal biomass. Distinctions between richer and poorer areas would have become more pronounced. Hunting may have become costlier because of difficulties in visibility and movement, but it may have become increasingly predictable if hunters learned to target richer areas and to anticipate prey movements. Late Palaeolithic hunters of the more undifferentiated pine-birch forests may have found hunting much more difficult and unpredictable than their Upper Palaeolithic reindeer-hunting predecessors. During the course of the ensuing Mesolithic, with the spread of temperate woodlands, costs of travel may even have increased, but predictability of prey location may have increased as well.

Attractive areas of higher resource abundance, diversity, and predictability would have existed throughout the Mesolithic, but they would have increased in prominence during the Late Mesolithic. At a large scale, areas with longer growing seasons and less snow would have had higher overall resource productivity. At a smaller scale, resource diversity would have been greatest around the larger lakes and marshes and along stretches of rivers in areas of high topographic relief.

Another component of environmental attractiveness, in addition to overall productivity and diversity, is the degree of year-to-year climatic variation. More stable areas are likely to have attracted repeated use over a long period, due to their predictable productivity. In temperate deciduous forests seasonal changes in growth, flowering, fruiting, and shedding are more pronounced than for any other major ecosystem (Roehrig and Ulrich, 1991). Winter is a period of scarcity and a bottleneck to survival. The timing of the onset of spring, with increased temperatures and snowmelt, may be one of the most critical factors determining productivity. Over the long term, areas with an early and predictable spring warming may have been more attractive than those of lesser reliability.

Two measures of spring onset are average March temperatures and average number of frost days (during which the temperature drops below freezing) per year. The first gives a general monthly picture of seasonal climate and the second provides some additional information about daily variations from this average. Data from climatic records of twelve stations in and near the study area are presented (Fig. 3). Fig. 4 shows that the two climatic measures are strongly correlated: stations with highest average March temperatures (Karlsruhe, Freiburg, and Stuttgart in the Rhine lowlands and Neckar Valley) have few frost days, and those with lowest average temperatures (Oberstdorf in the Alpine foothills and Freudenstadt in the Black Forest) have the greatest number of frost days. Note, however, that stations in Oberschwaben (Ulm, Munich) have about as many frost days as Freudenstadt, despite having significantly higher average March temperatures.

Yearly variations in these measures can be expressed by the variance/ mean ratio of each. As Fig. 5 shows, the variability in average temperature is strongly correlated with the mean: the coldest regions also have the greatest year-to-year variability around this average. With frost days, on the other hand, the situation is reversed (Fig. 6). Although the correlation is not as strong, in

Figure 3. Climatic stations in the study area.

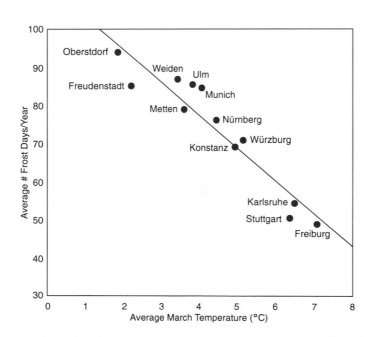

Figure 4. Correlation of average March temperature and average number of frost days.

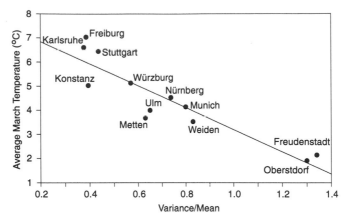

Figure 5. Correlation of average March temperature and variance/mean ratio of March temperature.

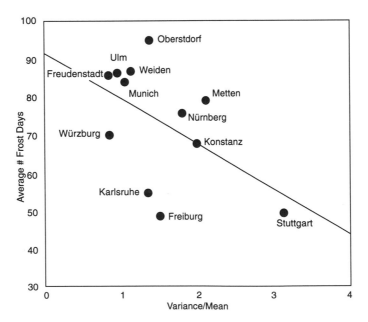

Figure 6. Correlation of average number of frost days and variance/mean ratio of the number of frost days.

general the warmest regions tend to have the highest variability, and contrasts between regions with similar means tend to increase as the average decreases. Among the warmer areas, Stuttgart in the Neckar Valley is much more variable from year to year than Karlsruhe or Freiburg in the Rhine lowlands, and Konstanz on Lake Constance is much more so than Würzburg in the north. As a general summary, the Rhine lowlands from Freiburg northwards stand out as a predictably warm region with early spring thaws. The two other warm regions, Lake Constance and the Neckar Valley, are less reliable, with greater possibilities of late frosts. The Black Forest and the Alpine foothills are reliably cooler, with late spring onsets. Intermediate in all respects are Oberschwaben and the Alb, although the former is the warmer of the two.

Another aspect of reliability is the degree to which different regions are correlated with each other. Do longer, colder winters in one region coincide with those in others? One way of assessing this is to examine the intercorrelation of climatic measures among stations over a given period. An examination of March temperatures (Fig. 7) indicates that all stations are highly correlated, with coefficients ranging only between 0.80 and 0.99+. In terms of average monthly conditions, this is clearly all one climatic region. An examination of the number of frost days, on the other hand, allows some distinctions to be made (Fig. 8). Several groupings of highly correlated stations can be created: (1) the Rhine lowlands, and Neckar and other valleys (Karlsruhe, Stuttgart,

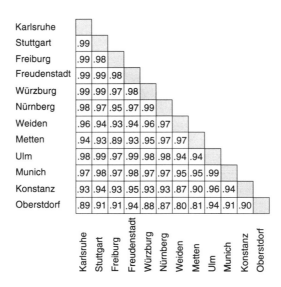

	Karlsruhe	Stuttgart	Freiburg	Freudenstadt	Würzburg	Nürnberg	Weiden	Metten	Ulm	Munich	Konstanz	Oberstdorf
Karlsruhe												
Stuttgart	.99											
Freiburg	.99	.98										
Freudenstadt	.99	.99	.98									
Würzburg	.99	.99	.97	.98								
Nürnberg	.98	.97	.95	.97	.99							
Weiden	.96	.94	.93	.94	.96	.97						
Metten	.94	.93	.89	.93	.95	.97	.97					
Ulm	.98	.99	.97	.99	.98	.98	.94	.94				
Munich	.97	.98	.97	.98	.97	.97	.95	.95	.99			
Konstanz	.93	.94	.93	.95	.93	.93	.87	.90	.96	.94		
Oberstdorf	.89	.91	.91	.94	.88	.87	.80	.81	.94	.91	.90	

Figure 7. Correlation matrix of yearly variation in average March temperature.

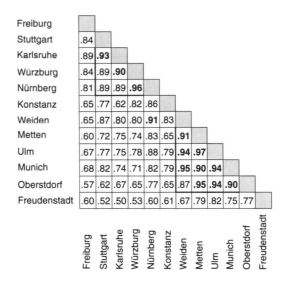

Figure 8. Correlation matrix of yearly variation in number of frost days.

Würzburg, and Nürnberg); (2) the Alb, Oberschwaben, and Alpine foothills (Weiden, Metten, Munich, Ulm, and Oberstdorf); (3) Lake Constance (Konstanz); (4) the southern Rhine (Freiburg); and (5) the Black Forest (Freudenstadt). The risk of late frosts in each of these areas varies from year to year somewhat independently from the rest. Any measures used by foragers to counteract such risks, such as mobility or exchange, would have been most effective if they crossed the boundaries of these subareas, into regions where conditions in a given year might be different.

Chapter 4

Sites on the Landscape: The Late Palaeolithic

4.1. INTRODUCTION

Although the Late Palaeolithic has not been the object of concentrated research, its temporal position and general typological characteristics have been
clearly documented in several stratified caves and rockshelter sites in the Swabian Alb. It overlies Magdalenian deposits in at least three sites–Zigeunerfels,
Dietfurt, and Helga-Abri–and underlies Early Mesolithic levels at these same
sites as well as in two additional sites–Jägerhaushöhle and Fohlenhaus. It also
occurs stratified beneath Early Mesolithic deposits at the open-air site of
Henauhof Nordwest on the Federsee. It dates to the periods of the Alleröd and
Younger Dryas, approximately 11,800–10,300 b.p.

Typologically, the Late Palaeolithic is similar to the contemporary Azilian
in France and the largely contemporary Federmesser assemblages of the North
European Plain. Backed points and backed blades, together with short scrapers,
round scrapers, and burins, dominate the assemblages (Fig. 71). In comparison
with the preceding Magdalenian, from which it is often difficult to distinguish,
the Late Palaeolithic is characterized by smaller artifacts and fewer distinct
types of retouched tools, as well as by far fewer objects of portable art and
adornment. Organic artifacts, such as bone needles, harpoons, and points, are
also rare.

The site records of southwest Germany for the Late Palaeolithic derive
from a variety of sources. Recent excavations since the 1960s provide the most
useful information. A number of earlier excavations were carried out but have

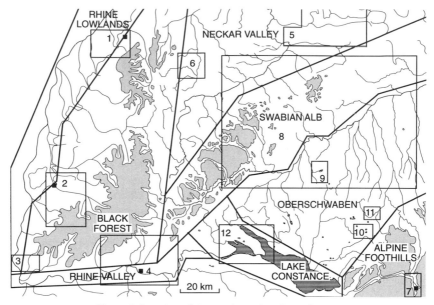

Figure 9. Location of site concentrations in study area.

been differentially reported; in addition, the collections are often no longer available for study. By far the majority of sites consist of surface finds, a situation that contrasts markedly with that of the preceding Magdalenian. Although this contrast may derive in part from differences in land surface stability and site preservation between the two periods, it seems also to reflect a significant shift in settlement patterns. Late Palaeolithic sites in general appear to be more widespread across the landscape than earlier sites. In addition, both surface and excavated sites tend to have small, diverse lithic and faunal assemblages, giving the overwhelming impression of small groups, brief occupations, and high residential mobility (Albrecht, 1983). The following discussion will briefly present an overview of known sites, organized according to the eight major subregions discussed previously and focused on particular areas where work has been carried out (Fig. 9). The few sites and faunal remains are summarized in Tables 1 and 2.

4.2. RHINE LOWLANDS

Gersbach (1951) has reported on a number of surface sites along the Rhine in the north of the area near Baden-Baden, seven of which appear to be

Table 1. Late Palaeolithic Sites

Area	Sites	Period	Location	Finds
Rhine lowlands				
Baden-Baden region	7 surface sites	All mixed with Mesolithic	Sand dunes and hillflanks	16–940 artifacts
Freiburg area	1 surface site	Mixed with Mesolithic	Hillflank	600+ artifacts
Basel area	Isteiner Klotz cave	Mixed with Mesolithic	Hillflank	1150 artifacts, bones
	14 other caves	Late Palaeolithic only	Hillflank	Varied assemblage sizes
Rhine Valley	9 surface sites	Some mixed with Mesolithic	Valley floor and hilltops	Varied assemblage sizes
Neckar Valley	None known			
Eastern Black Forest	1 surface site with test excavations	Mixed with Mesolithic	Valley floor	500+ artifacts
Alpine foothills	Jehlefels rockshelter	Late Palaeolithic only	Hillflank	Hearth, artifacts, bone
	20 surface sites, some excavated	Late Palaeolithic only	Hillflanks, terraces, and hilltops	Varied assemblage sizes, hearths, postholes
Swabian Alb	Jagerhaushohle cave	Level 15: Late Palaeolithic	Hillflank	116 artifacts
	Fohlenhaus cave	Level 3: Late Palaeolithic	Hillflank	6+ artifacts
	Diefurt cave	Levels 12–15: Late Palaeolithic	Rock outcrop in valley	Artifacts, bones, human remains
	Zigeunerfels cave	Levels D–E: Late Palaeolithic	Edge of valley floor	Artifacts, bones
	Helga-Abri Rockshelter	Level IIF7: Late Palaeolithic	Hillflank	Hearth, artifacts
Oberschwaben	Henauhof Nordwest	Level 6: Late Palaeolithic	Lakeshore	See Chapter 8
	Henauhof West	Late Palaeolithic only	Lakeshore	See Chapter 11
	Numerous surface sites	Some mixed with Mesolithic	Lakeshore	Varied assemblage sizes
Lake Constance	Bo 11	Possibly mixed with Mesolithic	Lakeshore	Artifacts

Table 2. Late Palaeolithic Fauna

Resource	Henauhof NW/6	Henauhof West	Fohlenhaus	Zigeunerfels D	Zigeunerfels E	Helga Abri	Istein caves						
							1,2,3,4,5	8	9	10	11	12	14
Red deer	X	X	X	X			X	X		X	X	X	X
Roe deer	X		X			X	X	X	X	X	X	X	X
Boar	X	X					X			X			
Aurochs	X						X	X					
Moose				X									
Horse	X		X										
Ibex			X	X	X								
Bear			X	X			X						
Beaver				X			X			X			X
Hare			X	X	X		X						X
Wolf	X		X										
Fox			X				X						
Ermine			X										
Lynx							X						
Marten							X						
Fish	X			X	X	X	X	X					X
Shellfish							X						
Birds	X									X			X
Eggs						X							

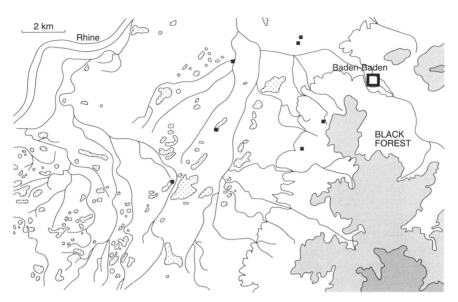

Figure 10. Late Palaeolithic sites near Baden-Baden.

clearly attributable to the Late Palaeolithic (Fig. 10). Five of these sites are situated on small sand dunes rising above the present valley floor, which would have formed dry, well-drained locations surrounded by marshes and meandering tributaries. The other two sites occur on the flanks of the hills overlooking the valley, on areas that would have been forested. All seven also contain Mesolithic materials, so it is difficult to draw inferences from the lithic collections. Nevertheless, it is notable that all but one of these sites produced small artifact collections (ranging from 16 to 74 finds) that were rather diverse, containing points, burins, scrapers, retouched and notched blades, and occasionally borers, along with unretouched flakes and blades. Despite the dangers of arguing from mixed collections of surface materials, it is difficult to view these sites as specialized camps for hunting or other activities. Because even the small surface samples are so typologically diverse, it appears more likely that they represent brief, residential occupations by small groups who carried out a number of different activities. The seventh site, located on a dune, had a diverse collection of 940 artifacts and may be interpreted either as a larger or longer-term occupation or as simply a palimpsest of many more reoccupations than the other sites.

To the south, near Freiburg, is another region where sites have been reported along the edges of the Rhine Valley and onto the heights of the Black Forest (Fig. 11). Only one of these is clearly datable to the Late Palaeolithic, lo-

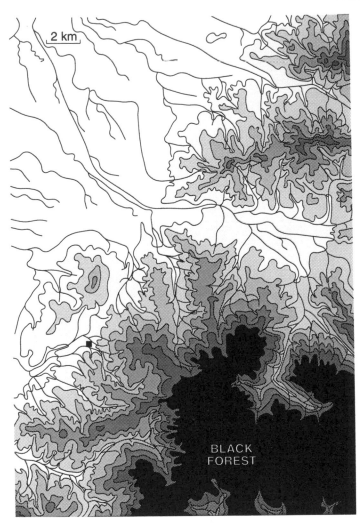

Figure 11. Late Palaeolithic site near Freiburg.

cated along a small stream on the gentle slopes of the hills. Its collection of over 600 stone artifacts contains diagnostic materials of the Late Palaeolithic and all stages of the Mesolithic, indicating that this was long a favored spot for occupation. The finds include a wide range of tool types, but most cannot be attributed to specific periods. The location would have provided easy access to both the forested heights and the marshy valley floor, and the stream itself may have carried salmon as well as other fish.

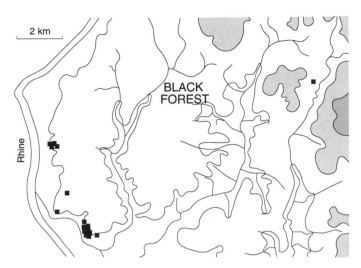

Figure 12. Late Palaeolithic sites near Istein.

Farther south the valley narrows considerably, just before the bend in the Rhine by Basel. Here, on a rock outcrop overlooking the river, at least 15 small caves (Fig. 12) were excavated beginning around the turn of the century (Lais, 1929; Mieg, 1904; Schmid, 1962). Most of these have since been destroyed by quarrying. All of them appear to have contained Late Palaeolithic materials and one, Isteiner Klotz, had Mesolithic occupations as well.

Among the stone tools in these caves, scrapers and retouched blades appear most abundant, followed by burins. Only Isteiner Klotz contained microliths as well. Cores, flakes, and blades were reported at a number of sites but were probably present in all, as these categories tend often not to be mentioned in early reports. The array of reported fauna is relatively diverse, including large and small mammals, fish, and shellfish. Although it is impossible to discuss the function of individual sites, this rock outcrop was clearly a focus of occupation, presumably for small residential groups exploiting the river, its marshy floodplain, and the hills beyond.

4.3. RHINE VALLEY

Farther upstream around the bend of the Rhine to the south near Säckingen is a series of reported sites that do not comfortably fit into the regional framework used here. The Rhine Valley in this area is narrow, not forming a broad marshy plain. The river itself flows more swiftly and cuts through bed-

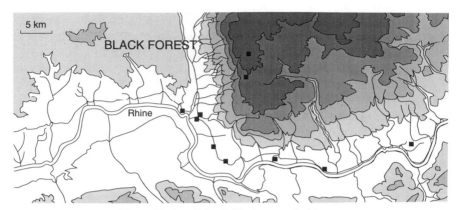

Figure 13. Late Palaeolithic sites near Säckingen.

rock at several locations, forming shoals and rapids. The climate of this area differs as well, being more influenced by the hills of the Black Forest and therefore cooler and wetter than the regions downstream.

Among the 24 sites reported (Gersbach, 1968), 10 can be attributed to the Late Palaeolithic (Fig. 13). All of these are surface lithic scatters with a diverse range of tool types. Six of these also contain Mesolithic materials, but 3 do not, and these latter also have diverse collections containing burins, scrapers, retouched blades, borers, and notched pieces, as well as cores, flakes, and blades. The sites tend to cluster along the edge of the valley floor, especially near tributary streams, but also at higher elevations in the hills above. Many are quite close to a historically known ford, where bedrock in the river outcrops and creates shoals.

4.4. NECKAR DRAINAGE

Although this region—the valley of the Neckar and the hills beyond—has one of the highest densities of surface lithic scatters reported, it is impossible to identify conclusively the presence of Late Palaeolithic materials here. Virtually all finds were made by amateur collectors, who have recorded site locations and gross tool categories, including numerous Mesolithic microliths, but no diagnostic Late Palaeolithic backed points and blades have been mentioned. It is difficult to imagine that this climatically favorable region was totally ignored during this period, but only future survey and collections research will be able to determine if this was the case.

4.5. BLACK FOREST

The Black Forest appears to have been essentially uninhabited during this period, which is not altogether surprising in light of its cool, wet climate and harsh winters. Nevertheless, much of this area lies hidden under forest cover and no surveys have been carried out, so it may be premature to infer a lack of occupation. Summer camps focused largely on hunting would be the most likely form that occupation of the heights would have taken.

Around the edges of the forest, however, lie traces of the Late Palaeolithic. As mentioned earlier, a few Late Palaeolithic sites occur up on the first range of hills along the Rhine near Baden-Baden, Freiburg, Basel, and Säckingen. On the eastern border of the Forest is one other known site of this period, actually situated at a low elevation within the narrow valley of the Nagold as it exits the hills (Fig. 14). From surface finds and test excavations, this site has produced over 500 artifacts of both the Late Palaeolithic and Mesolithic in an area of 2000 square meters. The collection includes a broad array of artifact types (Pasda, 1994). Among the raw materials are cherts from the local gravels, Jurassic chert from the Alb, about 40 kilometers away, and banded chert from Bavaria, 130 kilometers away.

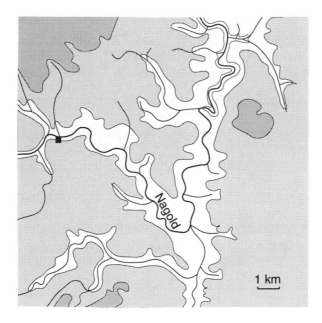

Figure 14. Late Palaeolithic site in the Nagold Valley.

4.6. ALPINE FOOTHILLS

Another region where vegetational cover hinders site visibility, the foothills of the Alps have nevertheless yielded Late Palaeolithic materials to a few
determined investigators (Reinerth, 1956). Along the upper reaches of the Iller
River near Oberstdorf, 20 sites were located and some were mapped and partially excavated during the 1930s. They range in elevation from 800 to 1400
meters and lie on gentle sloping prominences, terraces and hilltops, most within 200 meters of watercourses (Fig. 15).

Limited information is available for some of these sites. Site 2, discovered
during construction activities, measures approximately 40 × 60 meters. Excavations revealed several apparent hearths, marked by charcoal concentrations,
as well as some nearby sandstone blocks interpreted as seats or anvil stones.
The 1354 artifacts were concentrated around these features. Site 5 contained a

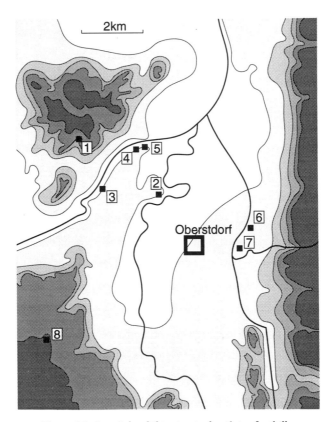

Figure 15. Late Palaeolithic sites in the Alpine foothills.

number of apparent postholes in regular alignments interpreted as remnants of huts. Site 1, Jehlefels, is a small rockshelter that contained a hearth approximately three meters from the back wall, around which lay the majority of the 683 lithic artifacts. Several concentrations of debitage from the same cores were interpreted as stone-working areas. Highly fragmented bone was concentrated between the hearth and the back wall.

The majority of stone raw material in these assemblages is alpine radiolarite, available in the local gravels. Most of the sites contain a variety of artifacts, including backed points, retouched blades, scrapers, burins, blades, and flakes. The higher elevation open-air sites tend to have smaller assemblages dominated by unretouched blades together with a few scrapers, burins, and points.

4.7. SWABIAN ALB

The primary sites of the Late Palaeolithic in the limestone Alb are four caves (Jägerhaushöhle, Fohlenhaus, Dietfurt, Zigeunerfels) and one rockshelter (Helga-Abri) (Fig. 16). Several other sites have components that have been variously classified as Magdalenian or Late Palaeolithic (Malerfels, Kleine Scheuer, Stadel, Spitalhöhle, Bärenfelsgrotte), but all have small mammal fau-

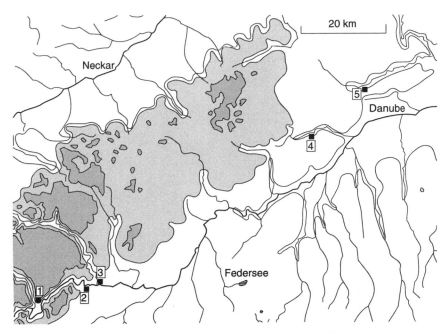

Figure 16. Late Palaeolithic sites in the Swabian Alb.

nas indicating cold conditions and so most likely predate the Alleröd. Therefore, they will not be considered here.

Jägerhaushöhle (Fig. 16, No. 1) is situated in the limestone cliffs approximately 80 m above the modern upper Danube. The cave, measuring 13 m wide by 12 m deep, faces southeast and is adjacent to a spring. Under eight Mesolithic cultural levels lies Level 15, attributed to the Late Palaeolithic (Taute, 1978). This level has been palynologically dated to the Younger Dryas (Filzer, 1978). Of 533 pieces of charcoal examined from this level, 532 were pine and one piece was maple (Schweingruber, 1978).

The lithic assemblage totals only 116 artifacts with very few retouched pieces, including several backed knives with retouched ends and a burin. A sandstone hammerstone was also found. No faunal remains were preserved.

Fohlenhaus (Fig. 16, No. 5) is the lower of two small caves in the dry valley of the Lone, a Danube tributary in the eastern Alb. The cave, measuring 7 m wide by 7.5 m deep, faces southwest and lies just 5 m above the valley floor. Intact deposits contained two Mesolithic levels overlying Level 3, which dates to the Late Palaeolithic (Taute, 1978). Only 6 lithic artifacts were found in this level: 1 backed knife, 2 micro-backed knives (< 6 mm wide), 1 atypical microlith, 1 denticulated piece, and 1 blade. Disturbed deposits in the cave contained 105 artifacts spanning the period from the Palaeolithic through the Neolithic; 2 of these were backed knives attributed to the Late Palaeolithic.

Dietfurt (Fig. 16, No. 2) is a tunnel-cave running east-west through a limestone block rising 25 m from the Danube valley floor. Beneath levels of Roman, Iron Age, Bronze Age, and Neolithic materials lie two Mesolithic levels and four (Levels 12–15, encompassing 70 cm of sediments) dating to the Late Palaeolithic (Dämmler, Reim, and Taute, 1975). The Late Palaeolithic lithic collections are small and include backed knives and points and a borer.

Although mammalian faunal materials have not been published, a total of 5407 fish bones have been reported in these levels (Torke, 1981). Most come from fish weighing less than 40 grams, but 155 derive from fish large enough (> 200 g) to be considered possible human prey. These latter include eight different species and represent 12–16 kg of live meat weight.

Notable among the finds are human remains: skull, teeth, phalanges. The skull shows cut marks consistent with scalping.

Zigeunerfels (Fig. 16, No. 3), a small (8 × 3 m) cave, lies just above the present valley floor of the Schmeie, a Danube tributary in the western Alb (Taute, 1972). Two Late Palaeolithic levels (D and E) lie beneath three Mesolithic and above three Magdalenian levels. Both levels have small lithic assemblages containing backed points and knives, short scrapers and burins.

Mammalian bones in both levels were highly fragmented and partially burned. Both levels had fish remains as well. Those from Level D, which have been analyzed, contained 64 bones representing 10–12 kg of live meat weight (Torke 1981).

Helga-Abri (Fig. 16, No. 4) is a small rockshelter situated about 20 m above the floor of the Ach, a Danube tributary in the eastern Alb (Hahn and Scheer, 1983). The shelter is 8 x 6 m and faces west. One Late Palaeolithic level (IIF7) of 25 cm thickness lies above two Magdalenian and below six Mesolithic levels.

The Late Palaeolithic level contains an ash-lens hearth containing pine charcoal. The small lithic collection includes several backed points, burins, borers, and numerous burin spalls.

4.8. OBERSCHWABEN

All of the known Late Palaeolithic sites in the morainic landscape of this region are open-air locations (Fig. 17). As discussed previously, both Henauhof Nordwest and Henauhof West on the southwestern shore of the Federsee have

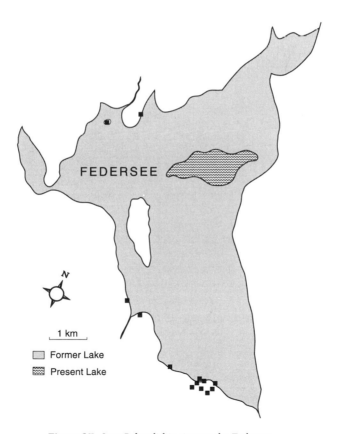

Figure 17. Late Palaeolithic sites on the Federsee.

components dating to this period. The southeastern shore of the lake also has a concentration of Late Palaeolithic sites, known through intensive surface collections (Eberhardt *et al.*, 1987). These sites, clustered around the complex shoreline adjacent to a major outflowing stream, have produced thousands of lithic artifacts, usually mixed with Mesolithic materials. The implements are made primarily of a brown chert that may outcrop within a few kilometers of the lake, but include Jurassic chert from the Alb, banded chert from Bavaria (about 200 kilometers to the east-northeast), and a chert from the upper Rhine, about 150 kilometers to the west-southwest, as well. A wide variety of types and debitage is represented in the collections. It is clear that this portion of the lake was visited repeatedly during this period, and that a variety of activities must have been carried out. Other surface sites of the Late Palaeolithic are known elsewhere on the former lake, primarily on the leeward, more indented parts of the western and northwestern shore. No other Late Palaeolithic finds are currently known in Oberschwaben, but a survey now under way may change this (Jochim, Glass, Fisher, and McCartney, in press).

4.9. LAKE CONSTANCE

Despite its favorable climatic conditions, few Late Palaeolithic sites have been found around this large lake. Intensive survey on the western shore has produced numerous Mesolithic and later materials, but those of the Late Palaeolithic are apparently scarce (Reinerth, 1953). Ongoing surveys may alter this picture, but in the meantime it appears that occupation was sparse in this area. One surface site, Bo 11, contains backed points and probably dates to the Late Palaeolithic. Interestingly, it contains banded chert deriving from 250 kilometers to the northeast, near Kelheim in Bavaria (Schlichtherle, 1994).

Chapter 5

Sites on the Landscape: The Early Mesolithic

5.1. INTRODUCTION

The Early Mesolithic, or Beuronien, lasted for approximately 2500 years, from 10,300 to 7800 b.p. The hallmark of this period is the abundance of microliths, which have been classified by Taute (1972/73) and used to establish a stylistic chronology. Three primary stages have been recognized in this scheme, derived from stratigraphic sequences in cave sites and supported by radiocarbon determinations: Beuronien A, characterized by isosceles triangles with obtuse angles, narrow, irregular trapezes, and lanceolate points with convex, dorso-ventrally retouched bases; Beuronien B, with isosceles triangles with acute angles and lanceolate points with concave, dorso-ventrally retouched bases; and Beuronien C, typified by backed bladelets, very small and narrow scalene triangles, bilaterally backed micropoints, and lanceolate points with concave, dorsally retouched bases. Since this sequence was developed, a poorly defined fourth stage, the "Earliest Mesolithic," has been recognized underlying the Beuronien A at a few sites.

Subsequent excavations have revealed that the distinctions between stages A and B are not clear, with forms typical of both often intermingled within stratigraphic layers. As a result, it is now common to use a simple, two-part division of the Early Mesolithic, ignoring the "Earliest Mesolithic," into Beuronien A/B and Beuronien C. Both stages have been found to be well represented in excavated sites, but only Beuronien A/B is common in surface lithic scatters. Several causes for this pattern have been suggested. Because of the extremely

57

small size of the diagnostic microliths of the Beuronien C, it may be that they are less likely to be seen and recovered during field-walking. In addition, changes in depositional conditions may have coincided with the onset of this stage, leading to less frequent burial and preservation of sites. Moreover, the duration of this stage is only about 500 years, much shorter than that of the Beuronien A/B (ca. 2000 years) and therefore it is likely that far fewer sites were originally created during this period. Finally, the differences in site numbers and locations may be real, reflecting adjustments to changing environments over the course of the Early Mesolithic.

Sites from this period are abundant and include many well-excavated caves, rockshelters, and even open-air sites as well as numerous surface lithic scatters. Compared to the Late Palaeolithic, these sites occur in a wider variety of locations and show a greater variability in assemblage size and composition. These data suggest considerable residential mobility with some indications of seasonal patterning. As is true for the preceding period, the quality of data varies substantially according to type of site, date of excavation, and standard of reporting. The following discussion of sites will be organized within the framework of the major regional subdivisions presented. Tables 3 and 4 summarize the sites and faunal remains of this period.

5.2. RHINE LOWLANDS

Field-walking in the region near Baden-Baden has revealed 18 sites clearly attributable to the Early Mesolithic (Gersbach, 1951). Although much more abundant than sites of the previous period, the Early Mesolithic sites occur in similar locations: dunes rising up from the valley floor and the flanks of the hills to the east (Fig. 18). Assemblages range in size from 1 to 940, but the larger ones contain materials from the Late Palaeolithic and/or Late Mesolithic as well. Of the 18 sites, 5 also have Late Palaeolithic materials, 5 also have Late Mesolithic artifacts, and 2 contain materials from all three periods. Microliths occur at all 18 sites, which is not surprising since they provide the means for dating the sites. All sites but 2 also have scrapers, followed in frequency by retouched blades, notched pieces, burins, and borers. Cores and unretouched flakes and blades accompany these finds at most sites.

Four sites with Early Mesolithic materials have been reported for the area to the south around Freiburg (Fig. 19; Vogelgesang, 1948). One of these sites, with an assemblage of over 600 artifacts, also has Late Palaeolithic and Late Mesolithic material. The other three include one small assemblage with microliths, scrapers, burins, cores, flakes, and blades located on a small hill rising out of the valley floor, as well as two isolated finds of microliths. One of the latter occurs in the hills back from the valley at an elevation of 1147 meters, and an-

Table 3. Early Mesolithic Sites

Area	Sites	Period	Location	Finds
Rhine lowlands				
Baden-Baden area	18 surface sites	Some mixed with Palaeolithic and/or Late Mesolithic	Sand dunes and hillflanks	1–940 artifacts
Freiburg area	2 surface sites	1 mixed with Palaeolithic and Late Mesolithic	Hillflanks, hilltop, valley floor	1–600+ artifacts
Basel area	Isteiner Klotz cave	Mixed with Palaeolithic and Late Mesolithic	Hillflank	1150 artifacts, bones
Rhine Valley	One cave, 15 surface sites	Some mixed with Palaeolithic and/or Late Mesolithic	Valley floor, hilltops	Varied assemblage sizes
Neckar Valley	200+ surface sites, incl.	Some mixed with Neolithic	Hilltops, hillflanks, terraces	
	Birkenkopf		Hilltop	11,000+ artifacts, pavement
	Rosi I	Beuronien B	Valley floor	1956 artifacts, hearths, bones, hazelnuts
	Rosi II	Beuronien ABC	Valley floor	2000+ artifacts, hearths, bones
	Rosi III	Beuronien BC	Valley floor	170 artifacts, hearths, bones
Eastern Black Forest	9 surface sites	1 mixed with Palaeolithic	Valley floor, hilltops	Varied assemblage sizes
Alpine foothills	None known			
Swabian Alb	Jagerhaushohle cave	Levels 13–8: Beuronien ABC	Hillflank	37–2341 artifacts per level, bones, shellfish, nuts
	Probstfels cave	Beuronien C	Hillflank	
	Falkensteinhohle cave	Beuronien C (?)	Hillflank	Large assemblage, bone, shell-fish, nuts
	Dietfurt cave	Levels 11–10: Beuronien ABC	Rock outcrop in valley	Lithic artifacts, bones, shell-fish, nuts

(continued)

Table 3. (*Continued*)

Area	Sites	Period	Location	Finds
	Inzigkofen rockshelter	Beuronien C	Valley edge	495 artifacts, bones, shellfish
	Felsstalle rockshelter	Beuronien C	Terrace	6290 artifacts, hearth, bones, nuts
	Schuntershohle cave	Levels 4–3: Beuronien ABC	Valley edge	481 artifacts, bones
	Helga–Abri rockshelter	Levels 11F6–1: Beuronien BC	Hillflank	1585 artifacts, hearth, bones, depression, nuts, eggshells
	Geissenklosterle cave	Beuronien A	Hillflank	Few artifacts
	Brunnenstein cave	Early Mesolithic	Hillflank	
	Fohlenhaus cave	Levels 2–1: Beuronien BC	Hillflank	216 artifacts, bones
	Hohlenstein Stadel cave and Kleine Scheuer Shelter	Beuronien A	Valley edge	Few artifacts, skulls
	Malerfels rockshelter	Levels 1a–b: Beuronien A	Hillflank	421 artifacts, bones
	Abri Klemmer Shelter	Early Mesolithic	Hillflank	
	Spitalhohle cave	Level VI: Beuronien AB	Hillflank	Few artifacts, bones, depression
	Barenfels cave	Level 1: Beuronien AB	Hillflank	Few artifacts
	Rappenfels rockshelter	Beuronien BC	Hillflank	1126 artifacts
	Various surface sites	Early Mesolithic	Hilltops, hillflanks	Varied assemblage sizes
Oberschwaben Federsee	Various surface sites	Beuronien ABC, often mixed with other periods	Lakeshore	Varied assemblage sizes
	Henauhof Nordwest	Levels 5–4: Beuronien ABC	Lakeshore	See Chapter 8
	Taubried	Beuronien A	Lakeshore	Microliths, nuts
	Siedlung Forschner	Beuronien AB	Lakeshore	Fishbones, point
Badsee/Obersee	Various surface sites	Early Mesolithic	Lakeshore	1 site with hearth, depression
Aitrach Valley	Various surface sites	Early Mesolithic	Valley floor, terraces	Varied assemblage sizes
Lake Constance	Numerous surface sites	Early Mesolithic	Lakeshore	Varied assemblage sizes

Table 4. Early Mesolithic Fauna

Resource	IST. Kl.	Rosi I	Rosi II	Rosi III/3	Rosi III/4	Jag. 13	Jag. 11	Jag. 10	Jag. 9	Jag. 8	Falk. L.1/3	Inz. L.1/3	Zig. C	Felsst.	Schunters	Helga Abri	Malerfels	Spi-Tal	Hen. NW 5	Hen. NW 4
Red deer	X	X	X	X	X	X	X	X	X	X	X	X	X	X		X	X		X	X
Roe deer	X	X	X	X	X	X	X	X	X	X	X	X	X	X			X	X	X	X
Boar		X	X	X		X	X	X	X	X	X	X		X	X		X		X	X
Aurochs	X	X	X		X	X	X	X	X	X	X	X		X	X		X			X
Moose																				X
Horse	X																		X	
Reindeer	X																			
Bear									X	X										
Beaver	X	X			X	X	X		X		X	X				X	X			
Hare	X	X				X				X	X		X	X		X	X	X	X	
Badger							X							X			X			X
Otter							X	X	X					X			X	X		
Wolf																	X	X		
Fox	X	X	X						X	X		X	X	X			X	X	X	X
Wildcat	X	X									X	X					X	X	X	X
Lynx											X	X								
Marten	X		X						X	X	X	X		X			X			
Weasel											X	X								
Fish	X	X			X				X	X	X	X	X	X		X	X	X	X	X
Shellfish	X							X	X		X	X								
Birds	X	X	X						X	X	X	X		X		X	X	X	X	X
Eggs																X				

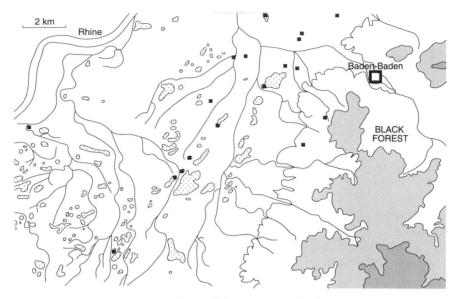

Figure 18. Early Mesolithic sites near Baden-Baden.

other is along a stream exiting the hills; both may represent simply losses while hunting.

Farther south, near the bend in the Rhine, only one cave, Isteiner Klotz, clearly has Early Mesolithic materials, mixed with those of the Late Palaeolithic and Late Mesolithic (Fig. 20). The assemblage contains 1150 lithic artifacts and an array of faunal materials, but the materials cannot be separated and assigned to specific periods.

5.3. RHINE VALLEY

In the narrow valley near Säckingen farther south, 16 sites with Early Mesolithic material have been reported, including 1 small cave and 15 lithic scatters (Fig. 21). Six of the open-air sites also contain Late Palaeolithic material and 2 also have artifacts from the Late Mesolithic. All of these sites have diverse lithic assemblages, with 4–6 general tool categories along with cores and unretouched flakes and blades. Most of the sites are strung along the entire length of the river in this area, both close to and set back from the river near tributaries. Two of the sites are located up in the hills above the valley floor. Assemblages throughout the Rhine lowlands and narrower upper Rhine include some material from the upper Rhine near Säckingen (Schlichtherle, 1994).

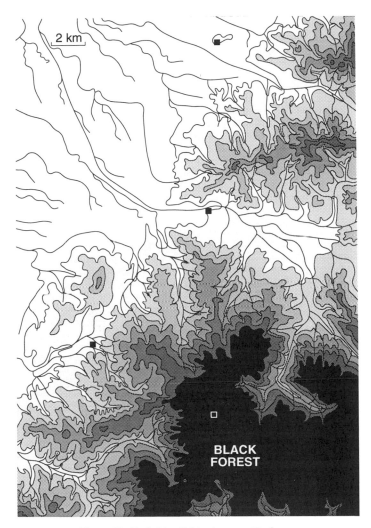

Figure 19. Early Mesolithic sites near Freiburg.

5.4. NECKAR DRAINAGE

The Neckar drainage, including its three tributaries the Fils, Rems, and Murr, has the highest density of Early Mesolithic sites of the entire region. Beginning in at least the 1920s, private collectors have combed the hills and valleys seeking surface finds, with much success. Over 200 lithic scatters have

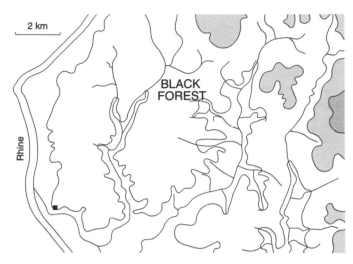

Figure 20. Early Mesolithic sites near Istein.

been reported, many of them clearly attributable to the Early Mesolithic. A good number also contain Neolithic materials, but artifacts characteristic both of the Late Palaeolithic and of the Late Mesolithic are extremely rare.

The number and types of artifacts at each site vary substantially, from an isolated microlith or a few flakes to hundreds or even thousands of finds including a diverse array of tool types. Part of this variation surely reflects collection intensity and surface visibility, but part must also reflect considerable differences in occupation intensity and functional role among these sites. Cer-

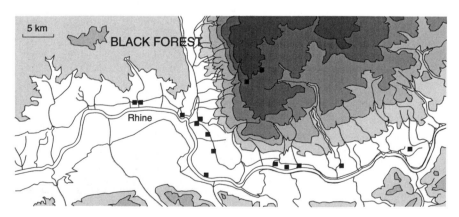

Figure 21. Early Mesolithic sites near Säckingen.

tain places on the landscape were repeatedly occupied, presumably over several millenia, while others must have witnessed far fewer occupations.

One of the most remarkable sites is Birkenkopf, which lies west-southwest of Stuttgart on a hill at an elevation of 471 meters. Collections from the surface were begun here in the 1920s and excavations carried out in the 1930s (Peters, 1941). Over 11,000 lithic artifacts derive from this work, including over 1300 retouched tools, 300 cores, and 600 utilized flakes and blades. Most of the raw material is Jurassic chert, available in the local river gravels. Microliths dominate the tools, followed by retouched blades, notched pieces, scrapers, burins, and a variety of other forms. In addition, a number of hammerstones and abraders were found. The excavation, which covered an area of about 100 square meters, located most finds within a 30 cm layer of sand beneath the topsoil. Part of this area was covered with a pavement of flat sandstone slabs. The collections contain a few Neolithic elements (projectile points, one polished axe) and either Magdalenian or Late Palaeolithic material (backed knives), but these differ in patina and material from the bulk of the collection (Taute, personal communication). The overwhelming majority of the material appears to belong to the Early Mesolithic, specifically the Beuronien B.

Although a number of sites are located relatively low in stream and river valleys, usually on terraces or low flanks above the valley bottom, the majority occur up in the hills, particularly on summits and on promontories over the valleys. A locational analysis of over 100 of these sites east of Stuttgart (Fig. 22) supports this generalization (Kvamme and Jochim, 1990). Compared to a random sample of points in the landscape, these sites were found to be situated at higher elevations than would be expected by chance alone. Moreover, the sites were

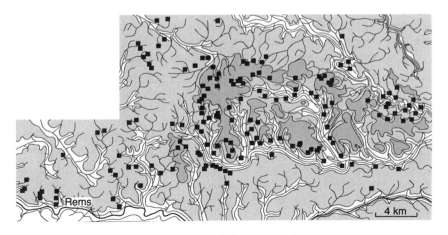

Figure 22. Early Mesolithic sites near Stuttgart.

found to be in locations of smaller slope, greater surrounding topographic relief, less topographic shelter, and wider viewsheds than chance alone would dictate. The topographic exposure and wide views afforded by these sites may, however, be illusory, for in this forested region the trees may have both provided shelter and blocked long-distance views. Another locational feature of these sites is their relatively large average distance to water, both horizontal and vertical; they are farther from streams than would be predicted by chance. This is surprising given the traditional characterizations of Mesolithic settlement distributions as close to water and the demonstrated importance of aquatic foods in their diets.

A major determinant of these patterns of site location may be modern site visibility. Sites low on the valley floors and close to water may simply lie buried under the alluvium and be undetectable by surface walking. As was discussed in Chapter 3, the Neckar and Danube systems underwent a long period of downcutting through most of the Mesolithic, exposing dry banks that have subsequently been buried by alluvial deposition. The recent discovery of alluvial sites along the Neckar near Rottenburg, to be discussed in the following section, indicates that such sites indeed exist. If this is the case, then the known sites in the hills represent just a portion of the overall settlement pattern.

It is tempting, on the basis of ethnographic analogies, to make some interpretive leaps to account for this sample of settlements. One scenario would suggest that the known sites represent largely special-purpose hunting camps, tied to residential bases in the valley bottoms. The typological diversity of so many of the lithic assemblages suggests that this is not the case, but rather indicates that a great variety of activities occurred in many of these sites. Furthermore, the location of a number of these sites on the very top of quite small, steep-sided hills is difficult to interpret as an ideal placement for hunting camps in the forest, where visibility would be difficult. Such camps might be better placed in locations close to valleys channeling game movements.

An alternative interpretation, taking into account the assemblage diversity and locational patterns, would be that these sites include both residential and more specialized camps. In the sample studied, the sites with larger assemblages tend to be located on flatter areas with less surrounding relief but in more exposed positions, suggesting a functional differentiation. If so, they might represent largely warm-weather occupations, when larger game might be likely to range upslope. During seasons when fishing was likely to be more important, perhaps late spring and early fall, occupation in the valley bottoms close to water might have been more profitable. Winter occupations are more difficult to envisage in this scenario. Large and small game should have been most important in the winter diet, and these prey would probably have been most concentrated in the lower elevations. At the same time, the valley floors may have held pockets of colder air and had deeper snow cover. Some of the narrower valleys may also have been wind tunnels and extremely unpleasant during winter storms. Locations low on the hill flanks, but protected in the forest, may have been optimal.

Supplementing these abundant lithic scatters are three recently discovered sites in the alluvium of the Neckar Valley near Rottenburg. Each occurs in the neighborhood of *Rottenburg-Siebenlinden*, and so they bear the designations Rosi I, II, and III (Fig. 24).

Rosi I, lying in the alluvial clay about one meter below the modern surface, was excavated over an area of 53 square meters (Hahn and Kind, 1991; Hahn, Kind, and Steppan, 1993). One main cultural level of approximately 50 cm thickness was discovered. Although the site had been disturbed by a later Iron Age trench, it could be determined that most artifacts lay in an oval concentration measuring roughly 5 by 6 meters. Two small hearths, 2.5 meters apart, were near the center of this oval and were marked by fire-reddened areas in the clay. Each had a diameter of 60–80 cm but contained no charcoal, which may have been washed away by gentle floodwaters.

The diverse lithic assemblage of 1956 artifacts contains 123 retouched pieces, 37 cores, and numerous flakes, blades, and shatter. Raw materials consist of chert available in the local gravels and white chert from the Alb, 20–30 km away. Microliths and microburins dominate the tools, followed by lateral- and end-retouched pieces, scrapers, notched pieces, burins, and other forms. The microlith types belong to the Early Mesolithic, predominantly Beuronien B, an attribution supported by three radiocarbon dates whose means range from 9110 to 8540 b.p. A fourth date of 8035 ± 75 was considered contaminated. A number of hammer- or nut-stones and a few sandstone grinding slabs and hand-stones were also found.

Numerous lithic refits and conjoins attest to the spatial integrity of this small site, despite the probable inundation that removed charcoal from the hearths. A tendency for larger lithic artifacts to be located around the periphery of the concentration suggests the existence of specific "toss zones" for larger debris, or simply the gradual dispersal of larger artifacts to the site periphery. In either case, this indicates an occupation of some duration.

Diverse organic materials were also found. The well-preserved faunal assemblage contains 1060 bones, which include remains of red and roe deer, boar, aurochs, red fox, beaver, squirrel, reindeer, and birds. The presence of reindeer (two metatarsal fragments) this late in the Holocene is surprising and has been interpreted as indicative of the presence of a remnant herd, perhaps in the Black Forest. Three antler adze blades and one bone awl complete the assemblage.

Finally, charred hazelnut shells were abundantly represented by over 1000 fragments, together with remains of wild raspberry, apple, and cabbage. They suggest a fall occupation, which agrees with faunal indicators of late summer/fall kills.

Rosi II lies 100–150 meters away from Rosi I on the lower terrace of the Neckar (Kieselbach and Richter, 1992; Richter, 1996). Artifacts were found in a 40 cm level approximately one meter below the modern surface, and include 2234 lithics, 2000 other rocks, and 350 bones. The lithic artifacts show a wide array of tool types, including microliths of the Beuronien A/B and C, as well as numerous cores, flakes, and blades. The one radiocarbon date (7795 ± 80 b.p.) seems too recent for this array of microliths. Cherts from both the local river gravels and the Alb, about 20–30 km away, dominate the assemblage.

Again, two hearths detectable as reddened areas of 60–80 cm diameter were found, as well as a third hearth in the form of a depression of one meter diameter filled with charcoal and fire-altered rock. Near the hearths is a pit, 30 cm deep and 80 cm in diameter. The bones include remains of red deer, roe deer, boar, aurochs, red fox, beaver, wild cat, marten, dog, and various birds. A few hazelnut shells were also found. Preliminary analysis of the faunal remains suggests a spring/early summer occupation. Based on the vertical distribution of materials and the pattern of lithic conjoins, two occupations were inferred. Several relatively discrete areas of lithic reduction and resharpening have been identified. The white chert from the Alb shows a slightly different treatment than the local material, indicative of greater economizing in its use (Kieselbach, 1996).

Rosi III is a nearby site of which 110 square meters have been excavated (Hahn and Kind, 1992; Kind, 1995). This site has three major occupation levels of 10–20 cm thickness, separated by 30 cm of sterile deposits. The upper level (II) dates to the Late Mesolithic and will be discussed later. Level III has two hearths. One, which is stone-lined and surrounded by stone and bone artifacts, has been interpreted as primarily a heating hearth. The other consists of a thick layer of fire-cracked rock, 120 cm in diameter, with charcoal underneath and surrounded by an area of heated clay with stones. This has been interpreted as a cooking hearth, and has proportionally more bones nearby. The 250 lithics are made of local cherts from the Neckar gravels, as well as some Jurassic cherts from the Alb. Retouched tools, which are relatively scarce, include a few microliths characteristic of the Beuronien C. Among the prey are red deer, roe deer, and boar.

Level IV contains microliths of the Beuronien B in a small assemblage of 150 artifacts. Bones include remains of roe and red deer, boar, aurochs, beaver, and dog. Hazelnut shells were also found. Deer are represented primarily by lower limbs, but include one skull with antlers attached, suggesting a late summer/early fall kill. Two of the antler tines had been cut off, presumably to be used as raw material for other implements.

One final find in this area deserves mention. During the 1950s construction along the upper Neckar revealed an aurochs bone with an obliquely blunted microlith embedded in it. Associated sediments have been palynologically dated to the Preboreal of the early Holocene. This find not only demonstrates the function of the small microlith as part of an arrow, used for even the largest game, but also indicates that hunting was indeed carried out on the valley floors.

It is clear that the Neckar drainage, apparently largely neglected during the Late Palaeolithic, became a focus for occupation during the ensuing Early Mesolithic. Whatever seasonal temperature uncertainties it presented may have been more than offset by its generally warm, dry climate, which would have encouraged the early immigration of hazel, oak, and other deciduous vegetation. These emerging temperate forests, if not too dense, would have provided excellent habitat for boar and deer, the rivers may have had numerous salmon and other fish, and hazelnuts would have been abundant.

5.5. BLACK FOREST

As in the preceding period, no sites definitely attributable to the Early Mesolithic are known from most of this region. As indicated earlier, however, a number of Early Mesolithic sites are situated on the hills overlooking the Rhine valley on the western edge of the forest. On the eastern flank, above the Nagold Valley, nine sites can be dated to this time (Stoll, 1932, 1933). One of these, which was also occupied during the Late Palaeolithic, is down in the valley on a terrace. The remaining eight, however, are all up on the heights above the steep-sided valley, in positions similar to those in the Neckar drainage (Fig. 23). Despite their elevation, these sites appear to be oriented to the river valley, because investigation of hilltops with similar soils away from the valley edges failed to discover sites. Retouched tools of these upland sites are dominated by microliths (70–80%), in contrast to the lowland site, which has approximately 32% microliths from the excavated assemblage.

Some sites are quite large lithic scatters (50 × 80 m, 60 × 80 m, 60 × 200 m, 80 × 250 m) and contain hundreds of artifacts, including a diversity of tool categories. Others have only a few finds from a small area. These patterns again could reflect differential collection, variations in reoccupation intensity, or functional diversity. The stone raw materials include local cherts, Jurassic chert from the Alb 40 km away, and one piece of radiolarite from Oberschwaben, at least 80 km away (Pasda, 1994).

5.6. ALPINE FOOTHILLS

This region has no definite occupations dated to the Early Mesolithic. Given the difficulties of surface visibility in this area of widespread forests and unplowed meadows, this lack of sites is not altogether surprising. Nevertheless, the absence of occupation may be real. The one area that has been systemati-

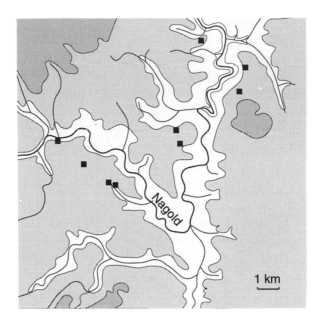

Figure 23. Early Mesolithic sites in the Nagold Valley.

cally walked, around Oberstdorf, contains repeated evidence for Late Palaeolithic occupation but none for the Early Mesolithic. Similarly, intensive fieldwalking in the foothills near Füssen to the east (which is outside of the study area examined here) produced a number of Late Palaeolithic finds but none of the Early Mesolithic (Reinerth, 1956).

5.7. SWABIAN ALB

This limestone plateau contains a large number of excavated caves and rockshelters, as well as a few lithic scatters, dating to the Early Mesolithic (Fig. 24). Most of these sites occur in the southern portion of the Alb along the Danube and its tributaries, rather than in the north, which belongs to the Rhine drainage and is somewhat higher in elevation, cooler, and wetter. The sites will be discussed briefly in a generally west-to-east direction.

Jägerhaushöhle (Fig. 24, No. 1) has six Early Mesolithic cultural levels stratified above the Late Palaeolithic level previously discussed: Level 13 (Beuronien A), Levels 12, 11, 10 (Beuronien B), and Levels 9, 8 (Beuronien C). These levels range in thickness from approximately 10 to 39 cm, and are separated by intervening levels (e.g., 11/12) of 10–20 cm thickness in which artifact densities are much lower.

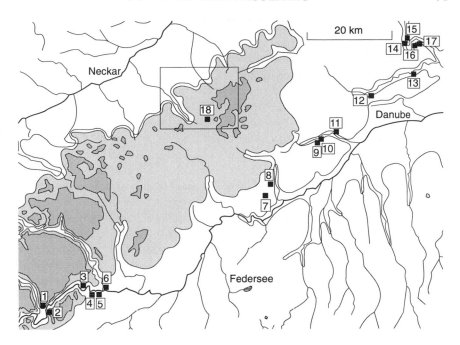

Figure 24. Early Mesolithic sites in the Swabian Alb.

Radiocarbon dates are presented in Taute (1978). The acceptable dates for the Beuronien B are 9600 ± 100 (Level 12) and 8840 ± 70 b.p. (Level 10), and for the Beuronien C are 8300 ± 70, 8140 ± 120 and 8060 ± 120 (Level 8). Pollen samples show a dominance of pine in Levels 13 to 10 and of hazel in Levels 9 and 8; in the latter, trees of the mixed oak forest are also more strongly represented. Charcoal identifications indicate a dominance of pine in Levels 13 to 9 and of hazel and oak (which first appear in some numbers in Level 10) in Level 8. A total of 82% of the tree charcoal contains fungal remains suggesting it came from gathered dead wood rather than felled trees.

The size of the lithic assemblages, which are dominated by the local Jurassic chert, varies widely, from 37 (Level 9) and 43 (Level 12) to 1200 (Level 13) and 2341 (Level 8), suggesting a varying intensity of occupation at different periods. Most notable about these assemblages is that, regardless of their size, the retouched tools (comprising 4–11% of each assemblage) are dominated by microliths. In the Beuronien A Level 13, microliths comprise 88% of the tools; in the Beuronien B levels they constitute 85%, and in the Beuronien C levels, 61%. If such implements were deposited largely as a by-product of arrow repair or manufacture, then this site appears to have been quite specialized, especially during Beuronien A/B times. Other tool forms, such as burins, scrapers, notched pieces, and retouched blades, consistently are represented by just a few examples until the Beuronien C, when retouched blades make up 27% of the assemblages. Although there is sufficient diversity within the total array of finds to prevent a simple interpretation of these levels as single-focus hunting camps, the lithic assemblages do indicate an emphasis on hunting-related activities and a scarcity of secondary processing of wood and hides or other tasks. Primary stone-working may also have had limited importance, given the relative rarity of cores (1–2% of each assemblage).

Faunal identifications are presented in Boessneck (1978a) and a summary is provided here. Only about 15% of the bones from all levels of the site could be identified, due to their heavily fragmented and highly calcined condition, but the bulk of those not identified are judged to come from large game animals. The identified bones of these levels are dominated by three big game species, red deer, boar, and roe deer, which comprise 59–100% of each assemblage by number. Smaller mammals play a variable role, ranging from 0 to 41%. Birds and fish are consistently of minor importance, absent in Levels 13 to 9 and comprising approximately 1% each in Level 8. It should be stressed, however, that these levels were not screened, so small bones may be underrepresented. Despite this caveat, the hunting of mammals, especially big game, appears to dominate the subsistence and agrees with the evidence from the lithic assemblages.

A variety of body parts have been identified for all three big game species, with no evidence that their occurrence is determined by bone density and preservation. Both boar and roe deer are represented by some high meat value parts (femur, pelvis), but the remains of red deer are dominated by parts of low meat utility, suggesting that these parts were either heavily processed for marrow and grease or were carried away. Boessneck does note that even phalanges were broken for marrow.

An additional component of the subsistence is the gathering of shellfish. Numerous fragments of river mussel shell, lacking valves, were found in Levels 10 and 8. Hazelnuts were also gathered at times, as witnessed by the remains of charred shells in these same levels. Finally, concentrations of pollen of round-leafed sorrel occur in Levels 11, 10, and 9 and have been interpreted as evidence of human gathering, although this is not certain, as they may derive from animal feces.

In sum, these levels of Jägerhaushöhle show a dominance of hunting and hunting-related activities in the faunal and lithic assemblages, especially in Beuronien A/B times. Late in the Beuronien B and into the Beuronien C other resources become evident (in a pattern not simply related to sample size) with the appearance of fish, shellfish, hazelnuts, and possibly other plants. The relative importance of microliths in the assemblages declines somewhat at the same time. Processing of animal prey appears to have been intensive. Seasons of occupation are only indirectly hinted, but summer/fall may be indicated by the plant remains. Infantile wild boar, which would suggest late winter/spring kills, were identified from this site, but not attributed to level.

Other finds from these Early Mesolithic levels include a number of fragments of bone tools of unidentified form, worked boar's tusk, one double-notched cobble, and various cobbles that may be hammerstones.

Probstfels (Fig. 24, No. 2) is a cave along the upper Danube that was excavated early in this century. Little can be said about this site except that it had a level attributed to the Beuronien C as well as some Late Mesolithic material.

Falkensteinhöhle (Fig. 24, No. 3), an extremely rich cave site, was excavated primarily by Peters in the 1930s but is much better known through the work carried out there by Taute in the 1960s (Taute, 1967b). The cave measures 10 by 15 meters and is situated 35 meters above the Danube. In the original excavation a single, undifferentiated Mesolithic level of approximately one meter thickness was determined and produced thousands of lithics and bones. Taute's subsequent work subdivided this into three arbitrary levels, since no stratigraphic breaks were apparent. These strata have been interpreted as spanning the period from the Beuronien C through the Late Mesolithic, but radiocarbon dates from all three of Taute's levels fall into the time period of the Late Mesolithic, and Taute indicates that the attribution of the lower third to the Beuronien C is not secure (Taute, 1978: 17). Among the charcoal, pine dominates in the lower third, while oak is more abundant in the upper two thirds. While attributable to the Boreal/Early Atlantic periods on these grounds, the lack of hazel, characteristic of the Boreal period (contemporary with the Beuronien C) is puzzling (Schweingruber, 1978).

The majority of finds from the earlier, massive excavation (200–250 cubic meters) was lost in the war, with only summary reports published on these collections. Taute's later excavation was much smaller but better controlled and reported. Given the problems of separating the finds by period, discussion here will focus especially on the lower third level of Taute's excavation, which is the most likely collection to be attributed to the Early Mesolithic.

The small lithic assemblage of 40 artifacts includes 14 retouched tools and cores, composed of a few microliths, scrapers, retouched blades, burins, and other forms, all made of local chert. The lack of dominance by microliths is also evident in accounts of the assemblage from earlier excavations, in which microliths account for only about 25% of the retouched tools, and scrapers and retouched blades are approximately of equal importance.

Approximately 38% of all the bones from Taute's excavation could be identified to species. In the lower third, large mammals comprise 73% of those identified and include red deer, boar and roe deer. High meat utility parts are noticeably absent, but Boessneck (1978b) suggests their presence among the unidentified fragments. Small mammals make up 14% of the finds, with birds

(2%) and fish (10%) the remainder. Reports from the earlier excavation confirm this dominance of large game as well as the significant proportion of fish compared to Jägerhaushöhle. This earlier work also reported hazelnuts and mussels among the finds, but it is not clear where in the stratigraphy they occurred. Taute found hazelnuts only in his middle third level.

Additional finds from the lower third include three fragments of bone tools. Although the early excavation retrieved numerous antler tools, these may be primarily Late Mesolithic in age, as Taute found worked antler only in the upper two thirds.

Dietfurt Cave (Fig. 24, No. 4) has two Early Mesolithic levels overlying the Late Palaeolithic deposits: Level 11 (Beuronien A/B) and Level 10 (Beuronien C), with a combined thickness of 40 cm. This site is not yet published, but microliths and cores have been reported from these levels. A total of 1661 fishbones were recovered, of which 407 could be identified to ten different species. The larger species were estimated to represent 26.6—31.1 kilograms of meat. Finds of rib heads next to the spinal column suggest filleting (Torke, 1981). These fish remains were also interpreted as representing catches at least in spring. Charred hazelnut shells were abundant in Level 10, perhaps indicating fall collection, and mussel shells without valves suggest the collection of shellfish.

Notable among the finds are ornaments. These include perforated fossil shells, fish vertebrae and teeth, and a deer incisor. The fossil shells derive largely from the Steinheim Basin, roughly 100 kilometers to the northeast, but some come from the Mainz Basin, roughly 200 kilometers to the north-northwest.

Inzigkofen (Fig. 24, No. 5) is a small rockshelter measuring 3 by 8 meters, located low in the valley of the upper Danube. Like Falkensteinhöhle, it was excavated in the 1930s by Peters and again by Taute in the 1960s. Peters made no differentiations within the approximately one meter thick cultural layer, but Taute subdivided it into arbitrary thirds, with the lower third being attributed to the Beuronien C. One radiocarbon date for this level is thought to be somewhat too early at 8720 ± 120 b.p. (Taute, 1978). Charcoal studies document a decline in pine and a rise in oak through the sequence.

The 495 stone artifacts in this level include 42 retouched pieces (8%), of which microliths are most abundant (31%), followed by retouched blades (21%), scrapers (19%), and a few notched pieces, one burin, one borer, and various other forms. There are 17 cores, comprising 3% of the assemblage.

Approximately 60% of the bones in the lower third level could be identified to species (Boessneck, 1978c; Lepiksaar, 1978). In this level, 53% of the identified bones come from larger game animals, 29% from small mammals, 2% from birds, 1% from frogs, and 11% from fish. All body parts are represented among the big game bones. Remains of both red deer and boar included infantile specimens, which suggest late winter/spring/early summer kills. Mussel shells also occur in this level.

Other finds include two pieces of worked boar's tusk, two bone points, two fragments of red deer antler, and a quartzite hammerstone.

Zigeunerfels (Fig. 24, No. 6) had small collections of Early Mesolithic materials stratified in three levels above the Late Palaeolithic levels previously discussed: Level C (Earliest Mesolithic, with a few microliths), Level B (Beuronien A, with several microliths), and Level A (Beuronien A/B, with microliths mixed with later Neolithic material). Level C also contains two bone pendants, consisting of perforated bone rectangles with regularly spaced incisions along both edges. The only reported fauna also come from Level C. Level A contained one fossil shell that derived from the middle Danube, at least 300 kilometers to the east, but since this level contains material of various periods, it is not certain that this find dates to the Early Mesolithic.

Felsställe (Fig. 24, No. 7) is a relatively long rockshelter located low on a terrace above a tributary of the Danube in the Alb. Excavation of 29 square meters in three blocks revealed a 5–10 cm level attributed to the Beuronien C (Kind, 1987). A radiocarbon date of 8190 ± 90 confirms its chronological position in the late Boreal period. The charcoal is dominated by pine but also contains much hazel as well as oak, ash, and beech.

A hearth was found, consisting of a small depression of 40–50 cm diameter filled with dark gravel and charcoal, baked together in a conglomerate. Chemical tests indicate the presence of animal fats in this conglomerate as well, suggesting the use of bone as a fuel in addition to wood. A number of lithic refits were found close to the hearth, indicating the occurrence of stone-working in this area. This inference is strengthened by the concentration of most of the 22 cores around the hearth as well.

A total of 6290 lithic artifacts was recovered, of which approximately 85% were smaller than one centimeter in longest dimension. More than 97% of the raw material was identified as local cherts; the remainder either derives from morainic gravels 5 to 6 kilometers to the south or cannot be identified. Traces of heating were found on 29% of the artifacts.

The assemblage of 99 retouched tools includes 42% microliths, 28% retouched blades, together with burins, scrapers, borers, and other forms. Also found were seven bone point fragments, nine other pieces of worked bone, two pieces of worked beaver tooth, two pieces of worked antler, one bone bead, and 13 fossil shells deriving from the Steinheim Basin, about 40 kilometers to the northeast. One additional find of note is a stone slab of 8 cm length bearing traces of red ochre and interpreted as a painting of the head of a bovid (Campen, Kind, and Luxmann, 1983).

Of the total of 1832 bone fragments recovered, only 177 (just under 10%) could be identified to species, due to their heavily fragmented condition. The big game species of red deer, roe deer, and boar make up 73% of the identified remains, followed by small mammals (16%), fish (10%), and birds (1%).

Analysis of tooth eruption and wear suggests kills from February to June, that is, late winter/spring/early summer. Many charred hazelnut shells were also found, which may indicate either late summer/fall gathering or the practice of storage. The apparent dominance of big game in the economy of this site is supported by a study of the unidentifiable bones. Among these, 953 could be classified according to size and 86% of these derive from mammals of roe deer size or larger. The large mammal body parts include those of both high and low meat utility.

Schuntershöhle (Fig. 24, No. 8) lies in the Alb seven meters above the valley floor of a small tributary of the Danube. This cave, which measures about 6 × 12 meters, was partially excavated several times in the 1930s, 1940s and 1960s (Taute, 1978). Two Mesolithic cultural horizons have been determined, but they are not consistently distinct. Level 4 has materials from the Beuronien A and Level 3 contains artifacts from the Beuronien B, C, and possibly Late Mesolithic. A number of finds, including most of the bones, could be attributed only to the Mesolithic levels in general.

The total lithic assemblage from all excavations of both levels was originally approximately 481 artifacts, but only 237 were available for analysis by Taute (1978). The 100 artifacts of Level 4 include 55 retouched tools, of which 58% are microliths and the remainder retouched blades, notched pieces, scrapers, and other forms. Nine cores were also present. Only 58 artifacts could be definitely attributed to Level 3, of which 15 are retouched tools. These include 27% microliths plus retouched blades, scrapers, and other types, together with seven cores. An additional 79 artifacts derive from either level; of the 16 retouched tools, 50% are microliths together with a burin and various other tools, as well as one core.

Helga-Abri (Fig. 24, No. 9) is a rockshelter in the Alb situated 20 meters above the valley of the Ach, a tributary of the Danube (Hahn and Scheer, 1983). Mesolithic materials are confined to two depressions filled with charcoal and fire-altered rock. Only one depression was complete and measured approximately two meters in diameter; the other was disturbed by earlier excavations. Six Early Mesolithic levels were determined: IIF6-5 (Beuronien B), IIF4-2 (Beuronien C/B), and IIF1 (Beuronien C). One radiocarbon date of 8230 ± 40 b.p. was obtained from Level IIF2. Pollen and charcoal determinations place these levels in the Boreal period.

A total of 1585 stone artifacts were recovered, ranging in number from 71 to 766 per level. Local cherts dominate the assemblages, but the predominant color varies among levels. Radiolarite from Danube gravels consistently forms less than 2% of each assemblage. The number of heated pieces increases from about 11% in Level IIF6 to 74% in Level IIF1. Retouched tools in each level include numerous microliths and retouched blades, together with occasional scrapers, borers, backed knives, and flakes, and cores in all levels but IIF3.

Level IIF2 has a hearth ringed and lined with stones. The intact depression also has a rectangular pit extending deeper than the floor of the depression. These depressions have been interpreted as small hut areas reused during frequent, brief occupations.

The fauna of all levels are similar: dominated by hare and beaver, together with red deer and fish. Other food remains include eggshells and charred hazelnut shells, which suggest occupations in both spring and fall, unless one or both foods were stored. Levels IIF2 and IIF1 contain four perforated fossil shells from the Steinheim Basin, roughly 40 kilometers to the northeast.

Geissenklösterle (Fig. 24, No. 10) is a cave in the Ach Valley in the same rock outcrop as Helga-Abri. The cave is situated approximately 50 meters above the valley floor. Above substantial Palaeolithic deposits is one level, In, with a few stone artifacts of the Beuronien A.

Brunnenstein (Fig. 24, No. 11) is a cave in the Ach Valley that was tested in 1957 and produced Early Mesolithic lithic artifacts, but nothing more is known of these finds.

Fohlenhaus (Fig. 24, No. 12) is a cave that has two poorly defined levels of Early Mesolithic stratified in the terrace above the Late Palaeolithic material previously discussed: Level 2 (Beuronien B) and Level 1 (Beuronien C) (Taute, 1978). A radiocarbon date for Level 1 was determined as 8140 ± 70 b.p. Among the unstratified finds of this much disturbed site were also microliths characteristic of the Beuronien A. Just 22 stone artifacts were recovered from Taute's excavations of both levels. These were dominated by microliths but include various other tools and cores as well. The assemblage of unstratified finds is larger (194) and contains 105 microliths together with scrapers, burins, and retouched blades. The only fauna recovered include the remains of a badger and numerous rodents, as well as perforated fish teeth, in Level 2.

Hohlenstein Stadel and Kleine Scheuer (Fig. 24, No. 13) are a cave and adjacent rockshelter low in the valley of the Lone, a now-dry Danube tributary. Frequent excavations since the beginning of this century concentrated on Upper Palaeolithic deposits. Three microliths attributed to the Beuronien A were found in the poorly defined Level 1 of the rockshelter. Most intriguing is the possible association of this evidence for Early Mesolithic use of the site with a find at the entrance to the cave: a pit containing the skulls of a man, a woman, and a child, partially covered with red ochre. Both adults showed wounds from blows to the head, and the vertebrae had cut marks, indicating removal of the heads from the bodies. All three skulls faced southwest. The female skull was surrounded by ornamental fish teeth of a type associated with Early Mesolithic materials at Dietfurt and Fohlenhaus. The molluscan fauna in the pit fill is typical of early Holocene sediments. Probst (1993) cites a date for these skulls of 9785 ± ?, consistent with an Early Mesolithic age. Clearly this feature testifies to some ritual practices and it has fueled speculation about sacrifice and a skull cult.

Malerfels (Fig. 24, No. 14) contains two levels (1a and 1b) of Beuronien A materials (Albrecht, 1984; Hahn, 1984). Early excavations by Peters focused on the center of the shelter, but these finds have been mostly lost. As the material from the most recent excavation is largely distributed in two square meters against the back wall of the shelter behind a large boulder, and shows little internal spatial patterning, it has been interpreted as a trash accumulation. Three radiocarbon dates were obtained from Level 1b: 9560 ± 250, 9075 ± 100, and 8605 ± 210 b.p. The oldest of these is most accepted, as it derives from the least disturbed section of the deposits. The charcoal is mostly pine, with oak also represented.

Lithic artifacts total 421, of which 66 are retouched. Microliths are most numerous among the tools (45%), followed by retouched blades, scrapers, burins, and other forms. Five cores were also found. Virtually all artifacts derive from local chert, but radiolarite from the Danube gravels is also present. Of a sample of 194 flakes, 74% showed signs of heating. One additional find was a perforated red deer incisor.

Bones were heavily fragmented, but 76% of the assemblage of Level 1b and 93% of Level 1a could be assigned to gross faunal categories. In contrast to many other sites, but similar to Helga-Abri, small mammals and fish dominate in Level 1b, and small and medium mammals in 1a. Red and roe deer are represented only by remains of distal limbs and crania, while boar body parts also include scapula and pelvis. The bird remains of Level 1b include five species of probable prey, both waterfowl and grouse, and at least six species are present in the fish remains.

Abri Klemmer (Fig. 24, No. 15) is a small rockshelter near Malerfels in which early excavations apparently discovered Early Mesolithic materials, but no additional information is available.

Spitalhöhle (Fig. 24, No. 16) is a small cave approximately 20 meters above the Brenz, a Danube tributary. Excavated in the 1950s, its Level VI has materials from the Beuronien A/B. The entire remaining lithic collection, however, is only 23 artifacts, but this small number includes a variety of retouched tool forms. Faunal material is presented in Table 4 and is notable for the dominance of birds and fish. The materials occur in an artificial depression of about five square meters between three large blocks and the back wall, a feature that has been interpreted as a hut or windbreak (Hahn, 1983).

Bärenfelsgrotte (Fig. 24, No. 17) is another small cave in the Brenz Valley, 15 meters above the valley floor and 150 meters from Spitalhöhle. Many artifacts from early excavations have been lost, but enough remain to document the presence of Beuronien A/B materials in Level 1. The small assemblage of 14 lithics contains a variety of retouched tool types as well as three blades that refit, indicating manufacturing activities in the cave.

Rappenfels (Fig. 24, No. 18) is a rockshelter in the northeast part of the Alb, excavated during the 1930s (Peters, 1935). The lithic assemblage, which

was originally described as a "late Tardenoisien," contains materials characteristic of the Beuronien B and C, as well as apparently Neolithic points and possibly some Magdalenian material. A total of 1126 stone artifacts was reported,
of which approximately 9% were retouched. Microliths made up about 20% of
the tools, and together with retouched blades, were the dominant types in a diverse assemblage. A rich assemblage of bone tools was also found, including a
number of smooth bone points.

A good number of open-air lithic scatters have been reported from the
Alb, particularly along the northern edge and in the southeastern portions. Although many of these have been attributed to the Mesolithic, they often lack
diagnostic artifacts and so the attributions are questionable in some cases; others, however, do seem to be Early Mesolithic in age. Fig. 25 shows 17 reported
sites in the area near Urach; also included in the map is Rappenfels. The distribution of these sites is similar to that of the open-air sites in the Neckar drainage: concentrated on high hills, plateau edges, or flanks over valleys. One
notable cluster is evident near Randecker Maar and Torfgrube, areas that would

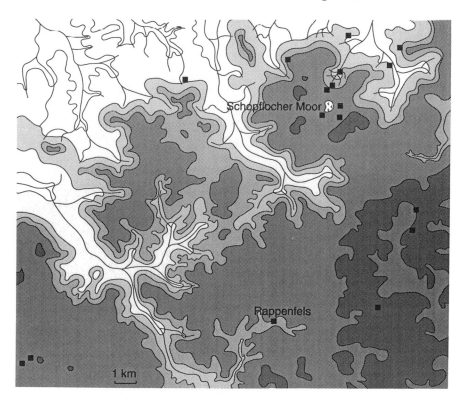

Figure 25. Early Mesolithic sites near Urach.

have provided some of the only standing water and marshes in an otherwise
dry, karstic landscape.

5.8. OBERSCHWABEN

The morainic area of Oberschwaben appears to have been frequently occupied during the Early Mesolithic, although the currently known sites are
concentrated in only a few regions. The Federsee contains the largest cluster of
sites, due largely to the long history of intensive work in this area (Fig. 26). All
of the known sites are open-air; most are surface lithic scatters, but a few have
been excavated.

A program of fieldwalking by Reinerth and others beginning in the 1920s
located 81 different sites around the former lakeshore of the Federsee. In later

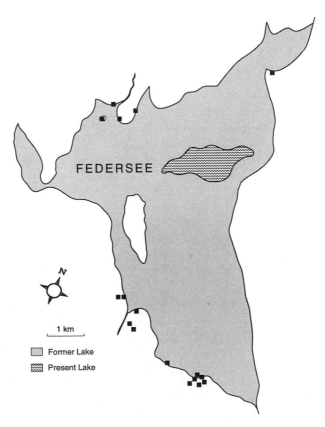

Figure 26. Early Mesolithic sites on the Federsee.

years this number was increased to over 100. Many of these produced only a few flakes and so could not be definitely attributed to the Mesolithic. Taute reviewed the existing collections in the early 1970s and found 17 definite Early Mesolithic sites, representing all three stages of the Beuronien (Taute, personal communication). Schmitt's (1984) later review of the material in the possession of four collectors produced a map of 43 Mesolithic sites or concentrations, representing only those that yielded more than ten artifacts per episode of field-walking. Subsequent work by Wagner (1975) and Eberhardt et al. (1987) documented additional finds at a number of the richer surface sites, many of which have diameters of 50–100 meters.

Several patterns have emerged from this research. First, most known sites contain a mixture of materials, not only of different stages of the Early Mesolithic but also frequently of the Late Palaeolithic and more rarely of the Late Mesolithic and Neolithic. It is clear that certain locations were repeatedly sought out and occupied. Second, the dominant stone raw materials derive largely from local outcrops and gravels, but assemblages frequently include substantial amounts of cherts from the Alb to the north, suggesting that groups were using both areas in their patterns of movement across the landscape. Third, the richest sites tend to be concentrated on certain areas of the lakeshore. These include the Aichbühler Bucht in the southeast, the southwest near Henauhof, the northwest by Moosburg, and the north by Seekirch. All of these areas share certain traits: their shorelines are convoluted with bays and peninsulas, they are the locations of inlet or outlet streams, and they are somewhat sheltered from the sweep of the dominant westerly winds across the lake. Such locations would probably have offered easy access to a variety of plant and animal resources, including excellent fishing in shallow water and around stream mouths, and would have been protected from the wind's full force during storms.

Several excavations augment our knowledge of sites in this area. In addition to the levels of Beuronien A/B and C at *Henauhof Nordwest* (see Chapter 8), a small excavation at *Taubried* in the southern lake basin away from the solid shore produced Early Mesolithic materials (Schlichtherle, 1980). Sealed in the lake deposits was an assemblage of a few microliths, a sharpened wooden spear, and many cracked hazelnut shells. Two radiocarbon dates on sediments (9370 ± 80, 9300 ± 80 b.p.) confirm the typological attribution of the microliths to the Beuronien A. The "spear," however, has recently been dated directly to the later Neolithic, and has been reinterpreted as a stake for a stationary net (Schlichtherle, 1996). The presence of these finds so far out from the solid shore documents the frequent shifts in water level during the Mesolithic and especially the low water phase of the Preboreal period. A brief, possibly fall camp on a temporary shoreline has been suggested to account for these finds.

During the excavation of the Bronze Age site of *Siedlung Forschner*, in the southern part of the old lake basin, some finds were made in sediments palynologically dated to the early Boreal period, contemporary with the Beuronien A/ B (Torke, 1993). These finds consist of the bones of a pike weighing 4–5 kilograms together with the remains of a smaller fish (1.4 kilograms) and a smooth bone point. The point was sharpened at one end and measured 6.7 cm long. These finds have been interpreted as the remains of line fishing using the point as a hook and the small fish as bait for the pike. A similar use might be proposed for at least some of the bone points found at Henauhof Northwest.

One other isolated find related to fishing was reported by Wall (1961). In otherwise fine-grained sediments dating to the Boreal were found wood, bone, and stones that may have been brought in by humans. Among the finds were a two-meter long smoothed and sharpened hazelwood spear and the remains of two large fish. These were found in a shallow bay behind a low gravel bank. Wall's interpretation of these finds is that fish sought out these protected shallows during spawning, where they could be driven toward a spear-holder with stones and sticks.

Mention has previously been made of the problematic site of *Tannstock*, excavated by Reinerth and reconstructed as having two occupations of small pit dwellings. Surface material from this sites comes from all periods of the Mesolithic as well as the Late Palaeolithic and Neolithic. Charcoal analyses pose problems for a Mesolithic dating of the pits, as the dominant species (ash and others) are quite different from the pollen evidence. Furthermore, as mentioned earlier, it is now considered likely that the "hut depressions" are the remains of tree falls. Unfortunately, this site was never fully published, so that a new assessment of the finds has not been possible. Mention was made of organic finds, including a bone point and faunal materials, in preliminary publications (Reinerth, 1929; Bertsch, 1931).

Other excavations were also carried out at the Federsee in the 1920s and 1930s, but they are equally poorly documented. Bertsch (1931) mentions remains of plants, animals, stone tools, and an antler axe from the lake sediments downslope from Site 3 by Moosburg, but little more is known and the upslope surface site contains material from both the Neolithic and Mesolithic.

Other, smaller lakes in Oberschwaben were also used during the Early Mesolithic, including both Badsee and Obersee in the southeastern part of the region (Fig. 27). The sites here are smaller (ca. 30 meters in diameter) and produced generally fewer artifacts than many of the Federsee sites, suggesting perhaps fewer occupations or smaller groups. One site on Obersee was reported to have had a small hut depression with a hearth (Reinerth, 1956). The assemblages of these sites are dominated by local radiolarite, but also contain considerable amounts of Jurassic cherts from the Alb.

Riverine settings were also occupied during the Early Mesolithic, as witnessed by finds from the Aitrach Valley (Reinerth, 1956). Here, in contrast to the patterns in the Neckar drainage, the sites are situated low in the valley on

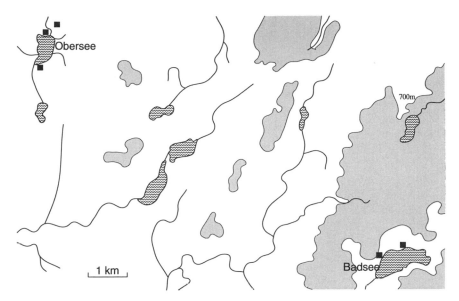

Figure 27. Early Mesolithic sites on the Badsee and Obersee.

slight rises and low terraces (Fig. 28). These sites are also smaller (diameter of 40 meters) than many of those on the Federsee, suggesting less frequent occupation. Microliths form less than 10% of the retouched tools in these collections, which are instead dominated by burins and scrapers. This may be due to the bias toward larger tools in surface collecting, the mixture of materials of different periods, or a functional difference between these sites and the cave and rockshelters where microliths are more common. The assemblages here are also dominated by local radiolarite but contain Jurassic cherts as well.

5.9. LAKE CONSTANCE

This region was heavily occupied during the Early Mesolithic. Reinerth (1953) has published a list of 76 surface lithic scatters attributed to the Mesolithic, discovered by fieldwalking around the shoreline. These are all concentrated around the west end of the lake quite close to the shore, either because investigations were largely confined to this area or because the western region is climatically more favorable, being somewhat warmer and drier than the east. Hahn (1983) notes that the known sites in this area all date to the Early Mesolithic, except for one site that also has a Late Mesolithic component (Schlichtherle, 1994). Many of the sites are located adjacent to inflowing streams or around marshy regions at the extreme west end of the lake (Fig. 29).

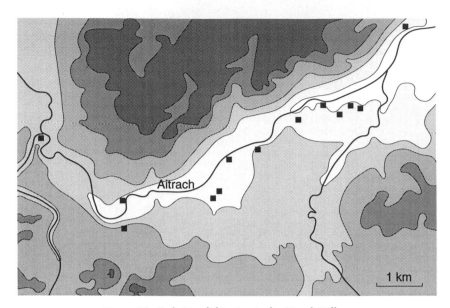

Figure 28. Early Mesolithic sites in the Aitrach Valley.

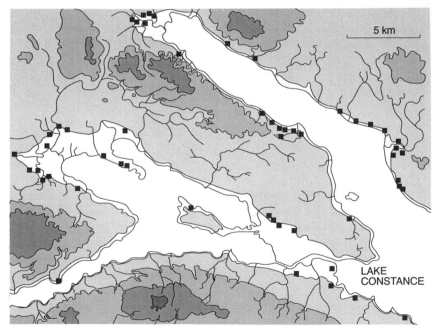

Figure 29. Early Mesolithic sites on Lake Constance.

The chert used in these sites appears to be relatively local, deriving largely from the limestone areas just west of the lake. However, there seems to be a clear pattern of distance decay in the distribution of this material, with sites farthest east, on the center of the north lakeshore, having relatively little of this material. Instead, Jurassic chert from the Alb, up the Schussen Valley to the north, is much more common. In addition, at least one Early Mesolithic site on the lake has a little material from the upper Rhine Valley, approximately 120 kilometers away to the west-southwest (Schlichtherle, 1994). From Reinerth's accounts it seems that microliths occur in relatively low frequencies in these assemblages, similar to those in the Aitrach Valley, but materials of the Neolithic may be mixed in with them, diluting the percentages. Many of the sites around the lake are relatively large, averaging 50 × 100 meters, suggesting repeated visits to favored locations.

Chapter 6

Sites on the Landscape: The Late Mesolithic

6.1. INTRODUCTION

The onset of the Late Mesolithic at around 7800 b.p. witnesses a major technological change in stone tool industries in this area. Extremely regular blades
manufactured by pressure-flaking now dominate assemblages and the heat-
treating of stone raw material declines in importance. Trapezes made from
these regular blades become the most characteristic microlith form, presumably used as transverse arrow points. Their appearance here is part of a conti-
nentwide process of diffusion, suggesting communication networks ultimately
linking most of Europe. Notched blades and long endscrapers occur in increased numbers among the retouched tools. Antler-working, particularly for
the manufacture of barbed harpoons and axes/adzes, assumes great importance. This period ends between 6500 and 6000 b.p., not long after the appearance of agricultural villages in the area.

One of the most curious features of the archaeological record of this region is the scarcity of Late Mesolithic sites in comparison to the Early Mesolithic (Jochim, 1990). In contrast to northern Europe—Sweden, Denmark,
north Germany, and Holland—where abundant Late Mesolithic sites have
been interpreted as reflecting a population increase at this time, southwestern
Germany, together with some adjacent areas, shows a marked decline. Even
taking into account the shorter duration of the Late Mesolithic (ca. 1300
years) in relation to the Early Mesolithic (ca. 2500 years), the relative scarcity
of sites is clear.

A number of different explanations for this paucity of sites has been suggested, including population decline (Taute, 1972/73), increased deposition masking sites (Hahn, 1983), and changes in settlement patterns leading both to the creation of fewer sites and to a shift in their location to areas of greater deposition (Müller-Beck, 1983; Jochim, 1990). The Late Mesolithic does coincide with a climatic change to the warmer and wetter Atlantic period. However, because the decrease in site numbers occurs in all of the subareas of this region, and in the entire variety of topographic situations utilized during the Early Mesolithic, it is difficult to accept that changes in depositional processes alone could be responsible. A fundamental change in population density and/or distribution certainly appears to be indicated for this period. Tables 5 and 6 summarize the sites and faunal assemblages of this period.

6.2. RHINE LOWLANDS

Only seven sites in the northern Rhine lowlands continued to be occupied from the Early into the Late Mesolithic. All of these are located on low dunes in the valley floor (Fig. 30). The hills at the edges of the valley bear no trace of material from this period. Given the small sample size, it is difficult to assess whether this distributional change reflects an alteration of settlement patterns, but this

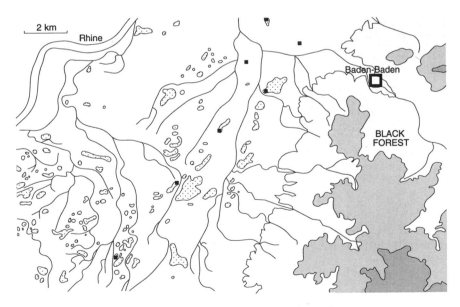

Figure 30. Late Mesolithic sites near Baden-Baden.

Table 5. Late Mesolithic Sites

Region	Sites	Period	Location	Finds
Rhine lowlands				
Baden-Baden area	7 surface sites	Mixed with Early Mesolithic	Sand dunes	1–940 artifacts
Freiburg area	1 surface site	Mixed with Palaeolithic and Early Mesolithic	Hillflank	1–600+ artifacts
Basel area	Isteiner Klotz cave	Mixed with Palaeolithic and Early Mesolithic	Hillflank	1150 artifacts, bones
Rhine Valley	2 surface sites	Mixed with Early Mesolithic	Valley floor	Varied assemblage sizes
Neckar Valley	Rosi III	Late Mesolithic only	Valley floor	Artifacts, hearths
Eastern Black Forest	None known			
Alpine foothills	None known			
Swabian Alb	Jagerhaushohle cave	Levels 7–6: Late Mesolithic	Hillflank	186–1424 artifacts per level, bones
	Bernaufels cave	Late Mesolithic	Hillflank	
	Teufelsloch cave	Late Mesolithic	Hillflank	
	Falkensteinhohle cave	Late Mesolithic	Hillflank	Artifacts, bones, shellfish, nuts
	Dietfurt cave	Level 9/10: Late Mesolithic?	Rock outcrop in valley	Artifacts
	Inzigkofen rockshelter	Late Mesolithic	Valley edge	271+ artifacts, bones, shellfish
	Lautereck rockshelter	End-Mesolithic	Valley edge	Small assemblage, bones
	Schuntershohle cave	Level 3: Late Mesolithic?	Valley edge	Few artifacts
Oberschwaben				
Federsee	Various surface sites	Often mixed with Early Mesolithic	Lakeshore	Varied assemblage sizes
	Henauhof Nordwest	Level 3: Late Mesolithic	Lakeshore	See Chapter 8
	Henauhof Nordwest 2	Late Mesolithic	Lakeshore	See Chapter 12
	Henauhof Nord 1	Late Mesolithic	Lakeshore	Artifacts, hearths
	Henauhof Nord II	Late Mesolithic	Lakeshore	Artifacts, hearths, bones, bark floor
Lake Constance	Bo 69	Late Mesolithic	Lakeshore	Artifacts

Table 6. Late Mesolithic Fauna

Resource	Hen.				Rosi III/2	Jag.		Falk.		Inz.		Lautereck
	NW/3	W	NW 2	N II		7	6	Mid 1/3	Up 1/3	Mid 1/3	Up 1/3	
Red deer	X	X	X	X	X	X	X	X	X	X	X	X
Roe deer	X		X	X	X	X	X	X	X	X	X	X
Boar	X	X	X	X	X	X	X	X	X	X	X	X
Aurochs	X	X	X		X			(X)	(X)			
Moose	X											
Horse	X											
Chamois						X	X					
Bear								(X)	(X)			
Beaver	X	X				X		X		X	X	X
Hare						X	X	X				
Badger	X					X					X	X
Otter						X						X
Wolf/dog	X			X								X
Fox						X			X		X	X
Wildcat	X					X				X	X	X
Marten	X					X	X	X	X	X	X	X
Weasel											X	
Fish	X	X	X			X	X	X	X	X	X	X
Shellfish						X		(X)	(X)	X	X	
Birds	X	X	X			X	X			X	X	X

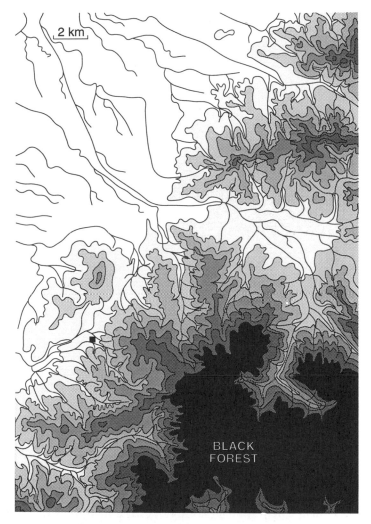

Figure 31. Late Mesolithic sites near Freiburg.

same change is seen elsewhere as well. As each site has an assemblage of materials from both periods of the Mesolithic, little can be said about their content, except that all have a diverse collection of tool and debitage types.

Similarly, in the area around Freiburg to the south, only one site has Late Mesolithic materials, and these are mixed with those of the Early Mesolithic and Late Palaeolithic (Fig. 31). This site lies on the low hill flanks along a stream as it exits the Black Forest. Farther south, only the cave of Isteiner Klotz

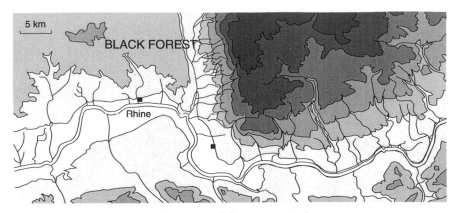

Figure 32. Late Mesolithic sites near Säckingen.

was possibly occupied in the Late Mesolithic, and this site too contains materials of the earlier two periods.

6.3. RHINE VALLEY

Finally, in the region around Säckingen only 2 Late Mesolithic sites are known, compared to 16 for the Early Mesolithic (Fig. 32). These 2 sites also contain Early Mesolithic materials and both are situated close to the river along the edge of the valley floor. Here, too, the adjacent hills appear to have been unoccupied.

6.4. NECKAR DRAINAGE

In contrast to the abundance of Early Mesolithic sites in this area, there is only one known site of the Late Mesolithic (Hahn, 1983; Kind, 1995). As most of the earlier sites were in upland locations, this lack of sites may reflect largely an abandonment of these higher elevation portions of the region.

The single known Late Mesolithic site is *Rosi III*, an open-air site in the alluvium of the Neckar Valley. The upper of the major levels of this site (Level II) has trapezoidal microliths characteristic of the Late Mesolithic and one radiocarbon date of 6845 ± 80 b.p. This level appears to have been completely excavated and consists of three hearths with concentrations of lithic material. Eight different nodules of chert have been identified by refitting: five of local material from the Neckar gravels and three deriving from the Alb to the south. All stages of reduction, from cortex flakes to finished tools, are represented by these nodules. In addition, some finished tools of other Jurassic cherts were brought to the site and discarded. Identified faunal remains include red and roe deer, boar, and aurochs.

6.5. BLACK FOREST

The area around the Nagold on the eastern edge of the Black Forest contains no known Late Mesolithic sites, in contrast to the 12 Early Mesolithic sites reported there. As was true along the western flank facing the Rhine, these upland areas appear to have been abandoned.

6.6. ALPINE FOOTHILLS

This is another area that lacks Late Mesolithic sites, although earlier materials were reported at least around the upper Iller River.

6.7. SWABIAN ALB

The Alb has a number of informative sites from this period, although far fewer than for the preceding Early Mesolithic. Noteworthy is the concentration of these sites largely in the western Alb along the upper reaches of the Danube. Despite considerable research, the central portion of the Alb has produced only one site with possible Late Mesolithic materials and the eastern Alb has none (Fig. 33).

Jägerhaushöhle (Fig. 33, No. 1) has two levels (7 and 6) of Late Mesolithic stratified above the earlier materials (Taute, 1978). One radiocarbon date of 7880 ± 120 b.p. was obtained from Level 7, which places it at the beginning of the Late Mesolithic. Pollen samples from these levels record much higher proportions of oak and other deciduous trees in comparison to earlier levels, and pine no longer occurs among the charcoal (Schweingruber, 1978).

The lithic assemblage of Level 7 contains 1424 artifacts, while that of Level 6 has only 186. In each, cores represent approximately 1% of the assemblage and retouched tools range from 4% (Level 7) to 13% (Level 6). Microliths play a small role in these assemblages, which instead are dominated by scrapers and various retouched blades. Burins are absent. Taute notes that the blades, especially in Level 6, are larger and much more regular than those of earlier levels and that the cores mirror this pattern.

In both levels, large mammals clearly dominate the identified bones, forming 78% of those in Level 7 and 95% of those in Level 6. These include

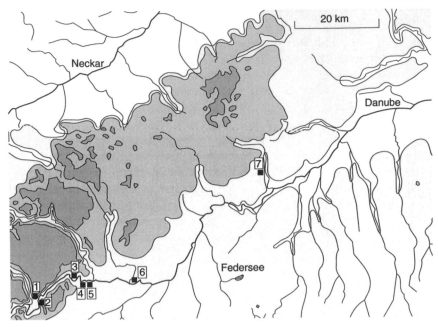

Figure 33. Late Mesolithic sites in the Swabian Alb.

chamois in both levels, which are the only reported chamois in the Mesolithic
in this area. They were probably winter visitors to the region, spending summers in the Alps and possibly the Black Forest (Boessneck, 1978a).

Other finds in Level 7 include a perforated deer incisor and a perforated
fossil shell (from the Steinheim Basin, about 100 kilometers to the northeast), a
fragmentary barbed antler harpoon, fragments of a bone point and other tools,
worked boar's tusk, two fragments of a polished stone axe (an artifact normally
associated with the Neolithic) and various hammerstones. Level 6 had one piece
of worked antler, as well as a concentration of pollen of round-leafed sorrel.

Bernaufels Cave and *Teufelsloch Cave* (Fig. 33, No. 2), also in the upper
Danube, appear to have had Late Mesolithic occupations, but all that is known
today is that Bernaufels contained a barbed antler harpoon.

Falkensteinhöhle (Fig. 33, No. 3) contained Late Mesolithic material that,
as mentioned earlier, Peters did not clearly distinguish from that of the Beuronien C. Taute's arbitrary upper third level, as well as possibly the middle third,
appear to be largely Late Mesolithic in age. These two levels have radiocarbon
dates of 7540 ± 120 and 7820 ± 120 b.p., respectively.

Taute's small lithic collections from the two levels contained few retouched pieces, but the large original assemblage from Peters's excavation produced approximately 9% retouched tools including roughly equal proportions

of microliths, scrapers, and retouched blades, together with burins, notched pieces, and other forms. Cores made up about 3% of that assemblage.

Taute's excavation produced a total of 610 bones in these two levels, of which approximately 38% could be identified. Large mammals, including boar, roe deer, and red deer, dominate these assemblages, constituting 65% by number of the upper third and 75% of the middle third levels. The remains from Peters's excavation of all levels contained a smaller percentage (51%) of large mammals but included the additional species of aurochs and bear. Small mammals comprise from 9% to 24% of Taute's assemblages (32% of Peters's), while fish range from 12% to 16% of the collections (17% of Peters's). Birds were not found by Taute, but Peters's collection contained one bird bone. Taute reported charred hazelnuts from the middle third level and Peters's excavation produced both hazelnuts and shellfish.

Perhaps the most outstanding feature of this site is its richness in other types of artifacts and ornaments. Peters found four complete or fragmentary barbed antler harpoons, two antler sleeves, numerous pieces of worked antler, bone awls, fragments of worked bone and boar's tusk, red ochre and stones bearing this pigment, a partially polished stone axe hafted in an antler sleeve (this was in the upper portion of the Mesolithic level), and 14 perforated shells and teeth. In his upper third level, Taute found fragments of worked antler, bone, and boar's tusk, and in the middle third, fragments of a decorated antler tool and worked bone. The shell ornaments, which probably date to the Late Mesolithic, have been traced to the Mainz Basin, 200 kilometers to the northwest, and the Mediterranean, probably transported via the Rhone over a distance of about 600 kilometers.

Dietfurt Cave (Fig. 33, No. 4) may have Late Mesolithic materials in the form of a trapeze and regular blades, but as these are mixed with Neolithic artifacts in Level 9/10 they could represent Neolithic finds as well.

Inzigkofen (Fig. 33, No. 5), like Falkensteinhöhle, has a rich Late Mesolithic that was originally not distinguished from materials of the Beuronien C by Peters. Again, Taute's upper two levels, which most likely represent Late Mesolithic occupations, will be focused on here. One radiocarbon date of 7770 ± 120 b.p. is available from the upper third level.

Among the 271 stone artifacts of the upper third level, 11% are retouched tools, which are dominated by scrapers and retouched blades. Only one microlith occurs in this level. The middle third level has an assemblage of 124 artifacts, of which 15% are retouched, but includes no microliths (although three microburins testify to their manufacture). Peters's larger collection, which included triangular and trapezoidal microliths, has been lost.

The faunal assemblages of the two levels are both dominated by large mammals, which make up 71% of the identified bones from the middle third and 81% of those from the upper third. Small mammals comprise 9–10% of the collections, fish 8–12%, and birds (both waterfowl and terrestrial game birds) 2–7%. Shellfish were found in both levels as well.

Peters reports only one perforated red deer incisor, but Taute's excavations produced a number of other artifacts as well. In the upper third level he found two barbed antler harpoons, one bone point, one perforated fox tooth, fragments of worked bone and antler, a sandstone hammerstone, and a sandstone chopping tool. The middle third level contained a fragment of worked antler and a worked boar's tusk.

Lautereck (Fig. 33, No. 6) is a small rockshelter situated low in the valley of a tributary stream where it enters the Danube (Taute, 1967a). Level E contains a Late Mesolithic (or "End-Mesolithisch") occupation with one radiocarbon date of 6440 ± 45 b.p., making it considerably later than the sites previously discussed. The small assemblage contains only one microlith and one macrolithic point, together with scrapers, retouched blades, and notched pieces. The blades are extremely regular and conform to the general technological patterns of the Late Mesolithic.

The faunal assemblage is dominated by fish bones, which make up 85% of the 830 identified bones. Large and small mammals make up 7–8% each of the assemblage and include a variety of species. Birds represent only 1% of the collection. Roe deer remains include all body parts, and the boar include one adult and one juvenile. The fish remains have been interpreted as representing largely spring catches (Lepiksaar, 1978). Additional finds include three bone points, one bone pendant, and one piece of worked boar's tusk.

Schuntershöhle, Level 3 (Fig. 33, No. 7) appears to contain a mixture of materials from both the Early and Late Mesolithic (Taute, 1978). However, the Late Mesolithic component appears to be minor, and is represented by only a few regular blades.

6.8. OBERSCHWABEN

In addition to the Late Mesolithic levels of Henauhof Nordwest, Henauhof West, and Henauhof Nordwest 2, excavations at two other sites in the Federsee have produced Late Mesolithic materials. Both were found during tests prior to the construction of a road and both occur in the southwestern basin, close to the Henauhof peninsula (Fig. 34).

Henauhof Nord I is located on a temporary shoreline of the Federsee, sealed in peat that has been palynologically dated to the Early Atlantic period (Schlichtherle, 1988). Together with a radiocarbon date of 7370 ± 55 b.p., this places it firmly within the Late Mesolithic. Excavations covering 181 square meters revealed a site poor in artifacts but rich in features.

The site has numerous concentrations of charcoal and burned rock, in places associated with thin layers of clay, which have been interpreted as short-

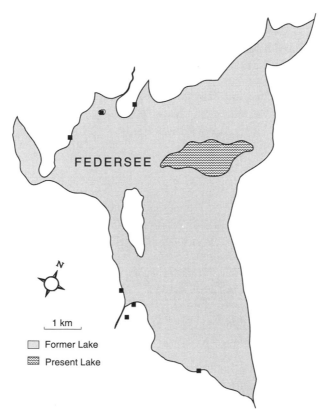

Figure 34. Late Mesolithic sites on the Federsee.

term hearths. There are also clusters of fire-cracked rock without associated charcoal, perhaps representing discarded heating stones. One additional hearth consisted of a flat piece of wood, 30–50 cm in diameter, covered with a 2–3 cm layer of clay and much charcoal.

Only eight stone artifacts were found, including six flakes, a core and a core-rejuvenation flake. Two pieces of wood were apparently worked, as they bear chopping marks. No bones were preserved. On the basis of indirect evidence, this site has been interpreted as a short-term summer fishing camp. The evidence includes the lack of charred hazelnuts despite good preservation, suggesting that it was not a fall occupation and that the normal spring high water may have precluded occupation of these marshy shores in that season.

Henauhof Nord II is located in the peat approximately 150 meters away from Henauhof Nord I (Kind, 1992). Excavations of over 280 square meters revealed an area of finds measuring 37 by 4–6 meters along a temporary shoreline. In one area a layer of birch bark measuring 2 × 1 meters, partially covered with a thin clay layer, was found, which may represent an activity or hut area created on the marshy ground. Four other patches of clay up to 70 cm in diameter were also found. Seven simple hearths consisted of 1–2 cm thick layers of ash and charcoal with diameters of 40–60 cm. In addition, the site contained many stones, some bearing heat traces, both scattered and in small clusters, that may represent heating stones.

A total of 450 stone artifacts were found, consisting primarily of highly regular blades together with three trapezoidal microliths and several other retouched tools. Most of the raw material is white chert from the Alb or Danube gravels, but no cores of this material were found, suggesting that the blades were produced elsewhere and brought in. One core and a few flakes of local radiolarite were also found.

Although bones were poorly preserved, some mammals could be identified. An additional find is a roll of birch bark filled with clay and gravel, which may be a net weight for fishing.

This site has been interpreted as a small, short-term camp with several reoccupations aimed at fishing and hunting. Given the activities represented and the lack of charred hazelnuts, the excavators suggest occupations in spring and summer. Examination of several branches of hazel from the site indicate that they were cut in spring.

Late Mesolithic materials are also represented among the surface finds around the former shoreline, but not nearly as frequently as those of the Early Mesolithic. Taute's examination of materials produced only six sites that definitely had Late Mesolithic occupations (Taute, personal communication), and these are concentrated largely in the northwestern and southwestern parts of the lake basin. Collections of over 5500 artifacts from surface sites around the Aichbühler Bucht in the southeast contained abundant Early Mesolithic material but none of the Late Mesolithic.

Elsewhere in Oberschwaben Late Mesolithic finds are also scarce. The Aitrach Valley and the lakes of Obersee and Badsee, for example, contain no materials from this period, although they did have Early Mesolithic finds.

6.9. LAKE CONSTANCE

Despite the intensity of fieldwalking, at least around the western shore, few Late Mesolithic sites have been located in this area. A favored region during the Early Mesolithic, it appears to have been practically abandoned during the Late Mesolithic, with only one site, Bo 69 near Fischbach, reported to have Late Mesolithic materials (Schlichtherle, 1994).

Chapter 7

Sites on the Landscape: Survey

7.1. INTRODUCTION

It is inevitable that my views of the late glacial and early postglacial prehistoric landscape be colored by my own fieldwork in this area. Consequently, it makes sense to describe this work and its findings in some detail in the next chapters. Between 1980 and 1991, I carried out surveys and excavations in the Federsee region, initially designed to test the predictions of my original model, but gradually evolving as new questions emerged. The focus on this prehistoric lake, now a peat bog, was dictated by four considerations: (1) the peat held the potential for excellent organic preservation, so crucial to questions about prehistoric subsistence economies; (2) no Mesolithic sites had been excavated and published for this area, despite the abundance of known surface lithic scatters around the former lake edges; (3) my original interpretative model suggested a definite seasonal role for sites on the Federsee (summer residential camps) but lacked data to test this proposition; and (4) the extensive studies of Neolithic and Bronze Age sites being carried out by German archaeologists promised not only a wealth of complementary data but also an active and enjoyable cooperative environment.

In order to facilitate finding buried materials, survey areas were situated just inside the former lakeshore, downslope from five higher, known Mesolithic surface sites on the solid ground (Fig. 35). Materials from shoreline occupations could have become sealed in the peat deposits by three possible means. Assuming that the focus of occupation was on the high ground, materials might have been purposefully discarded into the lake. Alternatively, materials may have eroded downslope after the occupation and become buried in the lake de-

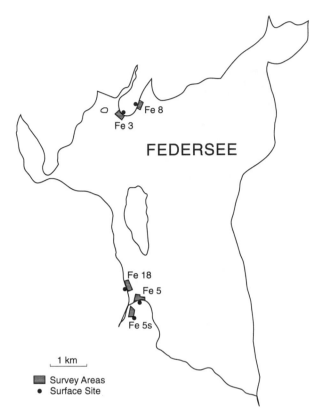

Figure 35. Survey areas on the Federsee.

posits. A third possibility is that the occupation itself may have shifted downs-lope in times of low water level, leaving remains to become sealed in lake sediments with subsequent rises in the water level. In all cases such remains could provide valuable insight into Mesolithic activities on the shore.

The survey involved the use of hand- and power-augers together with the excavation of a number of test trenches, allowing a definition of stratigraphic relationships and a sampling of subsurface deposits. Over 700 meters of former lakeshore, with a total areal coverage of approximately 30,000 m^2, have been investigated.

7.2. SITE FE-3

Site Fe-3 is located in the northwestern portion of the Federsee basin. The surface site, discovered by Reinerth (1929), lies in an agricultural field on the

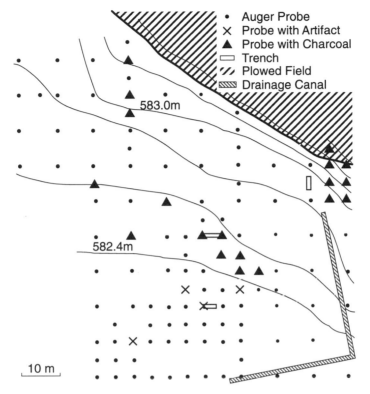

• Auger Probe
× Probe with Artifact
▲ Probe with Charcoal
▢ Trench
⁄⁄⁄ Plowed Field
▨ Drainage Canal

583.0m

582.4m

10 m

Figure 36. Site Fe-3.

southwestern slope of a peninsula jutting southward into the former lake. This site is one of many surrounding a small, protected bay adjacent to a stream outlet and appears to have offered good fishing opportunities. The number and type of finds collected from the site over the years is unknown, but include materials characteristic of the Early Mesolithic Beuronien (Taute, personal communication).

An area of 5600 m² in the meadow extending southwest from the solid shoreline was selected for investigation. The modern surface topography slopes gradually to the southwest from the somewhat steeper shoreline (Fig. 36). A total of 128 probes was made using a 6 cm diameter barrel auger. These probes were spaced 5 or 10 meters apart in a grid pattern. For each probe records were made of the type and depth of sediments encountered as well as of any finds of archaeological materials.

The general stratigraphic sequence throughout the area consists of inorganic deposits—sand, gravel, clay, or a mixture of these—underlying a peaty

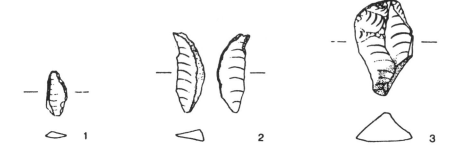

Figure 37. Artifacts from the survey: 1—microlith; 2—backed knife; 3—scraper.

topsoil. On the basis of the auger sampling, it was possible to record the surface of these buried mineral deposits, which is more complicated than that of the modern surface, showing a raised sand ridge separated from the shoreline by a narrow channel. Underlying the inorganic deposits of this channel in the northwestern part of the study area is a layer of peat extending beyond the 120 cm depth reached by the auger. The extent of this peat is unknown, as it was impossible to penetrate the gravels and sands to the full length of the auger in many of the probes.

Four of the auger tests produced chert artifacts on or in the sand sediments, all in the southern, downslope portion of the study area (Fig. 37). Three of these artifacts are small flakes (maximum length = 1.40 cm); the fourth is a microlith that suggests a chronological classification of the Early Mesolithic for these finds.

Many of the auger probes contained evidence of large amounts of charcoal in the sand deposits. The horizontal distribution of the charcoal suggests three areas of concentration: two in the upslope regions and one downslope between the shoreline and the area of lithic finds.

In order to explore the area further, three test trenches were excavated. Trench I was 5 meters long in an east-west direction and 50 cm wide and was located in the downslope area of charcoal concentration. The profile of its north wall illustrates the stratigraphic sequence: below the topsoil is a thin layer of sand with dense concentrations of charcoal, followed by sand and then gravel. Despite the charcoal accumulation in a discrete level, no artifacts were found in this trench.

Trench II, measuring 3 meters by 50 cm, was excavated in an east-west orientation farther downslope, adjacent to the area where lithic artifacts were found. The stratigraphic sequence here is somewhat more complex. Stratified within the peaty topsoil is a thin layer of yellow clay, gravel, and brick fragments, apparently representing a historic deposit from the hillslope. Below the peaty topsoil is a sequence of sand and gravel similar to that of Trench I. Trench II yielded no charcoal, but three chert artifacts were found in the sand: two flakes (maximum length = 2.58 cm) and a naturally backed blade showing both retouch and utilization.

Trench III, 2.5 meters by 50 cm, was excavated in a north-south direction in the upslope portion of the study area, adjacent to one of the charcoal concentrations. The stratigraphy shows sand and gravel underlying the peaty topsoil, with the sand content decreasing and the gravel content increasing toward the downslope end of the trench. No artifacts were found in this trench, and surprisingly, no charcoal was found either, suggesting a discrete boundary to the nearby charcoal concentration identified with the auger.

The work at site Fe-3 produced some understanding of the subsurface structure of deposits as well as limited evidence of Mesolithic occupational debris. Additional work in areas adjoining this study area may prove valuable in the future.

7.3. SITE FE-8

Site Fe-8 is also located in the northwestern region of the Federsee. Situated in a field on the eastern edge of the same peninsula as site Fe-3, site Fe-8 faces the open water of the main part of the lake. Also heavily collected since its discovery (Reinerth, 1929), the surface site has yielded artifacts characteristic of the Late Palaeolithic, Beuronien B, Late Mesolithic, and Neolithic (Taute, personal communication).

A rectangular area of 3200 m² adjacent to the shoreline was selected for investigation. The surface topography is one of a gentle slope eastward from an abrupt and very steep shoreline (Fig. 38). A 6 cm diameter barrel auger was used to make 37 probes spaced on a 10-meter grid. The subsurface stratigraphy as revealed by these samples is relatively straightforward. The highest shore regions, in the northwest and southwest of the study area, show topsoil overlying clays. The majority of the probes, covering those portions of the area farthest downslope, produced only humified peat. In a thin band parallel to the shore, just downslope from the solid shoreline, there occur deeply buried sand or sandy peat deposits underneath the peat.

As the probes produced no archaeological materials, only one trench was excavated perpendicular to the steep portion of the shoreline at its downslope edge. As the north wall profile of this trench shows, under the peaty topsoil is a dark gray clay with some charcoal, overlying a brown sandy peat. At the upslope end of the trench this sandy peat is significantly disturbed and mixed with the overlying clay sediments. It appears that the shoreline transitional deposits

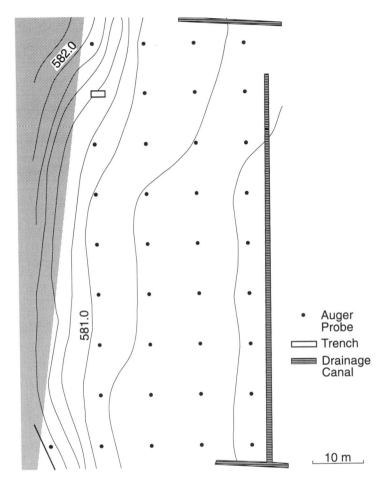

582.0

581.0

• Auger
    Probe
▭ Trench
▤ Drainage
    Canal

⌐ 10 m ⌐

Figure 38. Site Fe-8.

in this area have been disturbed by modern activities and subsequently covered with clayey fill. Three chert flakes were found in the trench, two in the topsoil, and one in the dark clay layer.

It was later learned from a nearby resident that archaeological excavations were carried out in this general area in the 1930s. The disturbed sediments, as well as the extremely steep shoreline slope, may reflect these earlier excavations. It is interesting in this connection that Bertsch (1931) refers to the occurrence of archaeological finds from site Fe-8, including many organic materials, in the lake sediments, an apparent reference to excavations by Reinerth conducted at this location. Unfortunately, the results of these excavations have not been published.

7.4. SITE FE-18

Site Fe-18, "Tannstock," is located in the southwestern portion of the Federsee on a small clay prominence projecting eastward into the lake basin. This is one of the richest sites discovered by Reinerth and has produced finds of the Late Palaeolithic, all phases of the Mesolithic, and the Neolithic (Taute, personal communication). Reinerth (1929) conducted excavations at this site and reported finding Mesolithic hut depressions, hearths, numerous lithic arti-facts, ceramics, and one smooth bone point. The exact context of these finds remains uncertain, as they have never been fully published, but several prob-lems are evident. The association of ceramics with the finds casts doubt on the purely Mesolithic affiliation. The placement of hearths against what are sup-posed to have been flammable brush walls appears unlikely, and it may be, in fact, that the oval "hut depressions" represent tree falls, an interpretation that would account for the mixing of chronologically different materials.

Because of its controversial interpretation, as well as the richness of its surface finds, site Fe-18 was selected for downslope investigation. Two factors were recognized at the outset, however, that posed potential stratigraphic prob-lems in the downslope area. First of all, the precise locations of Reinerth's ex-cavations are not known. Although he clearly concentrated on the high area of the prominence, the extent of his penetration into the lacustrine sediments is unknown. Even if his excavations were confined solely to the high ground, his backfill may have been partially dispersed over the lake deposits. Secondly, one of the many beach ridges or "dam-ways" known for the Federsee runs just east of the site parallel to the shoreline (Reinerth, 1929: 54). These ridges, at least some of which date to Mesolithic or Late Palaeolithic times, have been various-ly interpreted as natural beach deposits (Paret, 1951; Wall, 1961) and man-made dams and trackways (Reinerth, 1929; Göttlich, 1965). In all cases inves-tigated, they consist of sand and gravel overlying peaty sediments of the lake, and whether natural or man-made, they represent considerable disturbance to the shoreline sedimentary processes.

A rectangular study area of approximately 10,800 m^2 just east of the site was selected for investigation. A 20 cm diameter screw auger and a 6 cm diam-eter barrel auger were used to sample the sediments at 5 or 10 meter intervals with a total of 236 auger probes (Fig. 39). The surface topography shows a gen-tle slope to the east-northeast from a steep ridge in the southwest of the study area. This ridge runs from a high prominence on the west in a south-southeast-erly direction. This prominence and ridge are composed of dark gravelly clay

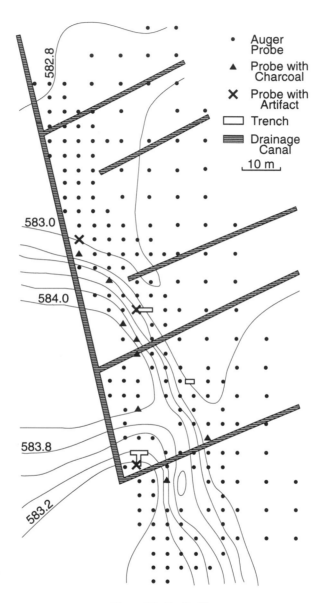

Figure 39. Site Fe-18.

down to the 120 cm limits of the auger, but at the edges this clay extends out over peaty deposits and becomes thinner, disappearing about 10 to 15 meters downslope. The rest of the study area shows only organic deposits down to 120 cm: a dark peaty soil overlying brown peat with many wood inclusions. The shape of the ridge suggests its identification as part of the "dam-way," but its composition—clays with no sand—is in accord with its interpretation as an extension of the prominence of the solid shore. The role of earlier excavations and backfilling in extending the distribution of these clay sediments is unknown.

Three of the auger probes contained archaeological materials. An endscraper of white chert was found just north of the ridge in the peat below the clay. South of the ridge three fragments of red deer metatarsal were found also in the peat beneath the clay. Finally, a small chert flake was found in the peat east of the ridge just beyond the clay distribution.

In order to explore this area further, a number of trenches and squares were excavated. All of them were placed in areas where the clay overlies peaty sediments. Three 1-meter squares in the region where the endscraper was found produced one chert flake and three pieces of large mammal bone, including a rib fragment. These occurred in peat beneath the clay, about 4 cm below several modern pottery sherds.

Two intersecting 2.5 by 1 meter trenches were excavated near the finds of red deer bones. These trenches produced only a red deer phalanx and a fragment of large mammal bone, both from the peat beneath the clay. A 5 by 1 meter trench in the downslope edge of the ridge yielded one irregular chert blade, one possibly worked quartzite piece, a tooth and part of a phalanx of wild boar, together with an upright piece of unworked wood 37 cm long and 8 cm in diameter. These were all in the peat beneath the clay. Finally, a 2.5 by 1 meter trench located to the southeast of the 5-meter trench produced no finds.

In addition to illuminating stratigraphic relationships beneath the surface, the work at Tannstock demonstrates that materials are to be found in the peaty sediments. The extremely low density of these finds and their stratigraphic proximity in some cases to modern materials indicated that further investigations were not warranted at the time.

7.5. SITE FE-5S

Site Fe-5s is located in the southwestern Federsee basin on the western edge of a peninsula jutting northward into the former lake. The surface site has produced artifacts characteristic of the Beuronien B and Late Mesolithic (Taute, personal communication). Its location adjacent to a former stream inlet suggests that it might have offered good subsistence opportunities in Mesolithic times.

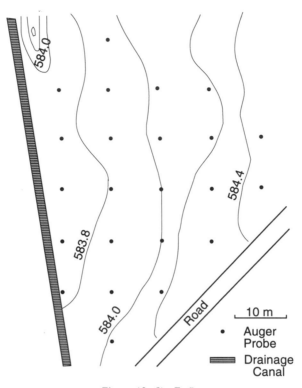

Figure 40. Site Fe-5s.

A 4600 m² area was delineated and tested with both the 20 cm and 6 cm diameter augers (Fig. 40). All of the samples contained only clay, a result consistent with the higher elevation (583.7–584.4 m) of this study area in relation to others tested. Lake deposits are to be expected farther to the west and north of this area. Despite the richness of the surface site upslope, the auger tests revealed neither artifacts nor charcoal in these clay deposits.

7.6. SITE FE-5

Site Fe-5, "Henauhof," is situated on the northern end of the same peninsula projecting northward in the southwestern portion of the Federsee. This large surface site has produced finds from the Late Palaeolithic, Mesolithic, and Neolithic (Taute, personal communication). Its richness and location suggested great potential and so a downslope study area of approximately 4000 m² was

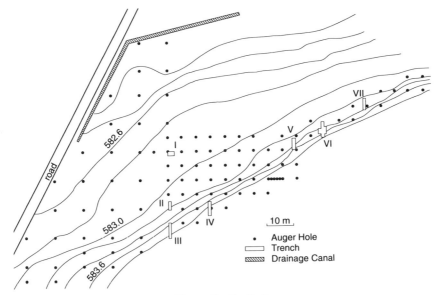

Figure 41. Site Fe-5.

surveyed. Both the 20 cm and 6 cm diameter augers were used to excavate 114 samples (Fig. 41).

The surface topography reveals a gentle slope to the northwest from the former shoreline, which is particularly steep in the southeastern portion of the study area. The subsurface topography is similar, composed of gravelly clays of the hillslope extending northward somewhat over the lake sediments, which consist of peat overlying sands in the nearshore area and solely of peat farther lakeward.

Three of the auger probes produced a total of five finds. A small microblade was found in the peat near the shoreline in about the center of the study area. Approximately 25 meters lakeward from this find one probe produced a bird vertebra and another probe, 5 meters away, contained a bovid mandible fragment, a large mammal vertebral fragment, and a perforated piece of bark. All of these finds were deep in the peat.

Seven trenches were excavated, mostly concentrated on the former shoreline zone. Trench I, farthest out in the peat near the auger finds, proved to have much wood and bark but no archaeological materials. Trench II, to the south, also showed only peat and produced only a tooth of a very large mammal (cow?) associated with modern glass in the top 20 cm. Trench III was located just south of Trench II, intersecting the clays of the old shoreline, and contained one bovid tooth in the peat and a layer of charcoal in the clay. Trench IV also intersected the shoreline 15 meters to the east and produced one flake in the topsoil. To the east another 25 meters, Trench V cut across the old shoreline and showed a more complex stratigraphy of clays, peat, and sand. This trench yielded 48 finds of bone and chert from both the clay and peat. The lithic artifacts included blades, flakes, one core, one microlith, and one retouched blade. The bones included those of large and small mammals and fish. Trench VI was 10 meters farther east and contained 160 finds of bone, ceramics, and chert in the peat and clay. The lithic artifacts included microliths, burins, scrapers, cores, flakes, and blades. Among the faunal materials were bones and antler of red deer and a variety of other large and small mammals and fish. The ceramics were mostly crude, undecorated body sherds but included a rim sherd suggesting affiliation with the Aichbühl Neolithic Culture. All of these finds will be discussed more fully later. Finally, Trench VII, located 15 meters farther east, also intersected the shoreline, but produced only three artifacts—a flake, a microblade, and a small mammal bone.

Of all the sites investigated, site Fe-5 certainly seemed the most promising. It showed an intact shoreline stratigraphy and abundant archaeological materials, both Mesolithic and Neolithic. The preservation of organic remains was excellent across a range of species sizes. It was decided to continue investigations at this site, now to be known as "Henauhof Nordwest."

Chapter 8

Sites on the Landscape: Henauhof Nordwest

8.1. EXCAVATION TECHNIQUES

Excavations at Henauhof Nordwest were conducted during the summers of 1981, 1983, 1985, and 1987. The excavation team ranged in size from 10 to 20 people and consisted of American, German, and Canadian students and volunteers. Excavation director in all seasons was M. Jochim, and the field directors were S. Gregg (1981, 1983), J. Hudson (1983), A. Stewart (1985), and T. Rudolph (1987).

The excavations were conducted using a 1-meter grid framework oriented to the survey grid of 1980. Each square was excavated independently according to natural levels. When possible, excavations were organized so as to provide broad exposures of surfaces across many squares at once. Within each natural level, arbitrary levels of 10 cm thickness were used to map finds. A total of 237 m^2 in a contiguous block plus isolated trenches were excavated to depths of 1–2 meters (Fig. 42). The high water table required that the water be channeled into several drainage pits at the edge of the excavations and periodically removed using hand and motorized pumps.

All artifacts were bagged, tagged, mapped, and labeled individually. One form for each 10 cm level of each square was used to map artifacts and features and to record artifact numbers, elevations, and soil information. All natural stones larger than 10 cm diameter (or concentrations of smaller ones) were recorded on these maps, as was all wood, hazelnuts, and charcoal. Wood was examined for signs of working and samples were taken for species identifica-

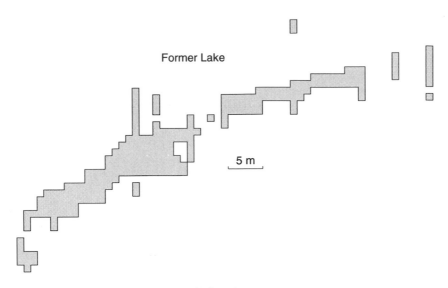

Figure 42. Henauhof Nordwest excavation area.

tion. As all hazelnuts proved to be present due to natural processes (few were broken or burned and none were concentrated in artifact levels), these were not saved. Samples of charcoal were taken for identification and radiocarbon determinations.

The three-dimensional coordinates in centimeters were recorded for all artifacts found in place. In addition, the dip and alignment of all artifacts with a long axis greater than 1 cm were recorded during 1981. This information was used to evaluate the role of downslope erosion in determining artifact distributions. All soils except the clays were water-screened through a 3 mm mesh and the locations of artifacts found were recorded according to 10 cm level and 50 × 50 cm quadrant. Samples of soils from each level were fine-screened and examined later for botanical remains and small artifacts. Profiles were drawn and photographed for all walls left in place, which included side walls and numerous baulks left temporarily standing during the course of excavations. Soil samples were taken from these walls for pollen and sedimentological studies.

Lithic artifacts were wrapped in tissue paper for bagging and transport in order to protect their edges for eventual later microwear studies. Wood, bone, and antler were kept moist in plastic bags. The bone and antler were allowed to dry gradually in the laboratory. Few pieces required stabilization for conservation; a few of the largest fragments of bone and antler were stabilized in a solution of white water-soluble glue.

The excavations reached the sterile, basal clay of the lake basin in 51 of the meter-squares. In the rest, excavations were stopped because of lack of finds or problems with the water table. The horizontal limits of materials were not reached in the excavations, but a number of concentrations in each of the levels were defined and a sufficient area excavated to permit description.

8.2. STRATUM 6

Stratum 6 represents a sand and gravel beach deposited by the high waters of the Federsee during the Younger Dryas period (Fig. 43). The large, deep lake was set in a mosaic landscape of steppe-tundra vegetation, scattered shrubs, and pine and birch trees. The beach surface was uneven, steeply sloping down into the lake from high ridges at the shore (Fig. 44). To this lakeside came hunters of the Late Palaeolithic, apparently camping on the dry slope above the site of Henauhof NW, to judge from surface finds from the field up-slope.

Two radiocarbon dates obtained on charcoal proved to represent contaminations from higher levels: 9370 ± 110 and 6480 ± 400 b.p.

The finds from Stratum 6 are horizontally concentrated in the southeastern corner of the excavation area on the highest portions of the sand, suggesting direct deposition on the exposed beach. They are vertically concentrated in the upper portions of the sand layer. Bones are heavily weathered but stone artifacts show different degrees of wear, with many having sharp edges. Direct deposition of the artifacts on the sand, with subsequent weathering and some

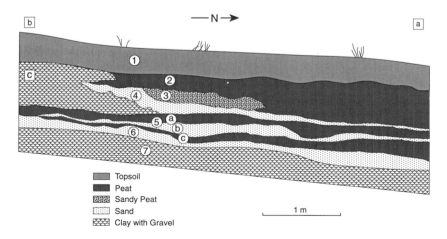

Figure 43. Henauhof Nordwest stratigraphy.

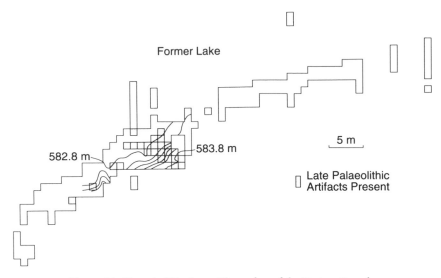

Figure 44. Henauhof Nordwest: The surface of the Stratum 6 sand.

trampling or rodent disturbance would best fit the distribution of the Stratum 6 finds.

8.2.1. Lithic Assemblage

The small assemblage from Stratum 6 contains only 85 lithic artifacts (Fig. 45). Cherts of various colors, including gray, greenish brown, and tan, are the most common raw material, followed by red radiolarite, banded chert, and other, coarse-grained material. All of these except the banded chert, which occurs naturally in Bavaria to the east, were presumably obtained in local gravels. The finer-grained radiolarite and banded chert are more frequently retouched than are the chert and coarse-grained material. Typological and technological characteristics of the assemblage are presented in Table 7.

8.2.2. Faunal Assemblage

The small faunal assemblage contains 92 bones, of which 19 (21%) could be identified to species. Table 8 presents the numbers and weights of the identified bones for each species as well as other taxonomic categories. Red deer and boar are represented each by four identified teeth, horse by three teeth, aurochs by a portion of a metapodial shaft and a distal fragment of a phalanx, and wolf by the distal end of a radius. Fish and waterfowl are also present.

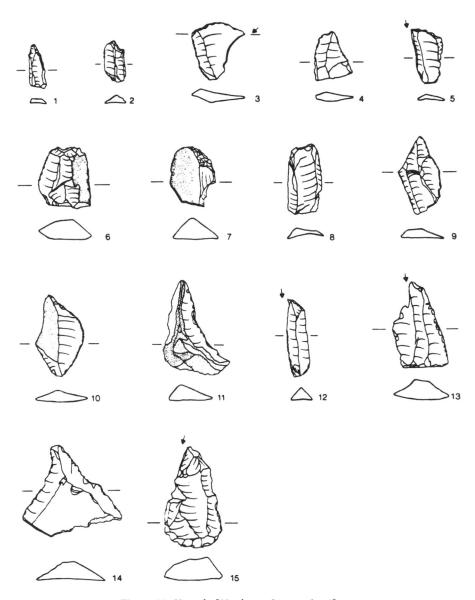

Figure 45. Henauhof Nordwest: Stratum 6 artifacts.

Table 7. Henauhof NW Lithic Artifacts

Category	Stratum				
	6	5	4+G	3	C
Microlith	0	2	49	11	8
Microburin	1	0	2	0	1
Backed point	1	0	2	0	1
Bilateral point	0	0	0	1	0
Backed blade	2	1	7	2	12
Notched piece	2	0	6	5	3
Borer	2	1	5	4	4
Burin	6	5	19	11	15
Burin-scraper	2	2	1	0	0
Scraper	3	4	15	4	9
Other retouched	3	8	16	10	13
Total retouched	22	23	121	48	66
Core	6	13	47	35	27
Chunk	10	7	90	52	43
Cortex flake	7	16	67	41	37
Core rejuvenation flake	4	7	25	11	11
Flake	26	58	356	202	194
Cortex blade	4	4	19	17	8
Core rejuvenation blade	2	3	11	12	11
Broken blade	11	27	123	65	72
Blade	4	21	69	43	40
Total lithics	97	179	929	526	509
Average weight (g)	2.49	3.22	2.41	2.86	2.74
# Heated	6	15	82	42	51
# With cortex	31	75	369	203	188
Average whole blade length (cm)	2.99	3.17	2.55	2.87	3.06

Although the sample is small, it presents a picture of a diverse subsistence emphasizing large mammals. The importance of horse, bovids, and red deer among the identified bones (and presumably in the categories of large and very large mammal) agrees well with the potential offered by the open parkland environment, while the boar suggests pockets of denser forest nearby. The few fish and waterfowl remains suggest a role for lacustrine resources in this lakeside camp.

8.2.3. Other Finds

Other finds from Stratum 6 include a perforated red deer canine, a fragment of a black fossil ammonite, and a fragment of fossilized marine shell, as well as one piece each of red and yellow ochre. Such finds are relatively common in Magdalenian contexts and emphasize the Palaeolithic nature of this as-

Table 8. Henauhof NW Stratum 6 Fauna

Category	Number	Weight (g)
Identified mammal		
Red deer	4	9.04
Boar	4	9.95
Aurochs	3	153.44
Horse	3	29.97
Wolf	1	3.78
Total	15	206.18
Unidentified mammal		
Very large mammal	16	162.61
Large mammal	20	47.62
Medium-large mammal	16	10.08
Small-medium mammal	1	0.08
Mammal	8	2.68
Total	61	223.07
Fish		
Pike	4	1.45
Other fish	1	0.13
Total	5	1.58
Total bird	1	1.77
Unidentified	10	3.79
Total	92	436.39

semblage. The ammonite may derive from the region north of the Black Forest, about 200 kilometers to the northwest of Henauhof Nordwest.

8.3. STRATUM 5

Stratum 5 was formed during the Preboreal, a period of generally low water levels of the Federsee. In the calm shallows at the Henauhof shoreline, peat deposition predominated, interrupted by an erosional episode that caused the deposition of the sand of Stratum 5b in a portion of the site. Toward the end of this period the water level dropped even lower, exposing the surface of this peat to prolonged weathering. The surrounding area at this time was covered by a relatively dense pine forest with stands of birch and scattered hazel in the few more open areas. The Federsee remained a magnet, drawing groups of Early Mesolithic people to its shores.

Five radiocarbon dates obtained on charcoal and wood agree with the pollen evidence in placing this level in the Preboreal period. These dates range from 10080 ± 100 to 9500 ± 130 b.p.

The archaeological materials of Stratum 5 are sealed in the peat. The vast majority occur in the black peat of Stratum 5a, forming a discrete vertical concentration of 10–15 cm thickness. This pattern of distribution suggests that the artifacts were deposited late in the Preboreal during the last phases of peat accumulation. The fact that they are sealed within the peat and well preserved suggests further that they accumulated when the peat was still marshy, before the lake recession that led to the intense humification of this stratum.

This wet depositional context argues against an interpretation of these materials as *in situ* remains of activities. Their vertical concentration and the excellent condition of both chipped stone edges and bone artifacts do not support their interpretation as the product of erosion downhill of upslope materials. It appears most probable that these materials were deposited largely as a result of purposeful discard into the marshy lake margins by occupants of an upslope camp.

There are many implications of such an interpretation. Discarded materials should be generally larger than those accumulating within an occupation area because the smallest objects would be more easily lost in the occupation area before discard or more difficult to see and accumulate for discard. The horizontal distribution of materials may show concentrations corresponding to episodes of discard, whereas downslope erosion should create more homogeneous distributions, with concentrations likely only in gulleys and depressions where water flow would be channeled and natural deposition of transported materials would occur. Direct deposition in an occupation area could also create artifact concentrations, but these should show internal compositional coherence according to the activities that created them and should be organized in relation to recognizable features such as hearths, structures, and topography. The concentrations created in a discard area, by contrast, should be associated with no cultural features, may show little organization in relation to one another, and may each be composed of a wide range of functionally unrelated materials.

The archaeological materials of Stratum 5 show all of these features. The range of lithic artifact weights (0.04 –28.71 g) is higher than that of the assemblage from Stratum 6 (0.03–13.65 g), which represents an accumulation on an activity surface. Similarly, the mean weight of lithic artifacts from Stratum 5 (3.22 g) is larger than that of Stratum 6 (2.49 g). Examination of lithic weights for the assemblages of the two strata show the greater importance of small chips less than 0.50 g in the Stratum 6 collection (32%) as compared to that of Stratum 5 (20%).

The horizontal distribution of the Stratum 5 finds shows a number of concentrations (Fig. 46) that are not restricted to depressions in the peat surface. Every concentration contains identifiable bones from a variety of different species and body parts together with various stone artifacts. No obvious functional relationship exists among the components of any concentration. Some areas contain large and small cobbles, some of which are fire-cracked, but these

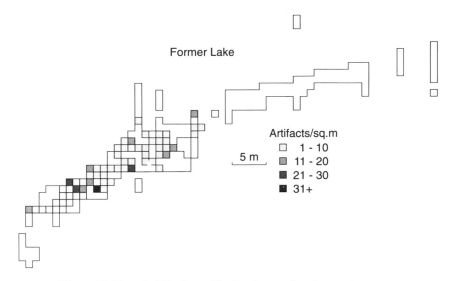

Figure 46. Henauhof Nordwest: The distribution of artifacts in Stratum 5.

form no spatial patterns, nor do the remains of charcoal. The only additional features visible in this stratum are natural accumulations of driftwood, most of which lies parallel to the former shoreline. Taken together, all of this evidence suggests that these materials were purposefully discarded into the marshy edges of the lake and consequently represent a restricted sample of the occupation debris of the lakeside camp.

8.3.1. Lithic Assemblage

A total of 179 chipped stone artifacts were found in Stratum 5 (Fig. 47). The raw materials are predominantly tan and gray cherts, followed by red and green radiolarite, black, gray, and dark red coarse-grained materials, and banded chert. Again, all are apparently available in local gravels except the banded chert. The finest-grained materials (banded chert, radiolarite) are more frequently retouched (24%) than is the chert (12%) or the coarse-grained material (0%—only debitage is present). Table 7 presents the typological and technological characteristics of the assemblage.

8.3.2. Faunal Assemblage

Stratum 5 produced a faunal assemblage of 206 bones, of which 88 (42%) could be identified to species. The greater proportion of identifiable bones in

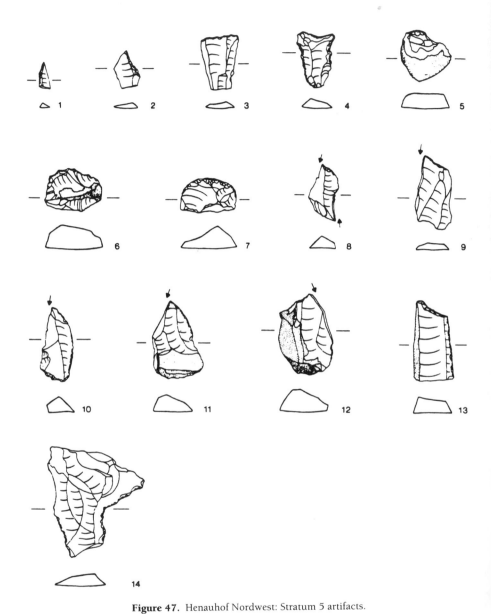

Figure 47. Henauhof Nordwest: Stratum 5 artifacts.

Table 9. Henauhof NW Stratum 5 Fauna

Category	Number	Weight (g)
Identified mammal		
Red deer	20	318.81
Boar	4	11.46
Roe deer	6	22.78
Aurochs	3	173.94
Horse	1	2.17
Hare	1	3.03
Red fox	11	14.29
Wildcat	3	6.11
Mole	2	0.19
Total	51	552.78
Unidentified mammal		
Very large mammal	1	11.52
Large mammal	18	70.61
Medium-large mammal	28	32.15
Medium mammal	3	2.43
Small-medium mammal	6	3.59
Small mammal	10	0.44
Mammal	14	9.51
Total	80	130.25
Fish		
Pike	15	17.68
Other fish	12	2.55
Total	27	20.23
Bird		
Mute swan	1	3.73
Tufted duck	1	0.38
Other bird	8	2.11
Total	10	6.22
Amphibian	2	0.05
Unidentified	36	2.53
Total	206	712.05

comparison to Stratum 6 may reflect both the better preservational qualities of the Stratum 5 peat and that many of the bones of this stratum are somewhat larger, discarded items. Table 9 lists the number and weight of bones according to species and other taxonomic categories.

Red deer remains dominate the assemblage and include fragments of a variety of body parts: skull, mandible, loose teeth, axis, scapula, humerus, radius, tibia, metapodial, calcaneus, and phalanx. No other vertebrae, ribs, pelvic remains, or femurs were found. As this is a very small sample (n = 20), the lack of these body parts may be of no significance, but examination of the identified remains of large and very large mammals (n = 19,) which presumably include red deer, shows a similar lack of these body parts and a dominance of shaft splinters of limb bones. This pattern of remains does not reflect the relative abundance of the various body parts in the skeleton: rare parts are represented along with numerous ones. It is also inconsistent with expectations based on differing bone density and survival of the various body parts, which is not surprising given the good preservational qualities of the peat and the excellent condition of bone in this stratum.

Because neither natural frequency nor survival probability adequately accounts for the pattern of body parts, behavioral causes may be responsible. The remains from Stratum 5 lack those body parts of high meat (and general) utility: the femur, sternum, ribs, pelvis, and thoracic vertebrae. Most of the parts with highest marrow utility are also missing, although fracturing for marrow extraction is clearly evident in some of the finds (tibia, radius, phalanges, and mandible) and is consistent with the relative abundance of long-bone shaft splinters.

Two possible interpretations are suggested by these data. Stratum 5 may represent the remains of brief occupations at a kill site, where red deer underwent primary butchering. The best meat- and marrow-bearing parts were taken away to residential sites leaving no remains, whereas the parts of lower value were processed for marrow and discarded. Arguing against this interpretation are three patterns in the data that suggest Stratum 5 to represent remains from a residential occupation. The Stratum 5 faunal assemblage, although small, contains a diverse set of identified species, not to be expected at kill sites occupied relatively briefly. Similarly, the small stone artifact assemblage is also diverse morphologically, and presumably functionally, whereas kill site assemblages, even with some meat processing, are likely to be relatively specialized. In addition, the finds of Stratum 5 have been interpreted as a purposeful dump connected with the primary site upslope. Such a dump area resulting from camp cleaning is more likely with longer-term residential occupations than with the briefer occupations of a kill site.

The alternative interpretation is that this stratum is, indeed, connected with a base camp or residential site with multiple activities. Low-value body parts were separated from those of higher meat and marrow utility and treated differently. That these low-value parts were processed for marrow suggests some degree of food stress. After this processing, the fragments were discarded into the lake edge. The higher-value parts, on the other hand, were presumably processed for both meat and marrow and perhaps bone grease as well. Their remains were then either too small to be collected for discard or were disposed of in a different location.

The remains of other mammals show patterns similar to those of red deer. Horse, bovid, boar, and roe deer are represented largely by cranial and limb elements, although one rib fragment each was found of roe deer and bovid. All large mammals appear to have been treated in a similar manner.

Among the carnivores, wild cat is represented only by limb elements (tibia, ulna, and phalanx). These were found within a small region of the site. In the same portion of the site were found 11 remains of fox, all concentrated in the same 1-meter square. The fox remains also consist only of limb elements together with their attachments: metatarsals, left and right femur, pelvis, sacrum, and scapula. It would appear that these carnivores were dismembered, perhaps in the process of obtaining their furs, and the unused limbs and girdles discarded in one location. The mode of disposal of other body parts, and the reason for their separation, is not known.

Only two of the 10 remains of birds could be identified to species: tufted duck and mute swan. Both of these waterfowl would have been natural inhabitants of the Federsee shores. Fish remains were more numerous; of the 27 bones, the only identified species was pike. Fifteen of the fish remains were concentrated within four adjacent 1-meter squares of the site, suggesting one episode of discard.

8.3.3. Other Finds

A number of pieces of worked bone and antler were found in Stratum 5. Most abundant were 12 fragmentary portions of bone points (Fig. 48). These display considerable morphological diversity, but all show to some extent the polished surfaces and fine parallel striations resulting from smoothing and shaping using chipped stone as scraping tools. Two point tips are oval in cross section and another is concavo-convex. Of the 8 shaft fragments, 2 are subrectangular, 4 are concavo-convex, and 2 are biconcave in cross section. One almost complete point consists of 4 fragments, all from the same excavation square, but 2 are from Stratum 5, one is from the bottom of Stratum 4, and one is from Stratum C. This point is biconcave in cross section along the shaft but oval in cross section through the tip. The stratigraphic distribution suggests some mixing of materials in this portion of the site. This was a high hump of the sand of Stratum 4; erosion and sand deposition on this high beach ridge may easily have disturbed somewhat the underlying peat of Stratum 5.

Other finds include one tiny fragment of horn, one fragment of the long-bone shaft of a medium large mammal worked to a rough point, and one smoothed (but highly weathered and exfoliated) fragment of the long-bone shaft of a large mammal. This latter find occurred in the sand layer of Stratum 5b, unlike most of the finds discussed here, and may have lain exposed to the effects of weathering on the beach. Finally, one fragment of red deer antler has one cut and beveled end; this may be part of an antler sleeve to hold a stone implement.

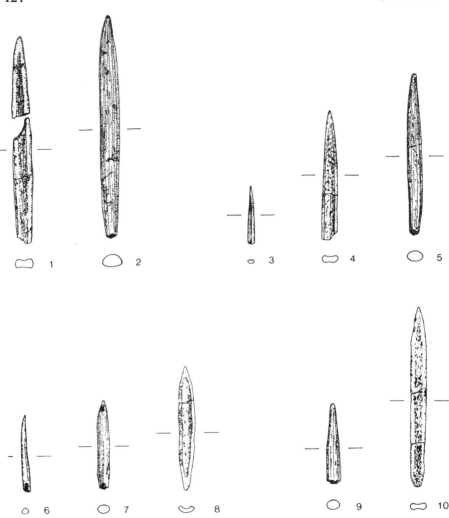

Figure 48. Henauhof Nordwest: Bone points (various strata).

8.4. STRATUM 4

Stratum 4 was formed during the Boreal period, a time of generally high water, causing erosion at the shoreline and deposition of the sand beach at Henauhof NW. The sand surface is uneven, with higher, flat areas separated by low gulleys (Fig. 49). The surrounding countryside at this time was heavily forested with pine, birch, oak, lime, and other deciduous trees. Hazel shrubs were

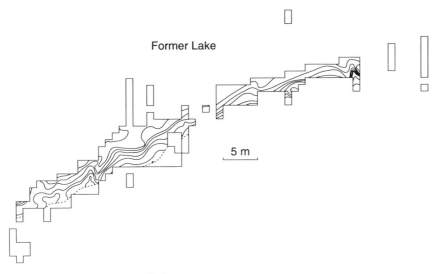

Figure 49. Henauhof Nordwest: The surface of the Stratum 4 sand.

abundant, leading to the natural accumulation of hazelnuts in the muddy shallows of the lake.

Three radiocarbon dates obtained on charcoal agree with the palynological placement in the Boreal period. These dates range from 8290 ± 90 to 8000 ± 185 b.p. A fourth date, 6660 ± 80, appears to represent contamination from the overlying Stratum 3.

The artifacts of Stratum 4 are distributed throughout the thickness of the sand. Such a distribution is consistent with an interpretation of: (a) downslope erosion and mixing of artifacts during formation of the beach, (b) intermittent occupations and *in situ* deposition of artifacts throughout the process of beach formation, or (c) single occupation and *in situ* deposition on the beach, with subsequent vertical dispersal of artifacts by trampling and rodent action.

Arguing against the first interpretation is the lack of significant rounding of lithic edges in the Stratum 4 assemblage: most of the pieces retain sharp edges. In addition, there are a number of conjoinable lithic artifacts in this assemblage, which would be unlikely in the case of downslope erosion of these materials from a larger upslope assemblage. Furthermore, artifacts transported downslope by erosion should be concentrated in gulleys and depressions, whereas the Stratum 4 finds are most numerous on the higher, flat surfaces of the sand. Significant transport of the materials might be expected to have caused patterned distributions in the orientation and inclination of the long axes of artifacts, but an examination of the materials demonstrates a random distribution of orientations and a normal distribution of inclinations around horizontal. Finally, the process of sand deposition involved some size-sorting, in that finer materials are relatively more numerous toward the top of the stratum. If artifacts were transported and deposited by the same processes, they should show the same sorting effect: given their size, they should be most abundant in the lower, more gravelly sand, and those artifacts near the top of the stratum should be smaller than those below. In fact, the artifacts are most abundant in the upper portions of the sand and show no tendency for decreasing size toward the top.

Consequently, *in situ* deposition, rather than downslope erosion, would seem best to explain the distribution of the artifacts in Stratum 4. Arguing against a single occupation episode as responsible for this deposition is the chronological span of artifacts in the assemblage, ranging from Beuronien B to possibly the Late Mesolithic. Moreover, materials from a single occupation dispersed by trampling and natural processes should show a sorting by size such that smaller materials are displaced downward to a greater degree than are larger materials. However, no such unidirectional trend in the vertical distribution of lithic weights is apparent.

It may be concluded that the artifacts of Stratum 4 represent the *in situ* remains from intermittent occupations at the Henauhof peninsula. The lack of clear vertical separation of chronologically significant microlith types suggests that these materials have become mixed. In addition, the horizontal distribution of the diagnostic microlith types indicates considerable overlap in the utilized areas of the beach at different time periods, preventing a separation of materials for analysis by time period. The pattern of conjoinable lithic artifacts suggests contemporaneity of some materials from much of the exposed beach surface (Fig. 50), further precluding a separation of materials from different episodes of occupation.

The Stratum 4 assemblage, therefore, represents an accumulation of materials over a considerable period of time. In such a situation, interpretations must be cautious. Little spatial patterning may be evident, although remains of features may be present. Associations of materials may be accidental and of no value in interpreting the activities with which they were originally connected. To the extent that each component occupation differed in its activities and residues, the resulting aggregate picture could be extremely misleading, suggesting, for example, a highly diversified subsistence on the basis of a mixture of different specialized occupations.

Interpretation of these materials must also take into account the fact that these artifacts are likely to represent only a sample of materials from each occupation. The extent of the upslope occupation is unknown, but was probably considerable in light of the density of surface finds. Activities leaving remains on the rather narrow beach may have been a small component of the total range

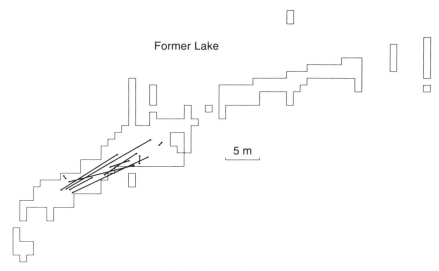

Figure 50. Henauhof Nordwest: Lithic conjoins in Stratum 4.

during any one occupation. It might be anticipated that activities directly associated with the lake edge—fishing, in particular—should be overly represented here, as should activities requiring areas clear of vegetation and away from habitations, such as the butchering of game and the preparation of hides. More "domestic" activities—food preparation and tool manufacture—may have been concentrated in an upslope residential area and underrepresented in the remains of Stratum 4. As a result, there may be reason to expect a certain redundancy in the materials deposited on the beach from each occupation, and the aggregate picture derived from the total assemblage may, indeed, accurately reflect the beachside activities of each.

8.4.1. Lithic Assemblage

Stratum 4 produced a lithic assemblage of 922 artifacts (Fig. 51). The types and proportions of raw materials are similar to those of Stratum 5: gray, white, and tan chert is most common, followed by red and green radiolarite, dark gray, black, and red coarse-grained material, and banded chert. The finest-grained materials, radiolarite and banded chert, were preferentially retouched, followed by chert and the coarse-grained materials. Utilized pieces comprise 12% of the assemblage and represent similar proportions of all raw materials. Table 7 presents the typological and technological characteristics of the assemblage.

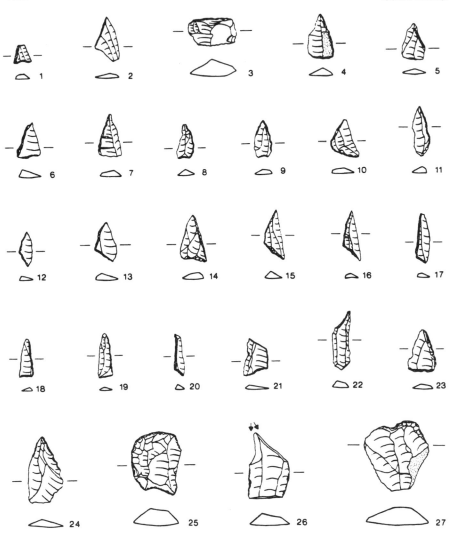

Figure 51. Henauhof Nordwest: Stratum 4 artifacts.

Only 10 sets of conjoinable lithics were found in this stratum. Most involved sections of broken blades and only one was a refit to a core. This suggests that core reduction was largely not carried out on the beach, despite the relative abundance of cores, which may reflect secondary discard, particularly as many of these are quite small and no longer usable. The frequency of refitted broken blades as well as the overall abundance of broken blades may indicate the effects of trampling of discarded blades on the beach.

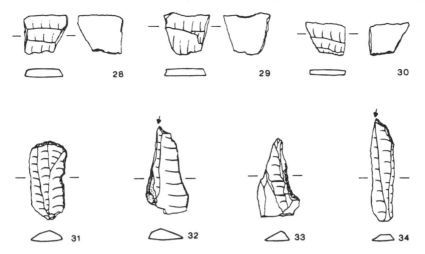

Figure 51. (*Continued*)

The horizontal distribution of the lithic artifacts shows three areas of concentration (Fig. 52). These areas coincide with the higher areas of the sand beach above the 582.5 m contour of the sand surface. The largest concentration is in the western portion of the site where the beach was flattest and most suited for activities. Each concentration has all typological categories of lithic artifact and although there are some proportional differences among the areas (cores

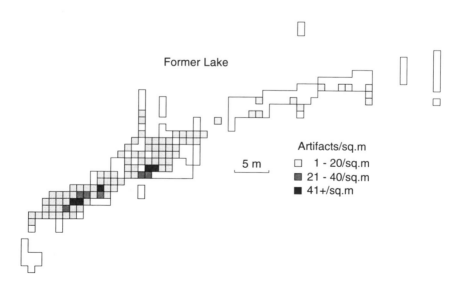

Figure 52. Henauhof Nordwest: The distribution of lithics in Stratum 4.

are relatively more abundant in the westernmost area and microliths and very small flakes are proportionately somewhat more abundant in the eastern two areas, for example), these differences are not statistically significant. Neither disposal patterns (with sorting of artifacts by size) nor activity area differentiation (with sorting of artifacts by function) can explain the distribution of materials in these three areas. Rather, it appears that these concentrations represent remains from a variety of activities over a long period, accumulated in the high flat beach areas most suitable for repeated use.

8.4.2. Faunal Assemblage

Stratum 4 produced a faunal assemblage of 811 bones with a total weight of 1355.93 g and an average weight of 1.67 g. This average is much lower than that of Stratum 5 and reflects both the poorer preservation of the sand and the fact that the Stratum 4 bones were not selected for purposeful discard. Bones identifiable to species (n = 117) comprise 14% of the assemblage, a much lower figure than for the larger bones of the Stratum 5 assemblage.

Table 10 presents the number and weight of bones according to species and other taxonomic categories. Among the bones identified to species, fish and waterfowl are most numerous, followed by roe deer, red deer, and boar. Other big game include horse, aurochs, and elk, while squirrel, badger, fox, and mole complete the assemblage. In terms of bone weight (and presumably meat contribution), however, big game—particularly red deer—dominate the assemblage. The abundance of cervid, large mammal, and medium-large mammal remains supports this conclusion.

The red deer and large/very large mammal remains contain a variety of body parts: skull, mandible, vertebrae, and hind limb bones. Missing from this collection are ribs, pelvis, sternum, scapula, and front limb bones. Because these are among the lower density bones, their lack may reflect the differential survival of bones on an exposed beach. Some behavioral causes may be operating as well. Many (but not all) of the most useful parts in terms of meat, marrow, and bone grease are absent. A pattern of primary butchering on the beach and secondary processing in an upslope habitation area could account for the systematic absence of high utility parts from the beach context. The lack of a single clear pattern in body part distribution may derive from the composite nature of this assemblage: repeated use of the beach with even slightly different butchering and disposal patterns, followed by differential preservation, would produce just such an aggregate assemblage with no single cause evident for the presence and absence of various body parts.

Other mammal bones show a similar pattern of body parts. Roe deer remains include a wide variety of parts but lack ribs, sternum, and vertebrae. Boar and bovids are represented almost solely by cranial elements, while horse, badger, and fox remains include only cranial remains. Elk is represented by a rib

Table 10. Henauhof NW Stratum 4 Fauna

Category	Number	Weight (g)
Identified mammal		
Red deer	21	387.05
Boar	17	95.81
Roe deer	24	52.56
Aurochs	6	136.89
Horse	2	3.72
Moose	2	61.71
Squirrel	1	0.25
Badger	2	2.07
Red fox	3	6.24
Mole	3	0.41
Total	81	736.71
Unidentified mammal		
Very large mammal	9	89.71
Large mammal	65	165.27
Medium-large mammal	201	203.06
Medium mammal	25	27.84
Small-medium mammal	31	14.09
Small mammal	74	6.27
Mammal	109	63.34
Total	514	569.58
Fish		
Pike	22	4.98
Wels	2	4.47
Other fish	39	10.74
Total	63	20.19
Bird		
Tufted duck	3	1.26
Coot	4	1.41
Teal	1	0.11
Goldeneye	1	0.29
Gooseander	1	0.58
Cormorant	1	1.11
Jay	1	0.17
Other bird	35	7.08
Total	47	12.01
Amphibian	10	0.38
Unidentified	96	16.07
Total	811	1355.93

fragment and a carpal. For the most part, mammalian body parts of lowest density and highest meat utility are lacking. Many of the bones have been broken to obtain marrow, including those such as the third phalanx with little marrow.

Among the fish remains, pike are most abundant, but wels, or European catfish, was also found. Vertebral bodies and some cranial elements dominate these remains. Birds include a variety of species of waterfowl: goldeneye, coot,

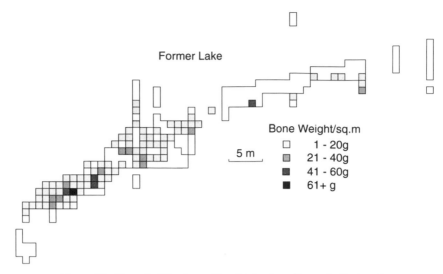

Figure 53. Henauhof Nordwest: The distribution of bones in Stratum 4.

cormorant, tufted duck, teal, and gooseander. Each of these is represented by one or a few identified bones. In addition, one bone of jay was identified.

The bones are distributed throughout the excavated area but do form noticeable concentrations (Fig. 53). Three of these areas coincide with the lithic concentrations already discussed. The others, farther east, are similar in that they occur on high prominences of the beach surface. No significant differences are apparent among these areas: all contain a great variety of species and body parts. The two western areas are richer in bone than the others, however. These patterns support the interpretation offered in the discussion of the stone artifacts. The concentrations apparently represent accumulations of materials from repeated use of these portions of the beach.

In sum, the faunal remains of Stratum 4 present a picture of a very diverse subsistence. Large game dominates the assemblage and include 6 different species. Small mammals, fish, and waterfowl are also well represented by an additional 12 species. Given the composite nature of this assemblage, it cannot be assumed that the Mesolithic subsistence was necessarily this diverse at any one time, but the aggregate picture of Boreal period subsistence is certainly one of considerable variety.

8.4.3. Features

Stratum 4 contains a good deal of charcoal and rocks. For the most part these two materials show similar distributions, away from the major concentrations of artifacts. In the middle of the excavated area are a number of rocks larger than 5 cm diameter at the periphery of the concentration of materials. These rocks occur on a high portion of the beach, are clearly intrusive in the sediment, and probably represent hearthstones scattered during repeated occupations. Some of these rocks show evidence of fire-cracking and many small pieces of charcoal were present in this portion of the site. Similar concentrations of rock and charcoal occur on the higher reaches of the beach at the peripheries of the other artifact clusters. The densest of the clusters—the two western areas—also have the largest and most abundant charcoal fragments. In the far western area there is a rough circular ash lens about 25 cm in diameter and 3–4 cm in thickness directly on the surface of the sand. This occurs at the edge of the major artifact concentration on the broadest expanse of flat beach and may represent a small hearth. Within 1.5 meters are seven large fragments of charcoal and a scatter of smaller fragments. Only 60 cm away from the possible hearth is a large stone, 23 cm in length, standing upright in the sand, while other, smaller rocks lie somewhat greater distances away. The upright stone shows no evidence of heating, but its top end has signs of battering, indicating perhaps its use as an anvil.

In contrast to these patterns, the unfired wood shows a different distribution. Except for a few fragments on the high beach, most wood occurs in the downslope portions of the beach, below the 582.4 m contour of the sand surface. Particularly in the north-central and northwestern regions of the site is a scatter of branches and twigs that seem to represent natural accumulations of wood. One large log remains from a fallen tree. Scattered in these concentrations are some charcoal fragments and stones, as well as occasional artifacts. Such areas may represent portions of the shoreline that were submerged or marshy, in which wood naturally accumulated and into which some materials from the site were discarded.

8.4.4. Other Finds

A notable characteristic of the assemblage of Stratum 4 is the abundance of worked bone. A total of 122 pieces are worked. Most of these (119) may be classified as "points," but this name masks considerable variability (Fig. 48). All but 2 are made of portions of deer metapodial shaft that have been cut and smoothed and have highly polished surfaces with fine striations from the scraping action of stone tools. The other 2 are made of antler and have rough, more porous surfaces. Seven of these artifacts are small in cross section, up to 3 mm diameter. Of these, 6 are shaft segments and 1 is a point tip. Five of the shaft fragments and the tip are oval or round in cross section; the other shaft piece has a concavo-convex cross section. The remaining 112 points are larger, with widths of 5 mm or more, and comprise 1 virtually complete point, 88 shaft fragments, and 23 point tips. The whole piece has a concavo-convex cross section, as do 23 of the shaft fragments. Another 32 of the shafts have biconcave cross sections, while 28 are oval in cross section. The remaining 5 shaft pieces are too fragmentary to determine. The cross-sections of the point tips include 14 oval, 5 biconcave, and 4 concavo-convex. As several refits indicate, biconcave and concavo-convex shafts may fit to oval tips; on the original artifacts the groove becomes shallower and disappears toward the tip.

The function of these points is not clear; the morphological diversity suggests a functional diversity as well. The smaller points may be needles, although no eyed basal ends have been found. The larger points may include projectiles or spear points used for fishing or hunting, although additional interpretations include portions of composite fishing gear and weaving implements. Virtually all of these points were found on the high sand beach in the same areas as the concentrations of other artifacts. This distribution, together with the overwhelming abundance of shaft portions over tips, suggests that they represent the remains of implements broken elsewhere and brought to the site for replacement. Hunting or fishing spears could have been broken during use—losing the tips—and the shafts brought back to camp still attached to wooden hafts. During replacement these shaft fragments would have accumulated with other artifacts on the beach. Arguing in favor of an interpretation as fishing implements rather than hunting tools is their abundance at this lakeside site. Henauhof NW, Stratum 4 has far more of these points than any contemporaneous site, including the upper Danube caves and rockshelters with good organic preservation. At all of these sites, hunting is clearly of great importance and fish remains are rare. Although hunting was apparently the dominant component of the subsistence at Henauhof NW as well, fish remains in Stratum 4 are relatively abundant, more so than at most of the Danube sites. Thus, indirect evidence suggests the use of at least some of these bone points for fishing, perhaps particularly well suited for fishing in the lake shallows. During use, such fish spears were apparently often broken. The evidence at Henauhof NW suggests that they were returned in their hafts to be replaced on the beach.

Other worked bone, although rare, also occurs in Stratum 4. One awl-like tool is a pointed shaft fragment, irregular in outline and cross section. Two proximal metatarsals of red deer were intensively shaped into hide-working tools. Each was split longitudinally and cut and polished through heavy use. One of these is decorated with a series of parallel cuts in clusters of three or four lines on both sides of the shaft, similar to Palaeolithic "hunting tallies" (Fig. 54). Two fox canines were perforated as jewelry (Fig. 55). In addition, five pieces of boar canine show evidence of cutting. Finally, three pieces of red ochre were found in the artifact concentrations.

Antler is a minor component of this assemblage. In addition to the two worked points, 13 pieces of unworked antler were found in Stratum 4. Six of

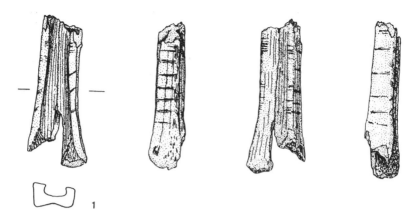

Figure 54. Henauhof Nordwest: Bone "hunting tally."

these are fragments of red deer antler and 7 are remains of roe deer. The roe deer antlers are unshed, suggesting kills between April and September or October. The few antler fragments are scattered throughout the excavated area.

8.4.5. Summary

Stratum 4 contains the largest assemblage from Henauhof Nordwest, representing the accumulation of remains from repeated Early Mesolithic occupations at the shore. The sand beach area appears to have been used for some primary butchering and processing as well as tool repair, among other activities. The flat, raised portions of the beach were the focus of repeated use, resulting in the concentration of diverse materials in these areas. Evidence suggests hearths may have been regular features on the beach, but the reoccupations scattered their remains. Large mammal hunting appears to have played a dominant role in the subsistence, but fishing and fowling were also practiced, and the abundance of bone points suggests a relatively significant role of fishing. The aggregate picture is one of considerable subsistence diversity, although this may be in part a result of the composite nature of the assemblage. Nonutilitarian items include ochre, perforated teeth, and a decorated bone, and only hint at the nature of these components of the material culture.

8.4.6. Stratum G

In the far western portion of the excavated area, the sand beach thins to form a narrow ridge extending westward into the lake basin away from the solid shore. Behind this ridge, on the upslope side, is a gravelly, sandy peat stratum

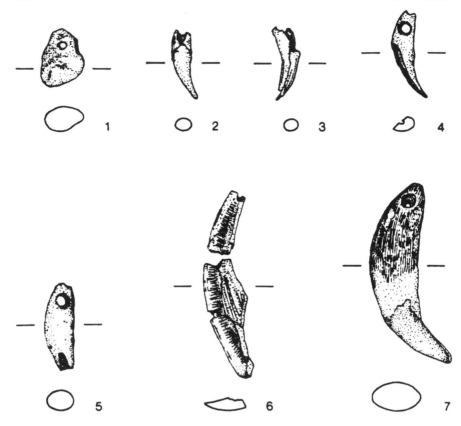

Figure 55. Henauhof Nordwest: Perforated teeth (various strata).

that is continuous with the sand (Fig. 56). This is Stratum G. It extends south to abut the solid shoreline. While the sand was forming, this region was apparently a shallow depression behind the sand ridge that remained marshy and gradually filled with sandy peat.

A very small assemblage was found in this stratum, which is contemporary with the materials of Stratum 4 and may represent objects discarded into this marshy depression. Seven pieces of chipped stone were found: one assymetrical backed point, one core, two whole blades, two broken blades, and one utilized flake. The faunal assemblage includes six finds. Identifiable to species were one rib fragment of red deer and one boar carpal bone. In addition there were limb shafts and a fragment of a maxillary among the mammal bones. One fragment of a bone point shaft and two pieces of red deer antler complete this small assemblage.

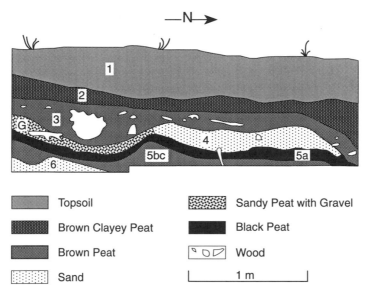

Figure 56. Henauhof Nordwest: Stratum G stratigraphic position.

8.5. STRATUM 3

During the Early Atlantic period, Federsee water levels dropped and peat formation became dominant around the shores. The forests surrounding the lake remained dense, but pine, birch, and hazel decreased in importance as oak, elm, lime, ash, and other deciduous trees increased in abundance. The marshy shores of Henauhof remained attractive to Late Mesolithic groups, who continued to return to this wooded peninsula.

The artifacts of Stratum 3 are sealed in the peat and most are concentrated within a discrete vertical horizon of 5–10 cm thickness. One radiocarbon date was obtained on charcoal from the cultural layer: 6720 ± 70 b.p. Preservation of organic materials in this stratum is excellent, suggesting that they accumulated in waterlogged peat. This in turn indicates that the materials represent items discarded into the marshy lake edges rather than *in situ* remains of activities. Their vertical concentration suggests a relatively brief episode of occupation and discard.

This interpretation is supported by the range of weights of lithic artifacts (up to 91.23 g) and by their mean (2.86 g), which are higher than those of Stratum 4. Small chips weighing less than 0.50 g are less important (32 %) than in Stratum 4. The mean weight of bones in Stratum 3 (4.58 g) is also considerably higher than that of Stratum 4, although this may largely reflect the better preservational conditions of peat in comparison to sand.

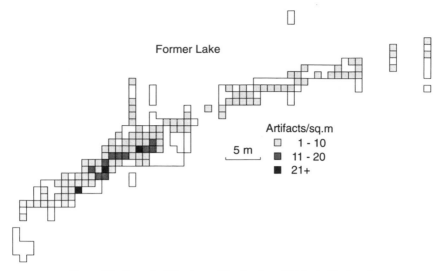

Figure 57. Henauhof Nordwest: Distribution of lithics in Stratum 3.

Also supporting this interpretation is the horizontal distribution of lithic artifacts in this stratum. Although concentrations are evident, the general pattern is one of a considerable scatter of artifacts, particularly throughout the central and eastern portions of the site (Fig. 57). Mixed together with the artifacts are abundant fire-cracked rocks and charcoal fragments, suggesting episodes of hearth cleaning and discard. Much wood is also present, none of which is worked, and apparently represents natural accumulations of trees, branches, and twigs in the marshy shore.

Thus, the Stratum 3 assemblage, like that of Stratum 5, represents materials discarded into the muddy shallows of the lake during a relatively brief period of occupation of the upslope area. It represents a well-preserved sample of Late Mesolithic materials, but a biased sample of the total assemblage of the entire site. It may be expected that larger and lower-value items will be overrepresented in this sample.

8.5.1. Lithic Assemblage

The lithic assemblage contains 526 artifacts (Fig. 58). The types and proportions of raw materials are quite similar to those of Stratum 4 and Stratum 5. As in Stratum 4, the finer-grained materials (radiolarite and banded chert) are preferentially retouched. Very few (n = 2) conjoinable pieces were found, supporting the interpretation of discard. The typological and technological characteristics of the assemblage are given in Table 7.

This Late Mesolithic assemblage lacks the trapezes considered to be characteristic of this period. While this lack is not unique (the Latest Mesolithic lev-

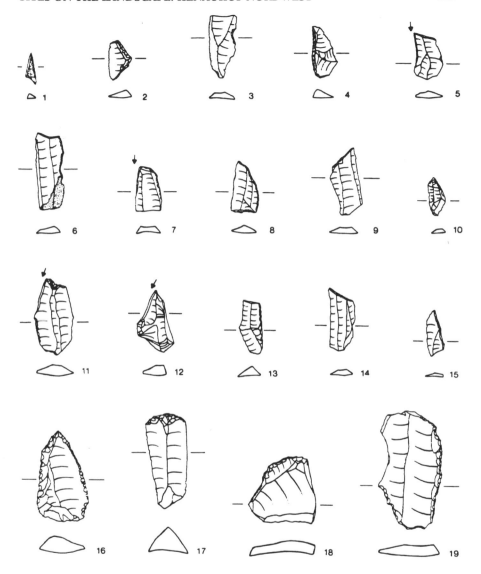

Figure 58. Henauhof Nordwest: Stratum 3 artifacts.

el of Lautereck Shelter on the Danube also has no trapezes—Taute, 1967), it does require some discussion. Other characteristics of Late Mesolithic assemblages in the area are an abundance of notched blades and a well-developed regular blade production technology. Henauhof NW, Stratum 3 shows both of these. Notched blades comprise 10 % of the small tool assemblage. Regular blades are common among both tools and unretouched blades. These observations, together with the firm stratigraphic, palynological, and radiocarbon dating, make a Late Mesolithic date certain. At the same time, this assemblage is small, it represents a biased selection of materials for discard, and it derives from a lakeside site of considerable resource diversity (see the next section). It may well be that trapezes were proportionately more numerous at the cave sites where hunting appears to have been more important. If so, then the sampling error resulting from the small size and selected nature of this assemblage may account for their absence at Henauhof NW.

Twelve lithic artifacts were found higher in the peat than the rest of the finds. These represent a later, Neolithic, occupation and include two bifacially retouched projectile points, one notched piece, five flakes, and four blades.

8.5.2. Faunal Assemblage

The faunal assemblage of Stratum 3 consists of 972 bones with a total weight of 4449.30 g and an average of 4.58 g. A total of 272, or 28%, could be identified to species (Table 11). This figure is much higher than that of Stratum 4 and reflects the larger size and better preservation of the bones in Stratum 3.

Red deer and large/very large mammal remains include virtually all body parts. Missing are the sternum, mandible, calcaneous, sacrum, atlas, ulna, and third phalanx, as well as some portions of other bones. No clear pattern of absence is discernible in terms of natural frequencies, bone density, or meat, marrow, or bone grease utility. It would appear that whole carcasses were being processed at the site and that all body parts were subject to collection and disposal into the lake edges. Roe deer show a similarly diverse array of body parts and were apparently treated in a manner similar to red deer.

Boar is represented largely by cranial elements, together with fragments of metatarsal, scapula, ulna, and phalanges. Aurochs remains include a tooth and fragments of phalanges. An incisor and a proximal tibia of horse were found, while elk is represented by a metatarsal shaft. Among the smaller mammals, badger remains are most numerous, including cranial elements and two virtually complete tibias. Beaver is represented by a humerus and a tibia shaft. Other finds include a marten mandible, a wildcat calcaneous, and one wolf canine.

The numerous fish remains include vertebral bodies and cranial elements. Pike is most abundant, but also identified are wels, or European catfish, and bream. Some of the wels remains come from a very large individual, approximately 1.6 meters in length. Four species of waterfowl were identified among the bird remains: grey heron, coot, teal, and pochard.

The bones of Stratum 3 are distributed horizontally throughout the excavated area (Fig. 59). The areas of higher bone density largely coincide with those of high lithic density as well. Such a pattern is consistent with the interpretation of these materials as discarded, mixed items. There are some differences in the distribution of bones by species. Fish bones, for example, are most

Table 11. Henauhof NW Stratum 3 Fauna

Category	Number	Weight (g)
Identified mammal		
Red deer	84	2224.51
Boar	46	501.87
Roe deer	73	358.91
Aurochs	3	21.36
Horse	3	30.86
Moose	1	15.91
Beaver	4	51.65
Badger	6	25.24
Marten	1	2.21
Wolf/dog	1	5.28
Wildcat	1	0.65
Mole	3	1.49
Total	226	3239.93
Unidentified mammal		
Very large mammal	12	182.64
Large mammal	88	483.33
Medium-large mammal	106	127.63
Medium mammal	28	62.27
Small-medium mammal	11	4.24
Small mammal	65	7.82
Mammal	83	47.95
Total	393	915.88
Fish		
Pike	23	19.03
Wels	14	37.68
Bream	1	0.05
Other fish	95	60.75
Total	133	117.51
Bird		
Coot	3	0.99
Teal	1	0.33
Gray heron	1	1.19
Pochard	3	1.92
Other bird	47	21.78
Total	55	26.21
Amphibian	8	0.25
Unidentified	157	149.56
Total	972	4449.34

abundant in the regions of higher overall bone density, in the nearshore areas of the peat. Red deer bones, by contrast, are more abundant somewhat farther from the shoreline. Roe deer and boar bones are similarly distributed to those of red deer, while bird bones are similar in distribution to the fish bones. In other words, the larger mammal bones tend to be farther out in the peat than are the smaller fish and bird bones. It may be that these distributions represent sim-

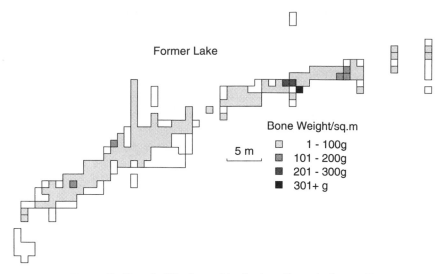

Bone Weight/sq.m

□   1 - 100g
▨   101 - 200g
▩   201 - 300g
■   301+ g

5 m

Figure 59. Henauhof Nordwest: Distribution of bones in Stratum 3.

ply a size-sorting as a result of discard: larger bones were tossed somewhat farther than smaller bones. Support for this interpretation is provided by an
examination of the average bone weight per 1-meter-square. The squares with
higher average weights are not the same as those with most bones, and they
tend to be farther from the shoreline as well. Wave action may also have played
a role in this size-sorting.

8.5.3. Features

Many pieces of fire-cracked rock were found in Stratum 3. These are scattered in a diffuse pattern, apparently representing discard from hearth-cleaning
episodes. It is interesting to note that their distribution is similar to that of the
larger bones, 2–4 m from the shoreline. Most of the charcoal shows a similar
distribution as well. This stratum also contains much natural wood, distributed
throughout the site, both close to and far from shore. This distribution is expected of natural wood accumulations in the marshy lake shallows. In addition
to numerous branches and twigs, there are several large tree trunks lying perpendicular to the shoreline, representing trees that fell into the lake from the
solid shore.

To summarize, the patterns of remains reflect the operation of both natural and cultural processes. Driftwood accumulation and tree falls resulted in
the distribution of natural wood throughout the stratum. Purposeful discard of
materials into the lake shallows caused a scattering of artifacts throughout the

peat as well, but patterns of discard caused a sorting of these materials by size. Most of the lithic artifacts, together with the small bone, including most of the fish and bird remains, were discarded in the nearshore region. Larger bones, fire-cracked rock, and charcoal from hearth cleaning, by contrast, were tossed somewhat farther out into the lake. The distribution of other materials—bone points and antler—supports this interpretation.

8.5.4. Other Finds

Antler is very abundant in Stratum 3. The number of finds is 350, but many of these are conjoinable fragments of larger pieces. Most of these (n = 341) are red deer antler; the remainder are from roe deer. These two deer species shed their antlers at different times of the year: red deer in spring, roe deer in fall. Un-shed antler from two different individual red deer, consequently, suggest kills sometime between September and April. One pair of roe deer antlers, found in the same portion of the site as these red deer antlers, was still attached to the skull but just in the process of being shed, suggesting a kill in September or October. Fragments of unshed roe deer antler suggests a kill between April and September. In addition, two shed roe deer antlers were found in this stratum.

The distribution of the antler is relatively concentrated in several areas of the site (Fig. 60). In general, the antler lies rather far from shore, in the same areas as the large bone, rock, and charcoal. Given the large size of the antlers, this distribution is consistent with the interpretation of this region of the site as a large-object toss zone.

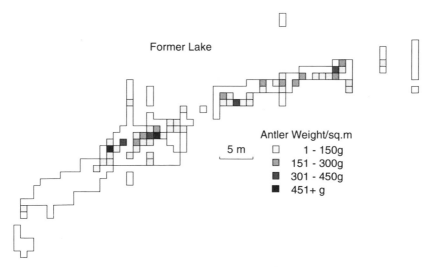

Figure 60. Henauhof Nordwest: Distribution of antler in Stratum 3.

Figure 61. Henauhof Nordwest: Worked antler.

Some of the red deer antler was worked (Fig. 61). Four pieces of shaft show shallow cuts around part or all of the circumference, after which they were snapped. In one case, both pieces resulting from the cut were discarded with no signs of additional use. One antler tool appears to be a hide flesher (Fig. 62). It consists of a shaft that has a notched end and one highly polished face. Striations in this face are parallel to the long axis, suggesting the motion of use was in this direction. Two fragments of shaft have beveled ends, possibly representing portions of sleeves for stone tools. One point was made of antler; this is a fragment of shaft with an oval cross section and a very porous surface. Four perforated antler axes/adzes were found, all in the eastern portion of the excavated area. They show considerable diversity in size (Fig. 63). An additional perforated antler axe was also found higher in the peat and farther from shore than most of the finds; this seems to represent a later, isolated find. Four fragments of ceramics were also higher than other finds in this stratum and represent later deposits.

Bone points are also relatively numerous. A total of 50 fragments were found. These include 3 small possible needles with cross sections less than 3 mm.

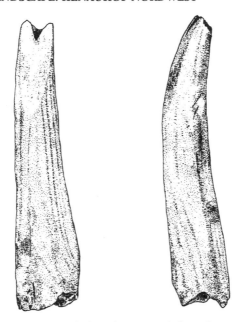

Figure 62. Henauhof Nordwest: Bone hide-working tool.

Two are shaft fragments and 1 is a point tip. One shaft and the point tip are oval in cross section; the other shaft is concavo-convex. Large points (cross section more than 5 mm) include 12 point tips, 34 shaft fragments, and 1 complete point. The whole specimen is pointed on both ends and is concavo-convex in cross section. These points are concentrated in the nearshore area, consistent with their small size. Although not as abundant as in Stratum 4, they are more numerous than in other contemporary sites. If they were used in lake fishing, this would be consistent with the relative abundance of fish remains in this stratum.

Other finds include four metapodia of red deer that have been split longitudinally and are highly polished, suggesting their use in hide-working. In addition, an apparent cache of four sets of metacarpals and carpals of red deer, representing two different animals, was found in the upslope edge of the peat in the western portion of the excavated area. This cache presumably constitutes raw material for the manufacture of bone tools. One fragment of boar's canine bears cut marks. Finally, there are three perforated teeth in this assemblage. One is a wolf canine, one a fox canine, and the third is fragmentary and cannot be assigned to species.

The last finds to be discussed are of considerable interest. These consist of two grinding stones made of a coarse-grained stone with one highly smoothed surface (Fig. 64). One is a large saddle-shaped grinder and the other is a smaller hand-stone. They occurred in the same 1 meter-square at the same

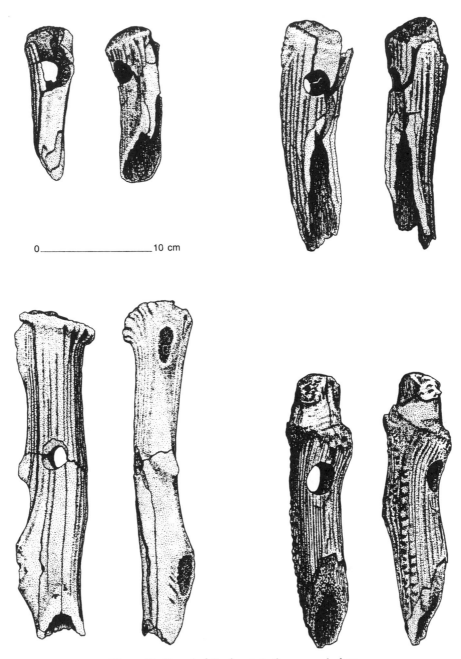

Figure 63. Henauhof Nordwest: Antler axes and adzes.

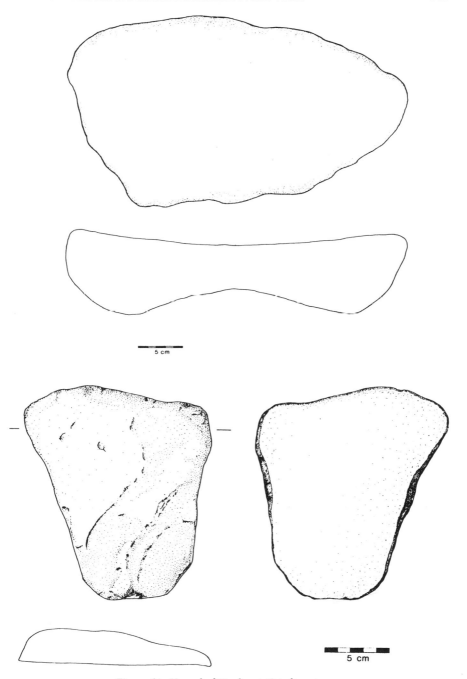

Figure 64. Henauhof Nordwest: Grinding stones.

elevation and together with many other artifacts. These are not typical Mesolithic artifacts. If they were, one might suggest that they were used to grind wild foods—nuts, berries, and so on. Rather, they are characteristic of the Neolithic, and their singular occurrence in this quite Late Mesolithic assemblage raises questions about the contemporaneity of Mesolithic and Neolithic in the area. Müller-Beck (1983) suggests such a contemporaneity between 7000 and 6500 b.p., precisely the period of occupation of Henauhof NW, Stratum 3. These Neolithic artifacts in this Mesolithic assemblage support this suggestion and indicate some form of contact between the two. If these contacts were peaceful and involved exchanges of grain for meat and labor (see Gregg, 1986), then such grinding equipment in a Mesolithic context would make sense. These finds suggest a need for additional research in this time period.

8.5.5. Summary

The Stratum 3 assemblage represents materials discarded in the lake shallows during the Early Atlantic period by Late Mesolithic occupants of the shore. A diverse subsistence was practiced, dominated by large game, but fish were relatively important, particularly given the large size of some of the fish. Antler-working was of considerable importance, as was hide-working. Episodes of hearth cleaning contributed much to the artifact scatter in the peat. Two grinding stones suggest contact with Neolithic groups and a role for grain in the subsistence economy. A later Neolithic occupation is represented by a small collection of ceramic and lithic artifacts.

8.6. STRATUM C

Stratum C is the till that has slumped downslope to overlie the lake sediments. Because this till now lies bedded within the peat of Stratum 3, this downslope movement must have occurred sometime during the Atlantic period, perhaps reflecting increased precipitation and erosion. Before this time, the till would have formed part of the surface of the slope above the lakeshore. Artifacts deposited on this surface from all periods of occupation were carried downslope with the till. Vertically the artifacts are dispersed throughout the till, suggesting considerable mixing during the process of transport. Horizontally the lithic artifacts are also distributed throughout this stratum, with some areas of higher concentration.

The artifacts from Stratum C, consequently, represent an aggregate assemblage spanning the period from the Late Palaeolithic into the Neolithic. The two radiocarbon dates obtained on charcoal from this stratum appear to relate to Neolithic components: 5920 ± 80 and 4540 ± 170. The Neolithic ceramics of this stratum are concentrated in the south-central portion of the site, but this portion of the shoreline was utilized in all other periods as well, so that no separation of the Neolithic materials can be made on this basis. As the different components cannot be separated, little interpretation is possible. The Stratum C materials do represent upslope activities and might be expected to differ functionally from objects deposited on the beach or discarded into the lake, but the composite nature of this assemblage obscures this difference. Moreover, the till could not be adequately screened, so that small items may be expected to be underrepresented in relation to the peat and sand stratum finds.

8.6.1. Lithic Assemblage

There are 509 lithic artifacts in the Stratum C assemblage. The raw material types are similar to those of the other strata. The finer-grained radiolarite and banded chert were preferentially retouched, followed by the cherts and the coarse-grained materials. The typological and technological characteristics of this assemblage are presented in Table 7.

8.6.2. Faunal Assemblage

The faunal assemblage includes 437 bones with a total weight of 877.24 g and an average of 2.01 g. This average is less than that of all strata except Stratum 4, and suggests some fragmentation and attrition of the bones in the process of downslope transport. Of this total, 102 (24%) could be identified to species. Table 12 lists the bones according to species and other taxonomic categories.

Among the bones identified to species, roe deer and fish remains are most abundant, followed by red deer, boar, bovid, and waterfowl. The fact that fish remains are proportionately less abundant in this assemblage than in any other may reflect in part the upslope origin of these bones, although preservational conditions and the difficulties of screening the till may also be responsible.

The bones of red deer and large/very large mammals contain a variety of body parts. Lacking are those of low bulk density, such as vertebrae and distal phalanges, and of low body frequency, such as mandible, skull, sacrum, sternum, pelvis, atlas, and axis. Consequently, if any regularity exists in the occurrence of body parts, this would appear to be due not to behavioral factors but rather to preservational conditions and sampling error. Roe deer remains similarly lack many of the low density parts, but also lack those of highest meat and general utility, suggesting that these parts were subject to different treatment and disposal. Boar remains include many cranial elements but in addition more post-cranial portions (pelvis, humerus, radius, calcaneous, phalanges) than the downslope strata. This underscores the selectivity of body parts underlying the deposition of materials in the shoreline location. Bovids are represented by

Table 12. Henauhof NW Stratum C Fauna

Category	Number	Weight (g)
Identified mammal		
Red deer	21	196.49
Boar	20	154.83
Roe deer	28	45.41
Aurochs	7	96.86
Mole	4	0.63
Total	80	494.22
Unidentified mammal		
Very large mammal	6	86.24
Large mammal	52	168.74
Medium-large mammal	57	57.15
Medium mammal	7	3.95
Small-medium mammal	9	4.31
Small mammal	31	2.99
Mammal	39	13.31
Total	201	336.69
Fish		
Pike	22	3.64
Other fish	6	0.87
Total	28	4.51
Bird		
Teal	1	0.12
Other bird	6	1.99
Total	7	2.11
Amphibian	8	0.42
Unidentified	113	39.29
Total	437	877.24

fragments of skull, mandible, teeth, metapodia, and vertebrae. The fish remains—largely vertebrae and some cranial elements—contain only pike as an identified species. Among the birds, only teal could be identified.

8.6.3. Other Finds

Despite the poorer preservational conditions of this stratum, worked bone and antler artifacts are not uncommon, perhaps because they were made largely from the very dense portions of deer metapodia. A total of 24 fragments of bone point occur in this assemblage. One is a small shaft fragment, oval in cross-section, that may be a portion of a needle. Among the 23 larger point fragments, 2 are nearly complete, 4 are point tips, and 17 are shaft sections. One complete point is oval in cross section, as are 2 point tips and 1 shaft fragment. The other nearly whole point is biconcave in cross section, as are 1 point tip and 9 shaft fragments. One of the point tips and 7 of the shaft fragments are concavo-convex in cross section.

In addition, this assemblage contains 1 cut fragment of a red deer metatarsal and a polished portion of a large mammal limb shaft. Antler tools include a piece of red deer antler with a cut and beveled end (perhaps a fragment of a sleeve for hafting stone tools) and a complete, perforated antler axe. One very fragmentary piece of unworked red deer antler was also found. As mentioned earlier, this stratum also contained 70 ceramic artifacts. Most of these are crude, undecorated body sherds. Two rim sherds are decorated with a series of notches, suggesting an affinity with the Aichbühl culture of the Neolithic. In addition, 1 sherd contained a lug.

8.6.4. Summary

Stratum C contains an assemblage from the upslope portion of Henauhof. This assemblage has components spanning the period from the Late Palaeolithic into the Neolithic that have been mixed in the process of downslope transport. Due to the processes of transport as well as presumably a period of original exposure on the surface, organic materials are not as well preserved as they are in the other strata. Screening of this stratum was not feasible, so that large finds may be overrepresented. Given these difficulties of chronology, preservation and recovery, the assemblage has limited interpretive value. It nevertheless testifies to the richness of the original upslope deposits and emphasizes the selective nature of the downslope assemblages.

8.7. STRATUM 1 AND STRATUM P

The topsoil contained materials of both prehistoric and historic origin. Along with modern ceramics, nails, glass, and saw-cut bones were found a number of finds apparently derived from the underlying strata. The burrowing of moles and rodents has been considerable, particularly in the peat, and has resulted in the upward transport of these prehistoric materials. Finds from original auger probes of the survey derive from either the topsoil or the underlying peat and are catalogued as coming from "Stratum P." Although the original stratigraphic context of these finds cannot be determined, they will be briefly described.

8.7.1. Lithic Finds

A total of 39 lithic artifacts were found in the topsoil and Stratum P. Retouched tools include 1 very short scraper and a large retouched flake. In addition were found 2 flake cores, 3 chunks, 21 flakes and 11 blades.

8.7.2. Faunal Materials

Faunal materials were much more abundant: 127 bones were found in Stratum 1 and Stratum P. These were much larger than those of the other strata, with an average weight of 6.59 g. Among the 46 bones (36%) that could be identified to species, bovids are the most numerous and include many clearly domesticated cattle remains. Other species represented are red and roe deer, wild boar, sheep or goat, dog, wildcat, and waterfowl. Obviously this small assemblage contains later prehistoric or historic materials.

8.8. STRATUM B AND THE IRON AGE FEATURE

To the southwest of the main site area a block of 8 square meters was excavated to explore stratigraphic relationships and to sample the sediments (Fig. 65). In this block a new stratigraphic unit, here called Stratum B, was found. This consists of a heavy brown clay with very little gravel, which overlies the till of Stratum C and the peat of Stratum 3 (Fig. 66). The origins of this clay are unknown. In the southern portion of this block of squares the clay is mixed with an organic, peaty deposit so that the stratigraphic relationships are not clear. From its general stratigraphic position, however, it must postdate both Stratum 3 and the slumping of the till of Stratum C. A radiocarbon date on wood within the stratum produced a date of 2400 ± 70 b.p., which would place it in the Iron Age.

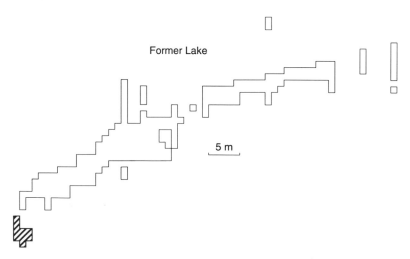

Figure 65. Henauhof Nordwest: Location of Iron Age deposits.

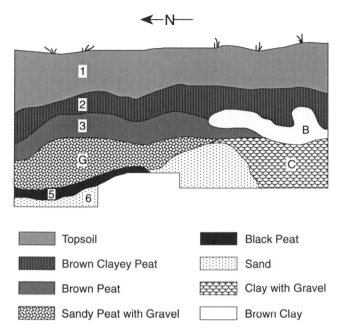

Figure 66. Henauhof Nordwest: Stratigraphic position of Iron Age deposits.

8.8.1. Feature

Most notable among the finds in this stratum are three sharpened wooden stakes (Fig. 67). One of these was upright in a small oval depression in the surface of the underlying till of Stratum C, and was in a rather poor state of preservation. The other two lay in the clay on the surface of Stratum C next to this depression. One was 37 cm long, 5 cm wide, and was sharpened by two intersecting bevels. The other was 89 cm long and 10 cm wide and was sharpened by cutting or chopping around the entire circumference of the point. The upright post was 5 cm in diameter and at least 50 cm in length.

Associated with the posts and flanking the depression were two large rocks. Both of these were reddened from heating. One was roughly triangular with a maximum diameter of 14 cm. The other was oval with a length of 25 cm. In addition there was a considerable amount of unworked wood in the depression and some large pieces of charcoal to the south of the depression.

8.8.2. Artifacts

There were 16 lithic artifacts associated with this feature: a short scraper, 3 whole blades, 2 broken blades, and 10 flakes. The raw materials include gray

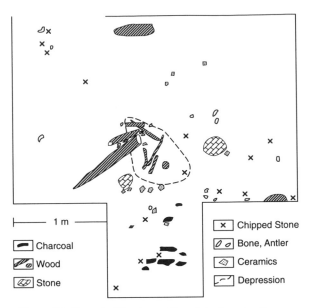

Figure 67. Henauhof Nordwest: Plan of the Iron Age feature.

and tan cherts (81%), red radiolarite (13%), and black coarse-grained material (6%). The whole blades are large, ranging in length from 3.30 to 4.42 cm, with a mean of 3.91 cm.

A total of 22 faunal remains were also found, of which 8 (36%) could be identified to species. These include pig or boar (4 teeth), red deer (2 teeth), roe deer (a distal tibia fragment), and squirrel (a femur). Other remains are shaft fragments from medium-large (4), large (7), and very large (1) mammals, as well as 2 fragments that could only be specified as mammalian. In addition there was 1 piece of red deer antler tine.

An additional find was a small tip of a point made of a black, semiporous stone. This point is square in cross section. The remaining artifacts are 14 body sherds of coarse ceramics that were in and around the oval depression. These differ somewhat in color from the Neolithic ceramics of Stratum C (Gregg, 1993).

These finds are clearly *in situ* remains of activities occurring on the firm shoreline during the later Iron Age. At that time the open water would have been quite far from Henauhof. Further excavations to investigate this area would be warranted.

Chapter 9

Change through Time at Henauhof Nordwest

9.1. INTRODUCTION

A major advantage offered by a stratified, multicomponent site is that it allows investigations of changes through time in behavior at the locality and, to some degree, in the wider region. In order to make inferences about behavioral changes, however, other sources of variation in the archaeological record must be controlled. As samples of prehistoric activities, the different assemblages from Henauhof Nordwest are not strictly comparable. Three factors affecting the formation and recovery of these assemblages—preservation, mode of deposition, and sample size—have imposed certain limits and patterns on these assemblages and therefore have caused specific types of variation among them.

9.2. PRESERVATION

First of all, preservational conditions clearly vary among the strata. Stratum 6 and Stratum 4 consist of sand beaches that were once partially dry. Artifacts deposited on these beaches were exposed to weathering and other natural factors of attrition. Moreover, human activity on these beaches would have caused damage by trampling. By contrast, the peats of Stratum 5 and Stratum 3 were wet at the time of artifact deposition. The artifacts were protected from weathering, decay, and the destructive effects of subsequent human activity. Although the top of Stratum 5 was exposed by lowered water levels after its formation, this occurred after the artifacts had been sealed in the peat.

155

Table 13. Preservational Differences among Strata, Henauhof NW

	Peat		Sand	
	Stratum 5	Stratum 3	Stratum 6	Stratum 4
#(Bone + antler)/# stone	1.15	2.51	0.95	0.89
% Identifiable bones	42.72	27.98	20.65	14.42
Mean bone weight (g)	3.46	4.58	4.74	1.67
#(Fish + birds)/# big game	0.38	0.44	0.09	0.31
# Broken blades/# all blades	0.49	0.47	0.52	0.55

As a result of these preservational differences, certain patterns of differences and similarities among the assemblages may be anticipated. Even if the activities occurring in each period had been identical, one would expect that, in comparison with the assemblages of Stratum 6 and Stratum 4, Stratum 5 and Stratum 3 would have assemblages with: (1) higher ratios of bone and antler to stone artifacts, (2) larger average bone weight, (3) more identifiable bones, (4) relatively more small, delicate bones of fish and birds, and (5) fewer blades broken by trampling.

Table 13 presents the results of comparisons among the assemblages in terms of these characteristics. For four of the measured traits the expectations are clearly upheld. The assemblages from the peat strata do, indeed, have relatively more bone and antler, more identifiable bones, more bones of fish and birds, and fewer broken blades. It should be noted that Stratum 4 has proportionately many more bones of fish and waterfowl that does Stratum 6, despite similar preservational conditions, suggesting a real difference in economic activities between the two strata.

Results of comparisons for mean bone weight are not as clear. The mean weight is highest for a peat level (Stratum 5) and lowest for a sand level (Stratum 4), as expected, but the value for Stratum 3 is lower than that for Stratum 6, contrary to expectations. This deviation reflects a contradiction inherent in the initial expectations. The good preservational characteristics of peat should encourage both less bone fragmentation (and hence larger bones) and survival of small, delicate bones. To the degree that fishing and fowling were important activities, small bones should be more important in the assemblage and should lower the mean bone weight accordingly. Stratum 6 has few fish and bird remains; Stratum 3 has many more, and has the lower mean bone weight as a result.

9.3. ASSEMBLAGE FORMATION

A second factor affecting the composition of the assemblages is their manner of deposition. The materials of Stratum 5 and Stratum 3 are interpreted as the products of purposeful discard into the marshy lake shallows, whereas the arti-

Table 14. Depositional Differences among Strata, Henauhof NW

	Discard		In situ	
	Stratum 5	Stratum 3	Stratum 6	Stratum 4
Mean bone weight (g)	3.46	4.58	4.74	1.67
Mean stone weight (g)	3.22	2.86	2.49	2.41
% Retouched tools	12.85	9.13	22.68	13.12
% Microliths/microburins	8.69	22.92	4.55	42.15
% Cores/chunks	11.17	16.54	16.49	14.75

facts of Stratum 6 and Stratum 4 are the *in situ* remains of activities on exposed beaches. This difference in deposition means that, even if activities remained unchanged through time, the assemblages should differ in a systematic way. Discarded materials are selected for disposal and should show an overrepresentation of large and low-value items. Specifically, it might be expected that, in comparison to Stratum 6 and Stratum 4, the discard assemblages of Stratum 5 and Stratum 3 should show: (1) a higher mean weight of lithic artifacts, (2) a higher mean bone weight, (3) a lower proportion of the small microliths among retouched tools, (4) a higher proportion of cores and chunks relative to flakes and blades, and (5) a lower proportion of retouched tools in the assemblage.

Table 14 presents the comparative figures for these characteristics of the four assemblages. Two of the expectations are clearly upheld. The discard assemblages have higher mean lithic weights and fewer retouched tools, as expected. The pattern of mean bone weights is not as expected and, as discussed in the previous section, appears to reflect the relatively high proportion of fish and bird bones well preserved in the peat of Stratum 3. Contrary to expectations, the percentage of cores and chunks shows little variation among the assemblages, suggesting that any selection of larger items for discard did not select solely for these artifact classes. One reason may be that a number of flakes in each assemblage are quite large, weighing as much or more than some of the small chunks; the technological classification does not adequately measure size or weight. More important, however, is the possibility that discard may not have involved only hand pick-up of materials. The use of scoops or containers of wood, bark, or basketry in cleaning and transporting debris would gather a mixture of large and small objects for discard. Thus, although some size-sorting seems to have occurred, many small flakes and bones are certainly included among the artifacts. Finally, the pattern of microlith proportions does not meet expectations and must be examined further in light of behavioral factors.

9.4. SAMPLE SIZE

Sample size is a third factor that will cause apparent differences among assemblages regardless of their underlying sets of activities. In general, the

Table 15. Sample Differences among Strata, Henauhof NW

	Stratum 6	Stratum 5	Stratum 4	Stratum 3
# Bones	92	206	811	972
# Identified species	6	12	19	19
# Retouched tools	22	23	121	48
# Tool types	10	12	43	22

smaller the sample, the lower the diversity of contents, as rare items have a low probability of being included in a small assemblage. In addition, proportions among component items can vary greatly among small samples of the same parent population. These considerations should encourage caution in interpretations. Both the lithic and faunal assemblages of Henauhof Nordwest vary greatly in size among the strata. It might be predicted, consequently, that diversity of species will increase with the number of identified bones and that the diversity of tool types will increase with the number of retouched tools.

Table 15 presents the comparisons of these measures of diversity in relation to sample size. The diversity of tool types does, in fact, vary generally with the number of tools: the largest lithic tool assemblage (Stratum 4) is also the most diverse, although the magnitude of differences among assemblages is small and is greatly dependent on the gross typology used. To argue on the basis of this diversity that the activities that produced this assemblage were more varied than those of other periods is unwarranted. Similarly, the diversity of species among the identified bones is also generally correlated with the sample size. Stratum 3 and Stratum 4 have more identified bones and more species than do Strata 5 and 6 (see Fig. 79). These data alone cannot be used to suggest differences in diversity of the subsistence base among strata.

9.5. BEHAVIORAL VARIATION

Against the background of these patterns of variation caused by differences in preservation, formation, and sample size, the assemblages can be compared in order to determine behavioral differences among occupations. Two general aspects of behavior will be examined: the organization of raw material procurement and technology, and the relative importance of different activities.

9.5.1. Lithic Raw Material Procurement and Technology

A remarkable feature of the Henauhof Nordwest assemblages is the uniformity of lithic raw material use in all periods. Cherts, radiolarite, coarse-grained materials, and banded chert occur in virtually every assemblage. All but

Table 16. Stone Raw Material Percentages, Henauhof NW

	Stratum 6	Stratum 5	Stratum 4	Stratum 3
Chert	81	82	82	80
Radiolarite	14	11	11	12
Coarse-grained	2	6	6	7
Banded chert	2	1	1	1
Assemblage size	97	179	929	526

Table 17. Percentage of Each Raw Material Retouched, Henauhof NW

	Stratum 6	Stratum 5	Stratum 4	Stratum 3
Banded chert + radiolarite	29	23	18	12
Chert	22	12	12	9
Coarse-grained	0	0	7	3

Table 18. Percentage of Each Assemblage with Cortex, Henauhof NW

Stratum 6	Stratum 5	Stratum 4	Stratum 3
32	42	40	39

the banded chert, which derives from Bavaria to the east, occur in local gravels. Moreover, the relative proportions of these different materials are practically identical among the assemblages, regardless of sample size (Table 16). Among the local materials, cherts always predominate, comprising 80–82% of each assemblage, followed by radiolarite (11–14%) and coarse-grained material (2–7%). The constancy of these proportions suggests that they reflect the natural frequencies of these materials in the gravels. The nonlocal banded chert consistently forms a small component of the assemblages (1–2%), reflecting its greater cost and difficulty of procurement.

The degree to which these different materials are retouched is also relatively constant among the assemblages (Table 17). The finest-grained materials, radiolarite and banded chert, were preferentially retouched (12–29%), followed by the cherts (9–22%) and the coarse-grained materials (0–7%). This pattern indicates that raw material quality, in addition to availability, was a major determinant of use throughout the Mesolithic.

Another indication of the technological constancy through time at Henauhof Nordwest is the percentage of artifacts retaining cortex (Table 18). Between 32% and 42% of the pieces of each assemblage have cortex, and this, together with the small size of cores (Table 19), suggests that similar sources of small nodules were utilized and that lithic reduction was practiced to a similar degree in all time periods. There is a slight trend for cores to increase in size

Table 19. Core Dimensions, Henauhof NW

	Stratum 6	Stratum 5	Stratum 4	Stratum 3
Mean length (cm)	2.68	2.89	3.06	3.29
Median length (cm)	2.49	2.73	2.81	3.09
Minimum length (cm)	2.23	1.75	1.78	1.85
Maximum length (cm)	3.64	4.04	6.29	6.15
N	6	13	47	35

through time and, correspondingly, for the percentage of artifacts with cortex to decrease, at least within the Mesolithic strata (5–3).

Blades comprise a relatively constant percentage of each assemblage, ranging from 22% to 31%. The length of whole blades varies somewhat among the assemblages, with means ranging from 2.51 cm (Stratum 4) to 3.17 cm (Stratum 5). Histograms by percentage for blade length (Fig. 68) show the distributions underlying these differences. Stratum 5 has very few short blades, whereas Stratum 4 has a preponderance of blades less than 2.50 cm long, and Stratum 3 has a much more even distribution of blade lengths than the other strata. Given the similar range of blade lengths among these strata, it is not clear what these differences mean, although two factors may be relevant. Stratum 4, with the predominance of small blades, is *in situ* rather than a discard deposit; size-sorting for discard may have led to an underrepresentation of all small artifacts in Stratum 5 and Stratum 3. In addition, among the characteristic artifacts for the Beuronien C, one of the main periods of deposition for Stratum 4, are small backed bladelets. Their manufacture may have coincided with a general technological emphasis on smaller blades.

Another aspect of technology that deserves consideration is the approach to formal tool manufacture. Microliths, for example, are considered to be the hallmark of the Mesolithic, but their relative abundance at different sites and periods is quite variable. At Henauhof Nordwest they are rare during the Late Palaeolithic, increase in frequency thereafter through the Beuronien C stage, and then decrease in the Late Mesolithic. Although functional and depositional factors may be relevant here, it is important to note that this temporal pattern is not unique: it is similar to that seen at the stratified site of Birsmatten Basisgrotte in northwest Switzerland. If microliths are interpreted as components of highly portable and easily repaired tools (see Bleed, 1986; Zvelebil, 1986), then these changes in frequency may reflect changes in technological organization and mobility.

An additional indicator of changing technological organization is the relative importance of combination tools. Such tools, for example, combination burin-scrapers, are costly to manufacture but represent portable, multipurpose implements, and may have been quite advantageous in situations where

**Table 20. Combination Tools as Percentage
of All Tools, Henauhof NW**

Stratum 6	Stratum 5	Stratum 4	Stratum 3
9	9	1	0

mobility was at least seasonally high and specific tool needs were difficult to anticipate. Such tools are generally rare in the Mesolithic but more common in the Magdalenian. At Henauhof Nordwest their relative frequency decreases from the Late Palaeolithic into the Early Mesolithic (Table 20), perhaps reflecting decreasing long-distance mobility or increasing predictability of tool needs.

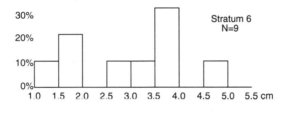

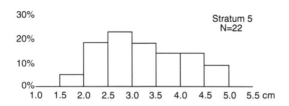

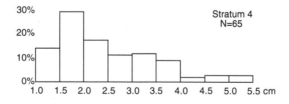

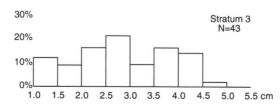

Figure 68. Henauhof Nordwest: Histograms of whole blade length by level.

9.5.2. Activities

Activities vary among sites and levels of sites for a variety of reasons. In comparing the different assemblages of Henauhof Nordwest, three main determinants of activity variation must be kept in mind. Environmental change is one such determinant. The main occupations at the site span the period from the Late Pleistocene to the Early Atlantic. During this time there were fluctuations in temperature and rainfall, successional changes in vegetation, and alterations in animal communities. Opportunities and constraints facing human populations would have varied as well, and should have affected the activities reflected at the site.

A second determinant is seasonal and functional variation in settlement. Hunting camps should differ from base camps and winter camps from summer. If Henauhof Nordwest changed its role within the settlement system during its periods of occupation, this would affect the activities occurring at the site.

Finally, the Palaeolithic and Mesolithic show long-term changes in technology and tool typology. To the degree that artifacts involved in these changes are used to examine activities at the site, assemblage differences among the levels will appear to represent activity differences.

The evidence available to investigate activities at Henauhof Nordwest consists of the lithic, bone tool, and faunal assemblages. Relative proportions among species or tool types may suggest relative importance of different foods and activities, but a number of cautions must be kept in mind. Sampling and depositional factors can influence relative proportions of species, so that inferences about relative dietary proportions must be cautious and treated as hypotheses. Relative importance of different tool types is subject to the same problems but, in addition, the connection between specific artifact types and specific activities is neither direct nor well understood. The comparisons that follow will be general and designed to suggest hypotheses for future work. Where possible, several types of evidence will be used simultaneously.

9.5.2.1. Stone Tool Manufacture

As mentioned earlier, the low frequency of small chipping debitage and of lithic refits in all levels suggest that significant amounts of stone-working were not performed on the shore. The occurrence of this activity at the upslope site is indicated, however, by the presence and rather high frequencies of cores and core-modification debris. In an effort to assess the relative importance of stone-working at the site, the percentages of cores, cortex flakes and blades, and core-modification flakes and blades may be examined in the different assemblages. As Table 21 indicates, there is very little difference in these percentages among the strata. There is consequently no basis for inferring any changes

Table 21. Primary Lithic Reduction Products, Henauhof NW

	Stratum 6	Stratum 5	Stratum 4	Stratum 3
Cores	6	13	47	35
Cortex flakes	7	16	67	41
Core rejuvenation flake	4	7	25	11
Cortex blade	4	4	19	17
Core rejuvenation blade	2	3	11	12
Sum	23	43	169	116
Sum as % of assemblage	24	24	18	22

in emphasis of lithic reduction through time at this site. The importance of stone-working, like the use of raw materials and the intensity of reduction, appears similar throughout the occupations at Henauhof Nordwest.

9.5.2.2. Bone- and Antler-Working

Another aspect of technology for which Henauhof Nordwest offers some evidence is bone- and antler-working. Antler occurs in Strata 5, 4, 3 and C, but 96% of all pieces are found in Stratum 3. Part of the explanation for this pattern may be the preservational and depositional context of this assemblage: the generally large pieces of antler were selected for discard into the peat, where they were well preserved. Nevertheless, the similar conditions of Stratum 5 did not lead to a similar accumulation of antler. Moreover, Stratum 4 does show reasonably good bone preservation and a large faunal assemblage, but very little antler. As there are no obvious gross environmental reasons for this concentration of antler only during the Late Mesolithic, seasonal and organizational factors have to be considered and will be discussed in the following section.

Bone tools, by contrast, are much more abundant in Stratum 4, primarily in the form of bone points, despite the better preservational conditions of Stratum 5 and Stratum 3. As these points are virtually all broken they suggest tool repair rather than manufacture, but their presumable replacement on hafts with complete points indirectly implies bone point manufacture at the site as well. No bone debitage from such manufacture has been found, however. It is interesting that the bone points are most numerous in this Stratum 4 assemblage, which also has proportionately the most microliths, suggesting that the repair of various types of projectiles was a major activity during this occupation.

The stone tool class most commonly thought to be involved in both antler and bone work is burins. The chisel end can be used for cutting grooves and the edge of the spall scar for smoothing shafts. From the bone and antler evidence at Henauhof Nordwest, consequently, one would expect burins to be proportionately most numerous in Stratum 4 and Stratum 3, but this is not the case. Among retouched tools, burins are most numerous in Stratum 6 and least so in Stratum

4. When burin-scrapers are considered as well, in fact, Stratum 4 and Stratum 3 have fewer burins than the other strata. When burins and burin-scrapers are examined as percentages of all lithic artifacts, rather than retouched tools, this pattern holds. As indirect evidence for bone- and antler-working, the percentage of burins does not agree with the organic remains. Explanations for this lack of agreement must examine the possibilities that burins were discarded in a manner differently from the organic products or that burins were used for a variety of other purposes as well. Microscopic analysis of wear patterns on burins would help shed light on this last possibility. Unfortunately, the sample of artifacts examined from all levels of Henauhof Nordwest showed significant chemical (carbonate) modification, preventing interpretations of use (Bamforth, 1991).

9.5.2.3. Hide-Working

Hide-working is another activity for which there is indirect evidence at Henauhof Nordwest. Fleshers and rubbing tools of bone and antler may have been used in the primary processing of hides. Unfortunately, the numbers of these finds are small: five were found in Stratum 3 and two were found in Stratum 4. In terms of a percentage of the preserved bone pieces, Stratum 3 has relatively more, but little significance should be attached to such small numbers. More indirectly, the abundance of stone scrapers might be informative about the importance of hide-working, but as these tools were most certainly used for such other activities as woodworking, they cannot confidently be used as a measure. Finally, the importance of sewing, as opposed to primary hide preparation, may be indicated by the abundance of bone needles and awls, but here again the numbers are small: Stratum 3 has three possible needle fragments and Stratum 4 has seven needle fragments and an awl-like tool.

9.5.2.4. Food Proportions

Somewhat more direct evidence is available for investigating the relative importance of different foods and food-getting activities: the food remains themselves. Problems of interpretation here are posed by differential discard and preservation. The relative proportions may be examined in terms of both numbers and weights of identified bones; determinations of minimum numbers of individuals have not been made. Bone numbers are sensitive to differential butchering and fragmentation, but will be useful for comparisons with other sites for which only bone counts are available. Bone weights may be more appropriate for evaluating the relative importance of different foods in the subsistence and will be emphasized when possible.

Big game is consistently dominant among the identified food remains of all assemblages, ranging from 91.3 to 96.6% by weight (Table 22). This domi-

Table 22. Role of Big Game in Assemblages, Henauhof NW

	Stratum 6	Stratum 5	Stratum 4	Stratum 3
Identified big game (g)	202.4	529.16	727.74	3153.41
As percentage of identified remains	96.6	91.3	94.6	93.2
Medium-large, large, and very large mammals (g)	220.31	114.28	458.04	793.6
Sum	422.71	643.44	1185.78	3947.01
Sum as percentage of total faunal assemblage	96.9	90.4	87.5	88.7

nance is supported by an examination of identified big game together with medium-large, large, and very large mammal bones as a percentage of all bones, which ranges from 87.5 to 96.9% by weight. The relative proportions of different species of big game, however, show considerable differences among the strata.

Horse occurs in all assemblages but is dominant in Stratum 6 and very rare in the others. Horses were a major prey during Magdalenian and Late Palaeolithic times in southwestern Germany (Weniger, 1982; Albrecht, 1983). Adapted to open country, they decreased in frequency and ultimately disappeared with the postglacial reforestation (von Koenigswald, 1972). Consequently, their significant decrease in frequency between Stratum 6 and Stratum 5, coinciding with the beginning of the Holocene, reflects their natural decrease in abundance with the environmental changes.

Bovids are another prey that were most important in the earliest periods and decreased during the Mesolithic, although not as early or as much. It is most likely that these represent aurochs remains rather than bison, which apparently became locally extinct during the late Pleistocene. Aurochs and horse together comprise almost 90% of the identified remains by weight during the Late Palaeolithic, while among the other bones of Stratum 6, very large mammals (presumably largely horse and aurochs) account for 37% of the assemblage. By the Early Atlantic of Stratum 3, horse and aurochs constitute less than 2% of the identified remains by weight and very large mammals less than 5% of the total assemblage.

Other big game species show trends through time in their exploitation as well. As horse decreased in importance, red deer increased and dominated all of the Mesolithic assemblages. Use of roe deer began in the Preboreal period and increased during the later times, while elk remains occur only in the later two strata. Boar was hunted in all periods, but its importance was greatest in the Early Atlantic, when moist deciduous forests dominated the vegetation.

The picture presented by these big game remains is one of significant subsistence change over the period of occupation, much of which appears directly tied to the late- and postglacial environmental changes. The Late Palaeolithic saw an emphasis on extremely large mammals, but prey size decreased during the course of the Mesolithic, particularly as roe deer increased in importance. These changes in prey emphasis also represent a shift to more dispersed animals that formed smaller groups, especially in the case of roe deer and elk.

Fur-bearers—beaver, hare, squirrel, badger, fox, marten, wolf, and wildcat—consistently played a small role in subsistence. By weight they range between 1 and 3% of the assemblages. There is a clear tendency for increasing diversity of these small mammals through time, from one species in Stratum 6 to five in Stratum 3. This increasing diversity is unrelated to the sample size of small mammal bones and is an indication of generally increased subsistence diversity, particularly during the Late Mesolithic.

Remains of birds consistently represent a small proportion by weight (0.4–1.0%). The relative abundance of their remains (1–6% of the bones of each assemblage), however, suggests that their dietary role may have been slightly more regular or more important than their weight indicates, particularly since bird bones are hollow and may be underrepresented in proportions by weight. This suggestion is supported by the diversity of species among the remains, particularly in Stratum 3 (four species) and Stratum 4 (seven species).

Fish remains also represent a small proportion by weight of each assemblage (1–3%), suggesting that their dietary contribution was small. On the other hand, fish remains consistently comprise a high percentage of the bones in terms of numbers of fragments, from 5 to 14%. Moreover, bone point fragments, possibly associated with fishing, occur in each of the Mesolithic assemblages and are particularly abundant in Stratum 4, which may indicate a more important role for fishing than bone weights alone imply.

A final category of food remains to consider is plant foods. Unfortunately, the finds at Henauhof Nordwest can shed little light on this poorly understood aspect of Mesolithic subsistence. Despite good preservational conditions, no remains of plant foods were found. Actually, their absence in the context of such good preservation may be meaningful. Hazelnuts, for example, are well preserved in the sediments, but unlike the finds at other sites to be discussed, none of the nuts shows signs of breakage, charring, or storage, even during the Boreal period when they were most abundant. It may be either that hazelnuts were not used during the occupations at Henauhof, perhaps because the site was occupied during seasons other than late fall or winter, or that hazelnut shells were discarded upslope rather than on the shore or in the lake.

The only artifacts likely to have been used with any certainty for plant foods are the grinding stones found in Stratum 3. Their probable use in the processing of grains, their similarity to Neolithic grinding stones, and the possible contemporaneity of this stratum with Neolithic occupation in southwestern Germany all suggest that these artifacts, together with grain, may have been obtained from farming groups in the region. A hypothesis worth further investigation is that some Late Mesolithic groups were involved in exchanges of meat or labor to farming villages in return for grain (see Gregg, 1986). If so, then wheat or other grains may have played a role in the diet of the Late Mesolithic inhabitants of Henauhof Nordwest. It is also possible that the antler axes and adzes that occur in the Late Mesolithic Stratum 3 were used as digging tools, perhaps for wild roots and tubers.

9.6. SUMMARY

Despite interpretative problems due to differences among the assemblages in preservation, deposition, and sample size, a number of inferences about behavior during the course of the Late Palaeolithic and Mesolithic may be drawn. One remarkable feature is the consistency of certain behaviors despite changes in environment and typology. The types, proportions, and intensity of retouch of various lithic raw materials are surprisingly uniform among all assemblages, as are the size of nodules and the degree of their reduction. The proportion of blades and their range in length also remain relatively constant through time. From the perspective of the organization of stone tool technology, this site appears to have occupied a constant role reflecting largely the *in situ* reduction of locally available nodules. This suggests that the site was a stable component of the settlement system, a residential base with a rather generalized subsistence economy, even though both the specifics of the site's economy and the overall regional settlement organization changed.

Against the backdrop of this technological uniformity are some patterns of technological change. Microliths increase in relative frequency from Late Palaeolithic to Beuronien C times and then decrease significantly in the Late Mesolithic. As the faunal remains suggest no corresponding changes in the role of hunting, for which microliths were at least primarily used, these typological changes must reflect differences in technological organization. Easily repaired composite hunting tools were apparently more important during Beuronien C times and the Early Mesolithic in general than they were during the Late Mesolithic. The emphasis on a composite tool technology in the Beuronien C is mirrored by a simultaneous emphasis on the production of smaller blades and the regular production of backed bladelets. In the Late Mesolithic new types of projectiles appear—transverse arrows using trapezes and barbed antler harpoons (although none of the latter were found at Henauhof Nordwest)—suggesting a change in approach to the manufacture of hunting equipment and perhaps in the organization of hunting as well. The implications of these changes clearly deserve further investigation. Similarly, the decreasing importance of combination tools from the Palaeolithic into the Mesolithic suggests an organizational rather than simply functional change that requires further research. In both cases, factors that may be important to examine include the degree of mobility, the predictability of tool needs, and the pattern of time use in manufacturing and subsistence activities throughout the year.

Certain aspects of subsistence activities are also remarkably constant through time at Henauhof Nordwest. Big game hunting was consistently the most important subsistence pursuit. Small mammals, birds, and fish made regular dietary contributions in all periods. Changes in big game types and proportions reflect, at least in part, changes in availability due to late- and postglacial environmental changes. One result of these changes was that smaller and less aggregated species became increasingly important, which would have had implications for hunting techniques and frequency.

Both fish and waterfowl may have contributed more to the diets than their weight proportions in the faunal assemblages suggest. The number of bones of these two resource groups, their dispersed horizontal distribution among the finds, and, in the case of waterfowl, the diversity of species, all indicate the regular procurement of these foods as important supplements to big game. In addition, an important role for fishing is suggested by the abundance of bone points, particularly in Stratum 4, and by the large size of some of the individual fish, especially the wels or catfish.

Little can be said about the role of plant foods, although in the case of hazelnuts, absence of evidence may indicate something about the seasons of occupation of the site. The grinding stones of Stratum 3 suggest the possibility that grains may have been obtained from farming groups and have contributed to the Late Mesolithic diets.

Slight indications exist for increasing subsistence stress through the course of the Mesolithic, in the form of increasing diversity of large and small mammals. This evidence is particularly strong for the Stratum 3 assemblage and may be related to other changes occurring during the Late Mesolithic. This period is characterized by a greater forest density and diversity, fewer sites, and a more restricted site distribution than the earlier Mesolithic, particularly the Beuronien A and B (Hahn, 1983; Müller-Beck, 1983). Moreover, it is with the Late Mesolithic that the greatest changes in lithic technology occur as well. All of these changes may represent a coherent system of interrelated adaptive responses.

Chapter 10

Sites on the Landscape: Henauhof West

10.1. INTRODUCTION

This site lies on a sand and gravel ridge connected to the solid shore approximately 200 meters west-southwest of Henauhof Nordwest (Fig. 69). During periods of low water this ridge would have been a corridor of dry ground surrounded on three sides by marsh, and with higher water it would have been a narrow spit jutting out into open water. The site was discovered by test trenches in 1987, at the suggestion of the landowner, who knew about the solid ridge in the midst of the spongy ground of his field. Excavations carried out in 1989 investigated a total of 83 square meters in a large contiguous block together with a few dispersed trenches.

On the ridge itself the stratigraphy consists of a peaty topsoil overlying a sandy soil occurring on top of the sterile sand and gravel of the ridge. On the flanks of the ridge the stratigraphic sequence is more complex (Fig. 70). Below the topsoil are peat deposits, formed later than the sandy soil on the ridge and overlying this soil as it slopes down and away from the ridge. Below the peat is a bright orange clay, followed by sand and gravel of the ridge and lake bottom. All sediments except the clay were screened through 3 mm mesh. Two archaeological levels were discovered in these sediments.

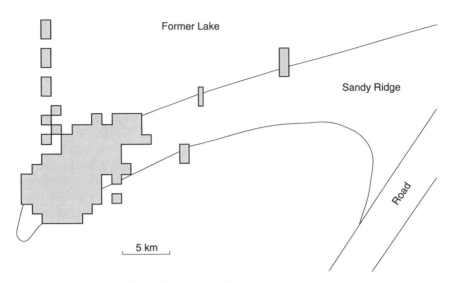

Figure 69. Henauhof West: Excavation area.

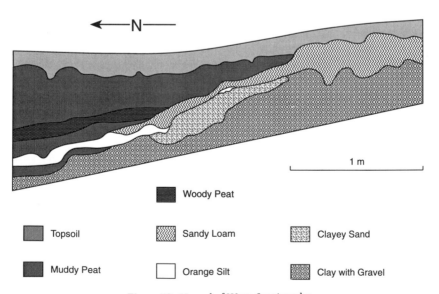

Figure 70. Henauhof West: Stratigraphy.

Table 23. Henauhof West Lithic Artifacts

	Stratum	
Category	Late Palaeolithic	Late Mesolithic
Retouched		
Microlith	1	0
Backed point	3	0
Backed blade	7	0
Truncation	2	0
Notched piece	1	0
Borer	2	0
Burin	6	1
Scraper	2	0
Other	5	0
Total retouched	29	1
Core	2	1
Chunk	3	1
Cortex flake	3	0
Core rejuvenation flake	3	0
Flake	51	8
Core rejuvenation blade	7	2
Broken blade	28	1
Blade	19	1
Total lithics	145	14

10.2. LATE PALAEOLITHIC

Most of the artifacts come from the sandy soil and from the clay around its edges on the flank. Dating of these materials to the Late Palaeolithic is based on lithic typology; radiocarbon samples proved to be inadequate, but a soil column has been submitted for palynological analysis, which should confirm the typological dating. The small lithic assemblage (Table 23), containing 145 artifacts, has a predominance of chert, followed by radiolarite, coarse-grained material, and banded chert. Retouched tools, which make up 20% of the assemblage, show a preponderance of backed knives and points (Fig. 71). Few cores and little primary debitage are present. A high proportion (37%) of the artifacts show obvious signs of having been subjected to heat.

A total of 883 bones was found in this level, most in extremely fragmented condition, with an average weight of 2.16 grams. The few that are identifiable to species (4, or 0.5%) belong to red deer and wild boar (Table 24). A total of 98% of the entire faunal collection has been determined to represent medium-large and larger mammals, and could have come from these two species.

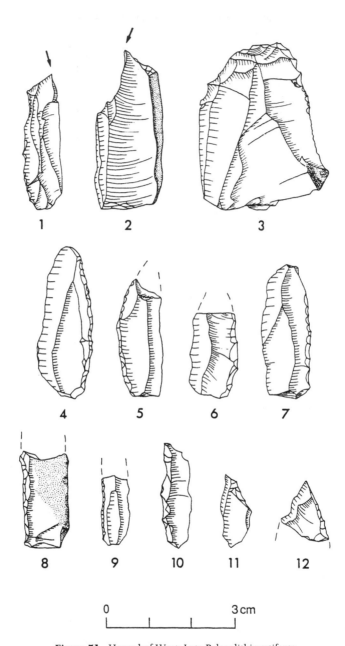

Figure 71. Henauhof West: Late Palaeolithic artifacts.

Table 24. Henauhof West Fauna

Category	Late Palaeolithic		Late Mesolithic	
	Number	Weight (g)	Number	Weight(g)
Identified mammal				
Red deer	3	15.17	1	30.97
Boar	1	0.51	1	5.31
Aurochs	0	0	3	41.11
Total	4	15.68	5	77.39
Unidentified mammal				
Large mammal	312	1341.87	66	802.87
Medium-large mammal	545	532.39	102	141.79
Medium mammal	8	5.59	9	9.25
Small mammal	4	1.42	2	0.24
Mammal	8	12.94	18	20.12
Total	877	1894.21	197	974.24
Fish	1	0.31	0	0
Bird	0	0	1	0.06
Human	1	0.95	0	0
Total	883	1911.15	203	1051.69

Among the identifiable body parts, a high proportion (74%) represent long-bone shaft fragments. One additional find is a piece of red ochre.

The artifacts occurred in clear concentrations (Fig. 72, 73). At the western end of the ridge were two large stones surrounded by many bones and stone artifacts that had been intensely heated. This may have been a hearth area where the artifacts were accidentally burned, but little charcoal remains to document this. A number of the stone artifacts can be conjoined, suggesting that they were broken in this area, perhaps through trampling (Fig. 74). In addition, the abundant bone suggests that this was an area of bone-fracturing, possibly using the large stones as anvils.

Two other concentrations exist: one of bone in the southeast part of the excavated area, and one of stone in the northeast. There is a tendency for stone raw materials of different sorts to cluster in different parts of the site, suggesting that some secondary stone-working occurred in different episodes in different parts of the site.

This level shows a number of contrasts with the Late Palaeolithic level of Henauhof Nordwest, suggestive of a different functional role for the two sites (Jochim, 1995). Henauhof West appears to represent a small, brief occupation focused largely upon the hunting and butchering of a few species of large game. Its faunal and lithic assemblages show a low diversity of species and tool types, and provide little evidence for activities other than those mentioned. In contrast, the Late Palaeolithic assemblage of Henauhof Nordwest contains evi-

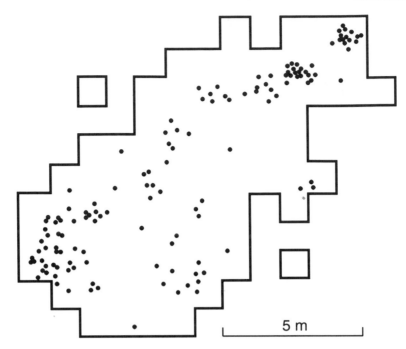

Figure 72. Henauhof West: Distribution of Late Palaeolithic lithics.

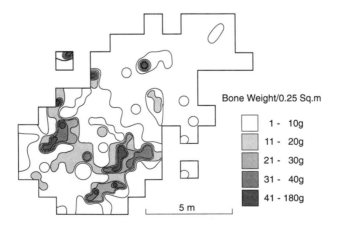

Figure 73. Henauhof West: Distribution of Late Palaeolithic bones.

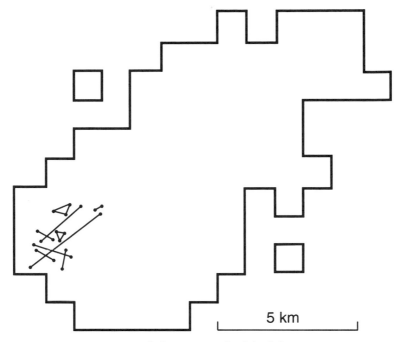

Figure 74. Henauhof West: Late Palaeolithic lithic conjoins.

dence for a much greater diversity of activities, and includes nonutilitarian items among the artifacts. It appears to represent a longer-term, residential occupation on the shores of the lake.

10.3. LATE MESOLITHIC

A small collection of archaeological materials was found in the peat overlying the sandy soil and clay. A bone sample from this level produced a date of 7090 ± 70 b.p. (BETA-23453), placing it in the Late Mesolithic.

The few lithic artifacts (N = 14) include one burin of banded chert, one core of radiolarite, and various flakes and blades, mostly of chert (Table 23). The low average weight (1.51 g) reflects the small size of most of the flakes.

The faunal assemblage of 203 bones contains identified remains of red deer, aurochs, and boar, as well as one fragment of bird bone (Table 29). Most of the collection (85% by number, 97% by weight) represents remains of large and medium-large mammals. The average weight of fragments is 2.92 g, much larger than that of the Late Palaeolithic level. Virtually all body parts are repre-

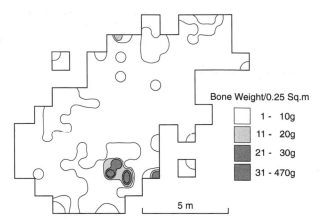

Figure 75. Henauhof West: Distribution of Late Mesolithic bones.

sented among the remains, with long bone shaft fragments constituting 63% of the identified parts. The bones are concentrated largely in the south-central portion of the site (Fig. 75).

Peat growth was apparently well advanced in this part of the lake basin by the time of the Late Mesolithic (Liese-Kleiber, 1988). Consequently, these materials were probably deposited by *in situ* activities on the ridge and its peaty edges. At most they represent ephemeral episodes of butchering and tool resharpening of what must have been extremely brief stays.

Chapter 11

Sites on the Landscape: Henauhof Nordwest 2

11.1. INTRODUCTION

On the former lakeshore about halfway between Henauhof Nordwest and Henauhof West lies yet a third site, Henauhof Nordwest 2 (Fig. 76). This site was discovered by test trenches placed along the old shoreline and appears to be quite separate from Henauhof NW on the basis of numerous sterile trenches lying between the two. A total of 72 square meters was excavated in 1991 and the sediments water-screened through 3 mm mesh.

The stratigraphy of this site is similar to that of Henauhof NW (Fig. 77). Below the topsoil lies a peat layer, below which is a layer of sandy peat with gravel. Below this are layers of black and yellow clay, yellow sand, and finally the gray clay of the lake basin. Artifacts were found in all layers, but the majority, approximately 75%, lay in the sandy peat.

11.2. LATE MESOLITHIC

A hearth was found in the sandy peat layer, composed of a roughly oval ash and charcoal lens on a thin layer of yellow clay and measuring 75 by 140 cm (Fig. 78). On one side of the hearth was a small concentration of stone artifacts, primarily radiolarite, and on the other side a concentration of bone and antler fragments. Several burned stones and bone fragments lay within the hearth itself. Two radiocarbon dates were determined on charcoal from this

Former Lake

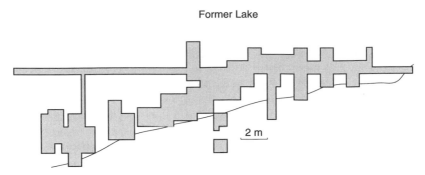

Figure 76. Henauhof Nordwest 2 excavation area.

level: 7260 ± 180 and 6940 ± 60 (BETA 46907, 46909), thus placing the materials in the Late Mesolithic.

   A total of 134 stone artifacts were found in this level (Table 25). The few retouched pieces include 2 microliths, 2 borers, 2 burins, and 3 scrapers. The Late Mesolithic attribution is strengthened by the presence of a trapezoid among the tools and of a number of very regular blades. The majority of the artifacts, however, consist of flakes and waste, together with two cores. The raw material percentages are: Jurassic chert (65%), radiolarite (21%), banded chert (3%), and a variety of other materials.

   Organic remains were well preserved, but very fragmentary (Table 26). Among the 156 bone fragments (together weighing a total of 456 g) were re-

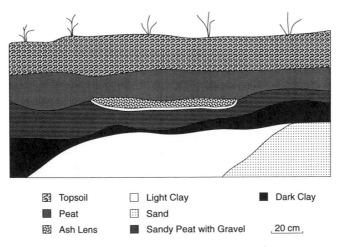

⧉	Topsoil	☐	Light Clay	■	Dark Clay
■	Peat	⊞	Sand		
⧈	Ash Lens	■	Sandy Peat with Gravel		20 cm

Figure 77. Henauhof Nordwest 2 stratigraphy.

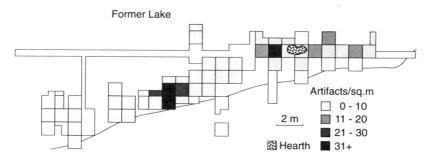

Figure 78. Henauhof Nordwest 2: Distribution of lithic artifacts.

mains of red deer, roe deer, aurochs, boar, beaver, birds, and fish. Red deer remains were most abundant, comprising 65% by weight; in addition, 21% by
weight were identified as remains of large or medium-large mammals, and
could also be remains of red deer. The identified body parts include primarily
cranial elements and extremities. One deer metapodial was worked as a hide-
scraper.

Also among the finds were 142 pieces of antler (665 g), including 130 of red
deer and 12 of roe deer. A few of the red deer antler fragments showed cut marks.
One unshed roe deer antler suggests a death between April and September.

Table 25. Henauhof NW 2
Lithic Artifacts

Category	Late Mesolithic stratum
Retouched	
Microlith	2
Burin	2
Scraper	3
Other retouched	2
Total	9
Core	2
Chunk	17
Cortex flake	15
Core rejuvenation flake	11
Flake	60
Cortex blade	1
Core rejuvenation blade	4
Broken blade	9
Blade	6
Total lithics	134

Table 26. Henauhof NW 2 Fauna

Category	Late Mesolithic stratum	
	Number	Weight (g)
Identified mammal		
Red deer	25	293.46
Boar	1	5.61
Roe deer	1	0.48
Cervid	10	5.56
Aurochs	1	7.44
Beaver	2	4.31
Total	40	316.86
Unidentified mammal		
Very large mammal	17	25.38
Large mammal	7	64.09
Small mammal	11	1.12
Total	35	90.59
Fish	20	7.59
Bird	3	1.95
Unidentified	58	38.63
Total	156	455.62

This site was apparently occupied only briefly by a small group during the Late Mesolithic. Based on the abundant antler remains, this occupation may have taken place in the late summer or early fall. The primary prey was red deer, but other resources were also taken. Among the activities that occurred were the working of stone, antler, and hides. A spatial analysis of the materials suggested that several distinct clusters could be identified (Bertrando, 1993). These include lithic reduction adjacent to the hearth, butchering and bone dumping centered approximately 10 meters from the hearth, and hide-working somewhat farther away. The preservation of these patterns supports the interpretation of a brief occupation with little disturbance of spatial associations.

Henauhof NW 2 shows a number of contrasts with the Late Mesolithic Level 3 of the nearby site of Henauhof NW. At the latter site, the finds represent materials of a larger occupation upslope, purposely discarded into the lake margins. This sample of discarded material consists of, on average, larger artifacts than those of Henauhof Nordwest 2. The diversity of stone and bone tools and of faunal resources is also much greater at Henauhof NW, a fact which, together with the creation of a clear rubbish disposal area, points to a longer and more diverse occupation at Henauhof NW. Apparently this peninsula was used frequently, in various ways, during the Late Mesolithic.

This site also shows several contrasts with the Late Palaeolithic site of Henauhof West, although both appear to represent short-term camps focused

largely on hunting. A comparison of the two assemblages indicated that Henauhof Nordwest 2 had proportionally greater amounts of cores and core modification debris and of utilized flakes and blades, and relatively fewer retouched
tools (Orphal, 1994). These differences may suggest that Henauhof Nordwest
2 had more primary lithic reduction and a more expedient technology. This, in
turn, may reflect a situation of short-distance movement within a settlement
system entailing greater sedentism at a residential base during the Late Mesolithic.

11.3. OTHER FINDS

In addition the the Late Mesolithic finds in the sandy peat, a number of
other artifacts were discovered in other layers.

11.3.1. Palaeolithic

An extremely fragmented bone hide-scraping tool was found in the yellow sand just above the clay of the lake basin. By comparison with the stratigraphy of Henauhof NW, this find may date to the Late Palaeolithic.

11.3.2. Early Mesolithic

In the black clay beneath the sandy peat were found several stone artifacts, including one microlith characteristic of the Early Mesolithic.

11.3.3. Bronze Age

Two concentrations of crude ceramic sherds were found in the peat layer
above the sandy peat. One of these actually occurred within a lens of smooth
yellow clay within the peat. The body sherds were quite thick and the rims were
undecorated. Two body sherds contained perforated lugs. Also in the peat, and
possibly associated with these ceramics, were 12 chipped stone flakes and
blades and 28 bone fragments, including remains of red deer and boar. These
finds may date to the late Bronze Age, as a worked wooded post, which was
found near one of the ceramic concentrations, was dated to 2910 ± 70 (BETA
48896). This post, measuring 60 cm in length, lay at an angle of 30–35 degrees
from vertical, began in the peat, and extended down through all layers into the
basal clay.

Chapter 12

Henauhof and the Federsee in the Regional Landscape

12.1. INTRODUCTION

The fieldwork at Henauhof Nordwest was originally motivated by two main goals. At the more general level, the research was designed to investigate the role of the Federsee in the Mesolithic land use patterns in southwestern Germany. The abundant surface finds around the former shores of this lake testify to the importance of this region in the settlement system, and the differences in habitat and site type in comparison to the sites of the Danube and its tributaries—lakeshore versus river valley, open-air versus cave or rockshelter—offered the potential of considerable differences in activities among the sites. The lack of well-published excavations and, more generally, of organic finds, however, limited our knowledge of the nature of activities performed there. Consequently, work was focused on the waterlogged peat deposits along the former shores, with the hope that such a good preservational context would provide the desired information.

A second and more specific goal of the fieldwork was to test the predictions of a theoretical model of hunter–gatherer subsistence and settlement patterns as applied to southwestern Germany (Jochim, 1976). Based on seasonal changes in the economic potential of different areas, it was predicted that the Federsee would have been most attractive to human settlement in the summer. During this season, fish and plants were expected to have been more important and large and small game less important in the diet than in other seasons.

In order to attain both these goals it is necessary to compare the finds at Henauhof Nordwest to those of other Mesolithic sites in the region. Underlying such a comparison is the assumption that, despite a variety of problems to be discussed, site contents will reflect site activities and that differences in contents among sites will reflect differences in their component activities.

12.2. PROBLEMS OF COMPARISON

Many of the problems involved in comparing different sites are the same as those complicating comparisons of different levels of Henauhof Nordwest. Because faunal materials are the most direct evidence of subsistence activities, conditions of organic preservation in the different sites must be given consideration. All of the caves and rockshelters to be used in the comparisons produced relatively large faunal assemblages. Jägerhaushöhle, for example, had a collection of approximately 8000 pieces of bone; these bones, however, were extremely fragmented and calcined through heating, allowing only 15% to be identified to species (Boessneck, 1978a). The conditions contrast with those of Henauhof Nordwest, where few bones were calcined and identifiable bones constituted between 14% and 42% of each assemblage. The differences in preservation between these two sites may create apparent differences in subsistence. It may well be that the low frequency of small, delicate bones of fish and birds at Jägerhaushöhle is in part due to the poorer preservational conditions at this site in comparison to those of Henauhof Nordwest. The bones from Falkensteinhöhle, by contrast, are much less calcined and, as a result, 38% of the 1963/64 collections could be identified to species (Boessneck, 1978b). It may be no coincidence that fish remains are relatively more abundant at Falkensteinhöhle in comparison to Jägerhaushöhle. At a third site, Inzigkofen, approximately 45% of the bones could be identified to species and here, too, fish remains are relatively more abundant than at Jägerhaushöhle (Boessneck, 1978c; Lepiksaar, 1978).

A second problem that must be kept in mind is that the processes of deposition underlying the various faunal assemblages may be quite different among the sites. The roofed areas of caves and rockshelters, where excavations have concentrated, may have been only a portion of the area actually used during occupation; the terraces and slopes in front of the cliffs may have been at least as important in terms of intensity of use. If so, the types of activities and debris may have varied across the entire site area and the cave or shelter contents, consequently, would be a partial, and perhaps biased, selection of the original site assemblage. Unfortunately, we have no information about the nature of this potential bias. If the shelter of the natural roof of these caves and rockshelters was a main reason for the use of these sites, then one might predict that a variety of repeated domestic activities—food preparation, tool repair—would have been performed inside. By contrast, activities requiring considerable space or producing much debris—primary butchering, hide-working, and purposeful debris discard—would have more likely occurred outside. If so, the assemblages from the caves and rockshelters may be complementary to those from Henauhof Nordwest, which appear to represent largely discard collections and the remains of extensive activities on the beach. On this basis, even if the activities at all the sites were identical, one would expect that the Henauhof Nordwest assemblages would differ from those at the cave and shelter sites in a systematic way. Henauhof Nordwest materials should be less diverse, should show a higher proportion of large items (including big game bones), and should have more evidence for primary butchering and hide-working. As the first two of these expectations are not met, there is good reason to suspect that the activities underlying the different sites are not identical.

A third problem confronting a comparison of the sites is that of sample size. Such measures as the diversity of faunal species, the presence of rare species, or the relative proportions of different species are all sensitive to sample size. The number of identified bones in each assemblage must be taken into account when comparing these characteristics.

Finally, differences in excavation techniques and reporting of finds will affect comparisons among the sites. It is not clear, for example, whether materials from Jägerhaushöhle or the recent excavations from Falkensteinhöhle and Inzigkofen were screened. If they were not, as seems to be the case, then small finds such as fish and bird bones may be underrepresented in their assemblages in comparison to Henauhof Nordwest. Nevertheless, since similar excavation techniques were used at all three cave and shelter sites discussed here, the relative differences among them may be significant: fish, for example, may have been much less important at Jägerhaushöhle that at Falkensteinhöhle or Inzigkofen. In addition, the faunal reports from the cave and shelter sites present information on numbers of bones and estimates of minimum numbers of individuals, but not bone weights. The information available for the Henauhof Nordwest assemblages consists of numbers and weights of bones, but not minimum numbers of individuals. Consequently, comparisons among the sites must be based on bone counts, which are sensitive to differential fragmentation and preservation among the sites.

12.3. GENERAL COMPARISON

Several characteristics of all of the Mesolithic assemblages at Henauhof Nordwest, regardless of underlying differences in preservation and deposition, set them apart from the cave and rockshelter assemblages. The general patterns of similarities and differences may help distinguish the nature of activities at the open-air, lakeside occupations from those at cave and shelter sites in the narrow valleys of the Alb. Given the various problems inherent in such comparisons, these patterns can only be suggestive of coarse differences, but do indicate some broad geographic distributions.

First of all, the proportion of big game among the identified bones is consistently lower in the Henauhof Nordwest assemblages (36–51%) than in those at Jägerhaushöhle (59–100%), Falkensteinhöhle (58–89%), or Inzigkofen (60–85%). Consequently, the role of big game hunting at Henauhof Nordwest appears to be less important than in these upper Danube sites that date to the Beuronien C and Late Mesolithic. This pattern is unlikely to be caused by differential preservation because big game bones are less likely than others to have been identified to species in the cave and shelter sites (Boessneck, 1978a). Moreover, the diversity of big game species in the Henauhof Nordwest assemblages (5–6 species per assemblage) is greater than that of Jägerhaushöhle (2–4 species per assemblage), Falkensteinhöhle (3–4 species per assemblage), or Inzigkofen (3 species per assemblage). The patterns are unrelated to sample size. In the central Alb the Beuronien C site of Felsställe also has a higher percentage (73%) and lower diversity (3 species) of big game than Henauhof Nordwest. It would appear that big game hunting was both less specialized and less important at Henauhof Nordwest than in the central and western Alb during this period of the Mesolithic. Sites of the Early Mesolithic in the eastern Alb, on the other hand, show lower percentages of big game (Spitalhöhle: 2%; Malerfels: 13%), and Lautereck, a Late Mesolithic site in the central Alb, has only 8% big game bones in its faunal collection. These small assemblages have 1–3 species of big game.

A second and related pattern is that the Henauhof Nordwest assemblages all have a greater proportion of fish remains among the identified bones than the sites of the western Alb. At Henauhof Nordwest the percentage of fish ranges between 31 and 33% in the Mesolithic levels, whereas at Jägerhaushöhle this figure ranges from 0 to 1%, at Falkensteinhöhle from 4 to 18%, and at Inzigkofen from 4 to 20%. By contrast, the Early Mesolithic site of Malerfels in the eastern Alb has 76% fish among its identified bones and the Late Mesolithic site of Lautereck in the central Alb has 85% fish.

A third pattern is that the Henauhof Nordwest assemblages all have proportionally more birds, primarily waterfowl, among the identified bones. The percentage of birds at Henauhof Nordwest ranges from 12 to 26%. At Jägerhaushöhle the comparable figures are 0 to 3%; at Falkensteinhöhle, 0–3%; at Inzigkofen, 2–8%; at Malerfels, 3%; and at Lautereck, 1%. Only at Spitalhöhle in the eastern Alb are birds proportionally more important, comprising 56% of the identified bones. At this and other Alb sites, however, most of the bird re-

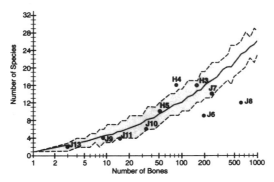

Figure 79. Comparison of Henauhof Nordwest and Jägerhaushöhle: Faunal diversity and sample size.

mains are not waterfowl, but rather land birds, including capercaillie, black grouse, and hazel hen.

A fourth pattern is that the overall species diversity of the faunal assemblages of Henauhof Nordwest is greater than that of sites such as Jägerhaushöhle. Within each site the number of identified species increases with the number of identifiable bones in the assemblage, but for any given sample size, Henauhof Nordwest is more diverse. The statistical significance of these differences may be evaluated using the method described by Kintigh (1984). Using a 90% confidence interval, it may be inferred that Henauhof Nordwest Stratum 4 is significantly more diverse and Jägerhaushöhle Levels 8 and 6 are less diverse than would be expected given their sample size (Fig. 79).

The conclusion from these patterns is that the Henauhof assemblages present a picture of a much more balanced, generalized subsistence than do the Alb sites. The sites of the western Alb appear much more specialized on hunting a few big game species. The sites of the central and eastern Alb, on the other hand, are more often specialized on fish or land birds. In addition, the Henauhof Nordwest assemblages include a greater diversity of larger mammals that is unrelated to sample size.

Two other, technological, characteristics distinguish the Henauhof Nordwest assemblages from the sites in the Alb. One of these is the importance of burins among the retouched stone tools. In the Mesolithic assemblages at Henauhof Nordwest, burins range from 16 to 23% of the retouched tools. By contrast, at Jägerhaushöhle and Inzigkofen these tools are extremely rare and at Falkensteinhöhle they comprise approximately 6% of the tools found. Given our poor understanding of the uses to which burins were put, it is difficult to interpret this pattern.

The second technological characteristic of the Henauhof Nordwest assemblages is their abundance of bone point fragments. Although similar points are known from several of the Alb sites, none of these has nearly the amount found in the assemblages of Strata 5, 4, and 3 at Henauhof Nordwest. The fact that several occur in the Late Mesolithic assemblage of Lautereck, in which fish are abundant among the faunal remains, supports an interpretation of their use in fishing. Hence, their abundance at Henauhof Nordwest may be related to the importance of fishing in the lake shallows.

12.4. SEASONALITY AT HENAUHOF NORDWEST

A comparison of the Henauhof Nordwest assemblages with those of the upper Danube sites must include an examination of evidence for season of occupation, as this was predicted to have differed among these sites. The only direct seasonality evidence available from Henauhof Nordwest is unshed antlers; these indicate unambiguously seasons of kills. Shed antlers, by contrast, may have possibly been collected at any time. Much indirect evidence, in the form of faunal constituents and proportions, is also available, but will be considered secondarily.

Unshed antlers were found only in the assemblages of Stratum 4 and Stratum 3, and so consideration of seasonality must be confined to these strata. Because these strata also produced the largest assemblages, the effects of sample sizes on other, indirect indices are also least.

The baseline for examining the indirect evidence of faunal proportions will be the sets of seasonal activities predicted by the original theoretical model (Table 27). Big game hunting was expected to have been most important in winter, followed by fall, spring, and summer. Fishing was complementary to this pattern: most important in spring, followed by summer, fall, and winter. Birds, modeled as migratory, non-resident waterfowl, were predicted to have been most sought in late winter/spring and in late fall/early winter. Plant foods were expected to have been most important in spring and summer, less so in fall, and least in winter. Finally, small mammals were predicted to have been of roughly equal importance year-round, but least so in early fall.

**Table 27. Predicted Resource Dietary Percentages
of Theoretical Model**

Resource	Late winter	Spring	Summer	Early fall	Late fall
Big game	81	31	34	47	62
Small game	12	9	14	6	8
Fish	4	27	21	14	4
Birds	2	3	0	3	3
Plants	0	30	30	30	15

12.4.1. Stratum 4

The Stratum 4 assemblage contains unshed antlers of roe deer, suggesting a kill sometime between April and September or October. Thus, an occupation during late spring, summer, or early fall is indicated.

In order to evaluate the faunal proportions in terms of this indication of seasonality, the assemblage must be compared to roughly contemporary ones. Stratum 4 has an aggregate assemblage spanning the Early Mesolithic Beuronien B, Beuronien C, and into the Late Mesolithic. A comparable aggregate from Jägerhaushöhle would consist of the assemblages of Levels 10 through 7. The sites of Falkensteinhöhle and Inzigkofen each contains a total assemblage that includes Beuronien C and Late Mesolithic components, and so are largely contemporary as well. Table 28 presents the percentage of bone counts for each of the sites used in the comparison.

If Henauhof Nordwest, Stratum 4 was indeed largely warm weather occupations, then one would expect that fish would play a larger role and big game a smaller role in its fauna than in cold weather occupations. As Table 28 indicates, this is clearly the case, and if these differences are not due solely to differences among the sites in preservation, deposition, and excavation, then these data support the interpretation of a warm-weather occupation at Henauhof Nordwest during the Boreal period. Various plant foods should also have been important during this season, but Henauhof Nordwest provides no evidence about their use. The absence of evidence for the use of hazelnuts in this assemblage despite good preservational conditions, however, may suggest that the occupation did not occur in late summer or fall. The high proportion of birds in the Stratum 4 assemblage is not as expected, but this may reflect deficiencies in the original model. Although the birds potentially utilized include migratory and resident waterfowl as well as resident land birds, the model of their changing seasonal use emphasized the migratory waterfowl and predicted their use only during late winter/early spring and late fall/early winter. Completely ignored were year-round and summer residents at lakes like the Federsee. The relatively high proportion of waterfowl bones and their relative species diversity may reflect hunting of such residents, perhaps during summer moult when

Table 28. Resources as Percentages of Number Identified Bones, Beuronien C and Late Mesolithic

Resource	Henauhof NW 4	Jagerhaus 10,9,8,7	Falkenstein all levels	Inzigkofen all levels
Big game	38	79	56	73
Small game	5	19	29	15
Fish	33	1	1	2
Birds	25	1	15	11

they were easiest to catch. Finally, the abundance of bone points in the assemblage may indicate the importance of fish spearing in the lake shallows, which would have been most productive when fish were spawning and least mobile. The pike and catfish of Stratum 4 spawn in the late spring/early summer and tend to remain rather inactive in shallow water during summer and into early fall. Hence, their abundance supports the interpretation of warm-weather occupations during the Boreal period at Henauhof Nordwest.

12.4.2. Stratum 3

The direct evidence for seasonality of occupation in Stratum 3 presents a different picture. Two sets of unshed red deer antler suggest kills some time between September and April. A fragment of unshed roe deer antler indicates a kill between April and September or October, and the pair of roe deer antlers just in the process of separating from the skull suggests a kill in September or October. One could argue from these data for year-round occupation, but an occupation during the early fall—September/October—could have produced all of these kills. Other, more indirect evidence can be examined in light of this interpretation.

For comparative purposes, other roughly contemporary assemblages must be used. Stratum 3 represents a Late Mesolithic occupation. Comparable assemblages would include Lautereck Shelter, Level C, the upper portions of the levels at Inzigkofen and Falkensteinhöhle, and Level 6 of Jägerhaushöhle. Table 29 presents the percentages of bone counts of various resource groups for these sites.

According to the original model, early fall should be a season when big game, birds, and fish were of intermediate importance and small game of least importance in comparison to spring/summer and late fall/winter sites. The assemblage of Henauhof Nordwest, Stratum 3 is consistent with these expectations. If these assemblage proportions are not due solely to the processes of deposition and preservation, then the assemblage of Stratum 3 may, indeed, represent an early fall occupation on the lakeshore. Since this is the season

Table 29. Resources as Percentages of Number of Identified Bones, Late Mesolithic

Resource	Henauhof NW 3	Jagerhaus level 6	Falkenstein upper 1/3	Inzigkofen upper 1/3	Lautereck C
Big game	51	94	68	78	8
Small game	4	3	28	12	7
Fish	32	3	0	3	1
Birds	13	1	4	8	85

when red deer antler is in best condition for working, the abundant evidence for antler collection and processing in this stratum is also consistent with this interpretation. The presence of the grinding stones may also be examined in this light. Grain could have been obtained from farming groups during and after the late summer harvest; early fall may have been a major season of exchange and grain-processing by the Late Mesolithic groups.

12.5. IMPLICATIONS

Clearly, many of the contrasts between Henauhof Nordwest and the Alb sites are due in part to differences in preservation, mode of deposition, and techniques of excavation. Nevertheless, the patterns are strong and coherent across a variety of data classes. On the basis of these patterns it can be suggested that activities on the Federsee shores at Henauhof were generalized and included fishing and fowling to a greater extent than at many of the Alb caves and shelters.

The original expectation that Federsee residential occupations would occur in summer appear to be upheld during the Boreal period when Stratum 4 was formed. During the Late Mesolithic the pattern of use of the Henauhof shore seems to have changed. The evidence suggests a residential occupation during early fall, when hunting was more important and fish and fowl less so. Antler-working was a major activity during this season, and processing of grain obtained by exchange with farming groups may have occurred as well. The sites in the western Alb appear to represent largely colder-weather camps, but Lautereck Shelter on the edge of the central Alb, with its emphasis on fishing, may represent a summer camp.

This shift in the season of residential occupation at Henauhof may reflect a more general organizational change occurring during the Late Mesolithic. Some evidence from Henauhof Nordwest suggests this to have been a period of greater subsistence stress than earlier, perhaps related to environmental changes or the influx of farming groups into the area. In this context, exchange of meat or labor for grain may have begun. If so, then such an exchange relationship would have required rescheduling of activities and perhaps a changed emphasis in hunting by Late Mesolithic groups. Alterations in settlement patterns may have followed as well. Aggregation around the shores of the Federsee may have been rescheduled from summer to fall as a result.

The Federsee in general seems always to have been a magnet for a variety of activities, as witnessed by the differences between the Late Palaeolithic sites of Henauhof West and Henauhof Nordwest, Level 6, and between the Beuronien A/B sites of Taubried and Henauhof Nordwest, Level 5. During the Late Mesolithic, however, settlement seems to have become more logistically organized. In addition to the evidence for longer-term residential occupation at Henauhof Nordwest, with its large discard area and evidence of caches, this portion of the Federsee witnessed a number of short-term, more specialized occupations at the sites of Henauhof West, Henauhof Nordwest 2, Henauhof Nord I, and Henauhof Nord II. These seem to have been variously occupied in spring, summer, or fall and to have had narrower focuses on hunting or fishing. These Henauhof shores document well the fluctuating use of one locale within the overall settlement patterns, as emphasized by Binford (1982).

Chapter 13

The Late Palaeolithic Landscape

13.1. RESOURCE PRODUCTIVITY, EFFICIENCY, AND RISK

Any consideration of the relative abundance, cost, and variability of specific resources in prehistoric environments truly deals with uncertainty. In the particular case of southwestern Germany at the end of the last ice age we confront habitats that no longer exist, with plant and animal associations that cannot be found today. Moreover, these habitats changed at irregular rates, probably with different effects on each potential resource. At best, we can use archaeological finds and modern studies to develop a general impression, in terms of rough rankings rather than spuriously precise quantification.

The late glacial period, corresponding to the Late Palaeolithic in archaeological terms, lasted approximately 1500 years (11,800–10,300 b.p.). In pollen studies it is conventionally divided into the warmer Alleröd and the briefer, cooler Younger Dryas periods. As discussed earlier, the entire period is characterized by a widespread pine-birch forest with some spatial and temporal variations in density and composition. Any open areas of shrubs, herbs, and grasses would have existed only at the higher elevations. Modern boreal forests provide somewhat of an analog, but differ in their higher latitude, longer winters, and greater seasonal extremes in temperature. The more temperate German forests were presumably more productive, but how much so, and in what form, is unknown. Certainly the diversity of plant species represented in the pollen records is low and they include none of obvious value as important human foods. Raw materials such as willow bark, pine pitch, and birch sap and bark would have been abundant, but it is difficult not to assume that the overwhelming majority of human foods were animals, just as they had been in the preceding steppe-tundra.

What animals were present in these forests? Archaeological finds indicate that the larger herbivores at least included reindeer, horse, red deer, mountain goat, aurochs, moose, roe deer, boar, and brown bear. Others possibly present were the giant deer (found during this time along the Rhine north of the study area) and chamois (found in southwest German sites both before and after the Late Palaeolithic). This community of up to 11 species of large herbivore contrasts considerably with that seen in modern boreal forests of Canada, where moose, caribou, and bear are frequently the only large herbivores. Unfortunately, our chronological control is too coarse to determine whether all these large herbivores were contemporaneous or not. Ten of these species—all but giant deer—were probably present throughout the entire 1500 years, because they occur in the area both before and after this period as well.

As a result, the Late Palaeolithic hunters would not have faced a new and unknown suite of resources; they were already familiar with all of the major prey. What *was* new was the gradually changing habitat in which these prey were found, the slowly differing relative proportions of each, and the changing behavior of each in the new landscape. In terms of optimal foraging theory, all of these large herbivores had already been in the optimal diet. The herds of reindeer and horse, which had presumably been previously highly ranked in terms of pursuit efficiency, were decreasing in abundance with reforestation. Animals particularly favored by these vegetational changes, on the other hand, would have included red deer, aurochs, and moose. Increasingly during the course of the Late Palaeolithic, these prey would have been the major food packages on the landscape. Whereas moose are relatively solitary most of the year, the other two probably showed periodic aggregations—of 5 or more for red deer and possibly up to 18 for aurochs (Mithen, 1990). According to Mithen's calculations, the ranking by pursuit efficiency of these animals would have been: (1) aurochs, (2) moose, and (3) red deer, paralleling body size.

A total of eight different species of big game are represented among the 12 assemblages with faunal remains. Any single site has between one and four of these (or 13–50% of the hunted species), suggesting some degree of seasonal or locational variation in hunting. Red and roe deer are by far the most common, occurring in 10 and 8 of the 12 sites respectively, followed by boar, aurochs, and bear. The average number of big game species per site is 2.3 (29%). Small game are represented in the faunal assemblages by seven species, and each site has from zero to four of these (0–57% of the hunted species), with a mean number of 0.9. Hare (at 5 sites) and beaver (at 4 sites) are the most common. Six, or 50%, of the sites have fish remains, 3 (25%) have birds, and only 1 (9%) has shellfish. No plant food remains have been found in sites of this period.

13.2. SETTLEMENT PATTERNS

Because both aurochs and moose are relatively tied to floodplains, lakes, and marshes, the lower river courses and the morainic area of Oberschwaben would have increasingly been the major focus for efficient hunting in the landscape. Red deer were probably more ubiquitous in their distribution, with some tendency for dispersal in the highlands during warm weather, and concentration at lower elevations during the colder months.

Thus, except during the height of summer, it is likely that all three major big game prey would have had overlapping distributions in areas of lower elevation near lakes and rivers. It is precisely in these areas that vegetational diversity would have been greatest, where many of the smaller mammals such as beaver would have been concentrated, and where waterfowl, fish, and shellfish would have also been found. This resource concentration created "hot spots" of productivity and efficiency in such areas, whereas their resource diversity made them the most reliable areas of subsistence as well. In this late glacial landscape we could expect to see a focus of occupation in Oberschwaben near lakes and rivers, in the Rhine lowlands, and along the lower Danube and Neckar—a focus very different from that during the preceding Magdalenian, when hunting of reindeer and horse would have concentrated on the high grazing areas of the Alb and morainic hills and the narrow valley corridors of animal movement (Weniger, 1982).

The distribution of known Late Palaeolithic sites fulfills these expectations to some degree. The two concentrations of sites along the marshy Rhine lowlands and around the Federsee had easy access to both the major big game species and a variety of smaller mammals, birds, and fish. The diversity of the few, relatively small faunal collections suggests that a focus solely on large mammals was too costly and risky, and had to be supplemented.

On the other hand, the cluster of sites along the Rhine near Säckingen is somewhat surprising. Because of the narrow valley and steeper river gradient, this would not have been a prime location for aurochs, moose, waterfowl, or beaver, some of the major prey of this period. Two features of this region, however, may have made it attractive. As a relatively narrow corridor, it may have funneled seasonal movements of some species—notably red deer—between the hills of the Black Forest and the lowlands, providing for some degree of hunting predictability in an otherwise rather unpredictable landscape. Topographic channeling may have helped compensate for the vegetational homogeneity. In addition, because of the configuration of the riverbed, this area was a center of salmon-spawning and fishing in historic times (Jochim, 1979). It may have provided a reliable focus of fishing during the Late Palaeolithic as well. The fast-flowing, clear water would have been particularly suitable for fishing with spear and bow and arrow, especially during the period of low water, from October to

April. Because salmon were historically absent from this portion of the Rhine from February through April, the most likely time for prehistoric salmon fishing in this area is fall and early winter (October to January).

Another surprise is the cluster of sites in the Alpine foothills, and the few sites in the narrow valleys of the uppermost Danube and its tributaries, which do not offer the low elevation and diverse resources of lakes and marshy floodplains. Here, too, the explanation may lie in the topographic channeling of animal movements by the narrow valleys, particularly important if game distribution is difficult to anticipate in the relatively undifferentiated forests. Given the rather high elevation, the Alpine valley of the Iller may have served as a base of residential occupation largely in summer, when deer would have been moving into the Alps and then out again in early fall.

The final surprise is the apparent paucity of occupation in both the Neckar Valley and the Lake Constance basin. Both are warm areas that offered a variety of resources. If the lack of sites is real, some explanation is required. The Neckar Valley is not as narrow and steep-sided as those of the upper Rhine, upper Danube, and upper Iller, and consequently would not have concentrated animal movements as predictably as the latter valleys. Both the Neckar Valley and Lake Constance are relatively warm regions but, as discussed in Chapter 3, both are more climatically variable and subject to unpredictable late frosts than the Rhine Valley. Perhaps these areas were simply less favorable—in terms of resource predictability, productivity, and diversity—and, in situations of low population densities, could be ignored.

The current picture of site distributions, in summary, indicates concentrations in the low, marshy areas of the Rhine and the Federsee, and in the narrow valleys of the upper Rhine, upper Danube, and upper Iller. Given the diversity of lithic assemblages in all areas, it appears that most sites represent residential occupations in which a variety of activities occurred. Only Henauhof West and some of the higher elevation sites in the Black Forest and Alps may reflect more special-purpose hunting camps. Subsistence may have been largely opportunistic and settlement patterns quite flexible, so that specific areas like the Federsee, with the sites of Henauhof Nordwest and Henauhof West, were used in different ways at different times. Nevertheless, some general trends of seasonal movement, influenced by environmental factors, may have been present. If the Alpine region was, in fact, occupied largely in summer, then in other seasons groups would have moved downslope to the north, into Oberschwaben. In the Alb, the presence of eggs at Helga-Abri suggests a spring occupation, perhaps indicating that the narrow valleys of the Alb were also largely warm-weather areas, with other seasons perhaps spent in Oberschwaben as well. If the upper Rhine was inhabited in fall and winter, then its occupants may have moved downriver to the north into the broad Rhine lowlands near Freiburg in summer.

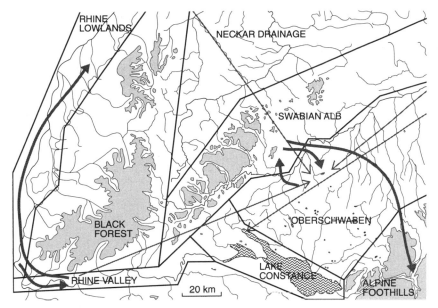

Figure 80. Possible seasonal movements (thick arrows) and long-distance exchange (thin arrows): Late Palaeolithic.

To a limited extent, such general patterns of seasonal movement may be reflected in the distribution of stone raw materials. In all areas, assemblages are dominated by locally available raw materials: Jurassic chert in the Alb, local brown chert at the Federsee, radiolarite in the Alps, local cherts in the upper Rhine, and jasper in the area near Basel. In addition, sites in each area contain some nonlocal material that tie them to other regions. The Alpine sites contain a small amount of Jurassic chert from the Alb, the Alb sites have radiolarite from Oberschwaben, sites in Oberschwaben have both, the sites in the upper Rhine contain some jasper from farther north in the valley, and sites in the northern Rhine lowlands have some material from the south (Fig. 80).

If these general patterns of movement are correct, they pose an interesting problem in light of the discussion of temporal variability in the environment. In each case, regions are linked that show similar patterns of climatic variability: the Alb, Oberschwaben, and the Alps on the one hand, and different portions of the Rhine Valley on the other. If climatic variability led to risk of late or early frosts, then any resulting subsistence unpredictability would not have been adequately dealt with through normal seasonal movements.

Exchange is another means of dealing with such risks by establishing social networks to facilitate occasional movement into other areas. Likely evidence for exchange comes from the sites of Henauhof Nordwest, Henauhof

West, and one surface site, Fe 87, all on the Federsee. These sites contain small amounts of banded chert from a source approximately 200 kilometers to the east-northeast, near Kelheim on the Danube. In addition, Henauhof Northwest also has an ammonite fossil possibly deriving from sources north of the Black Forest, roughly 200 kilometers to the north-northwest, and the site of Fe 87 has one piece of chert from the upper Rhine. In each case, the ties of exchange link these sites in Oberschwaben indirectly to areas clearly beyond the local region, areas that apparently offered different patterns of environmental variation. The one site on Lake Constance that clearly has Late Palaeolithic materials also contains a small amount of the banded chert from Kelheim.

13.3. SYNTHESIS

An economy and way of life that had been previously dominated by hunting probably remained so in the Late Palaeolithic. The gathering and passing on of information about animal behavior and its relationship to weather, season, and topography would have been clearly important and probably valued. If there was a sexual division of labor, it presumably did not take the stereotypic form of men hunting and women gathering, but may have taken a variety of other forms: both sexes hunting, but emphasizing different prey; one sex pursuing large game and the other procuring smaller animals; one obtaining land animals and the other fishing; one procuring food resources and the other concentrating on processing them. Modern ethnographies suggest that women would be the ones more involved in food processing, fishing, or small game capture, and there may be some biological basis for this pattern (Jochim, 1988), but the pattern is uncertain for the particular case of southwestern Germany of 11,000 years ago. Given the relative subsistence uncertainty, it is unlikely that sex roles were rigidly defined.

It may well be that the dominant hunting technique also changed. In the preceding Magdalenian, seasonal prey movements (of reindeer and horse) may have been relatively pronounced and fairly predictable, so that the hunters could focus on intercepting herds in fall and spring at particular points on the landscape (Weniger, 1982). The late glacial prey were much more dispersed throughout the forests, their movements were shorter and less predictable, and prey visibility was poorer as well. As a result, an intercept strategy was increasingly less likely to be productive. Walking through the forest to encounter prey probably became more important as a hunting technique.

This shift in behavior would also have affected settlement patterns. With the decline in herd species and the loss of predictable intercept points, group aggregation for cooperative hunting would have become less profitable. If hunting continued to play a major role in subsistence, the generally dispersed distribution of prey would have encouraged a dispersal of human populations. Local areas could rather rapidly have been depleted of the large herbivores, prompting relatively frequent movements. The only potential evidence for dwelling structures is a few postholes at one of the sites up in the Alpine foothills. A few of the sites consist of concentrations of materials around hearths. Large groups and long stays could have been supported only if subsistence shifted dramatically to emphasize fish and small game, which does not seem to be the case. The overlapping distribution of most resources for much of the year would have encouraged an organization around residential mobility rather than logistic mobility (Binford, 1980), so that most sites would be residential camps with a variety of activities represented. Special-purpose hunting camps might be expected especially in summer, focused on red deer.

Technology could have been affected in various ways as well. If hunting became less reliable and emphasized opportunistic encounters, then it would have been advantageous if weapons were multipurpose, easy to repair, and adaptable to different situations. Bleed (1986) refers to these characteristics as "maintainability" and suggests that such implements will tend to be lightweight and portable with a modular design that allows easy removal of parts for replacement. Repair of such tools should be ongoing, rather than concentrated during periods of "gearing up." One of the hallmarks of Late Palaeolithic technology is its simplicity in relation to that of the Magdalenian, with fewer well defined tool types, generally smaller artifacts, and a lack of complex bone harpoons that could not be easily repaired. Late Palaeolithic hunting technology appears to center on multipurpose, stone-tipped arrows and simple butchering knives, usable in a variety of situations. In the archaeological record, the evidence of tool manufacture and repair is widespread, occurring at most sites, and is characterized by diverse core types with little preshaping and relatively more flakes than carefully made blades (Fisher, 1990). Specific modes of reduction did, however, vary with raw material quality and availability. In the sites on the eastern flank of the Black Forest, for example, the local materials were treated more expediently than the Jurassic cherts from 40 kilometers away. The local materials showed less core preparation, more flake cores, and fewer retouched tools (Pasda, 1994). In addition, as a reflection of relatively high mobility, small portable tools and a diverse array of raw material types are represented at most sites.

It is likely that population densities were low, particularly if hunting played a (or the) major role in subsistence. As a result, marriage rules, if they existed, could not have been overly restrictive, because otherwise, suitable mates would have been too few and too distant. Marriage patterns would have been extensive, linking local groups across the landscape in broad networks. Such extensive social ties may have been reinforced by visiting and exchange. To carry further these speculations, the social networks could also have provided economic security, facilitating movement in times of hardship, such as particularly harsh winters, rainy summers, or local game depletion. To operate effectively in this manner, these networks would have had to cross the boundaries of occurrence of such hardships, to link different areas in the "geography of risk." Groups in Oberschwaben, for example, seem to have had ties to the northwest and east, and southwest.

Aggregations of people would surely have taken place, but not for economic reasons. More likely the desire to maintain social ties, arrange marriages, share information, conduct ceremonies, and simply have fun would have drawn people together. Given the dispersed distribution of most foods, these gatherings could not have been very large or have lasted very long. They would have been ephemeral events on the social landscape, perhaps generally held in late summer or fall when travel was easy and game fat and relatively easy to kill.

The imperatives of production and reproduction would have bound men and women together throughout the year, but in what sort of relationship it is impossible to say. Individual differences among men in hunting luck and skill may have been translated into differences in wealth, prestige, or number of wives, but such differences, based on a rather unpredictable resource base, would have been small. Few resources existed that could, with any regularity, be intensively harvested with concentrated effort. Thus, manipulation of labor and wealth would have been an unlikely path to social prominence. Moreover, the very unpredictability of foraging may have encouraged widespread sharing and the development of social mechanisms both to enforce redistribution and to hold social differentiation in check.

Finally, one might suppose that ideology stressed social cooperation in an uncertain natural world. Whether nature was perceived as hostile or benevolent, it was certainly not lavish or predictable, and so, perhaps, much effort went into acts of appeasement or control of natural forces. Competition between local groups may have had little importance, as few areas were exceptionally rich and reliably productive as to merit disputes. The evidence suggesting the practice of scalping at Dietfurt Cave is puzzling in this regard, and may represent either an isolated event or an aspect of ritual unrelated to competitive warfare. This evidence does serve as a reminder, however, that even the seemingly most homogeneous and egalitarian groups may have deep internal divisions and conflicts. The low degree of competition, coupled with extensive social networks, appears to have discouraged the formation of distinct social boundaries, resulting in a homogeneous material culture across the entire region.

Chapter 14

The Early Mesolithic Landscape

14.1. RESOURCE PRODUCTIVITY, EFFICIENCY, AND RISK

During the course of the Early Mesolithic, overall vegetational diversity increased, leading to a more varied mosaic of plant communities across the landscape. With the increasing deciduous component, seasonal differences in vegetational cover became more pronounced. In this more varied landscape, it is likely that animal distributions and movements of individual animal species became more restricted and predictable, according to the different requirements of each species. Some vegetational patches became more obviously richer than others. Forest density increased, causing greater difficulty in movement and visibility. Canoes were probably present to assist movement, as some sites appear on islands, in the Federsee, for example, but this device may have primarily assisted residential movement and fishing more than hunting. The amount of available graze decreased even more, with the result that horse and, to a much lesser extent, aurochs, declined in abundance. Boar and roe deer would have been particularly favored by these changes and increased in numbers, and red deer would have persisted as an important component of the environment; all three would have been quite widespread in their distribution. Moose may have decreased in abundance and become more restricted in distribution around the lakes of Oberschwaben and the Rhine lowlands.

These changes would have had profound effects on hunting over the course of the Mesolithic. Package size of the most common larger herbivores gradually decreased, at the same time as the costs of hunters' movement through the forests became greater. On the other hand, animal movements may have become somewhat more predictable, allowing some planning of ambush hunts. Overall, however, hunting probably gradually became a more expensive endeavor, favoring dietary diversification and technological changes to improve foraging efficiency. Potential plant foods—roots, nuts, berries—were increasingly abundant, but were doubtless relatively expensive. For example, Taladay, Keller, and Munson (1984) report a net acquisition efficiency of 592 kcal/hour for hazelnuts, a value that is substantially lower than the values generally reported for hunting and fishing, such as by Winterhalder (1981) among the Cree, which range from 1000 to 12,000 kcal/hour. Similarly, Keene's (1981) estimates of costs and yields of various resources in the temperate forests of Michigan suggest a low net acquisition efficiency for nuts in relation to that of fish and game. As dietary diversification occurred, small game, fish, shellfish, birds and some plants were all incorporated into the diet, but large mammals appear to have retained their dominance in the subsistence economy.

Big game prey are represented by eight different species, of which each of the 20 sites with faunal remains has from one to six (13–75% of the hunted species). The average number per site is 3.2 (40%). Red and roe deer are the most frequent, occurring at 18 sites each, followed by boar, which was found at 15 sites. Ten species of small game are represented among the faunal assemblages, with each site having between zero and eight of these (0–80% of the hunted species), with an average of 2.6 (26%). Beaver (13 sites), hare (8 sites), fox (8 sites), and wildcat (7 sites) are the most common. Eleven sites (55%) have fish, 11 (55%) have birds, 3 (15%) have shellfish, and 5 (25%) have hazelnuts.

In comparison with the Late Palaeolithic, these Early Mesolithic faunal assemblages do appear more diverse, with a higher average number of both big and small game species per site. In addition, more sites of the Early Mesolithic have other resources, such as fish, birds, nuts, and shellfish, in addition to the mammalian prey. These patterns may reflect the greater costs of big game hunting and the resultant diversification of the subsistence economy. There also seems to be more variation among sites, as suggested by the wider range of number of big and small game species per site in the Early Mesolithic, and by the relative abundance of small mammals, birds, or fish at some sites. This pattern of variation may derive from the wider range of locations exploited during this time, the greater seasonal distinctions in vegetational and snow cover and hence resource availability, or an organizational trend toward great differentiation of site function.

14.2. SETTLEMENT

The most striking feature of the Early Mesolithic record is the abundance of sites and their broad distribution throughout most of the study area. The large number of sites suggests higher mobility, higher population density, or both, in comparison to the Late Palaeolithic. Again, however, there is little evidence for dwelling structures. Birkenkopf in the Neckar drainage had a stone pavement. Several sites in the Alb (Helga-Abri, Spitalhöhle) and Oberschwaben (Obersee and possibly Tannstock) had oval depressions with and without hearths.

The wide distribution of sites indicates a more diffuse use of the landscape in accord with the broad distribution of the array of major resources. If the countryside was "filling up" with camps, however, it was not doing so in a homogeneous manner. Another notable feature of these sites is their diversity. These caves, rockshelters, and open-air camps occur in a variety of topographic situations: river and stream floodplains and terraces, dunes in the Rhine floodplain, the shores of large and small lakes, high plateau edges along valleys, and the summits of hills. Only the higher elevations in the Alpine foothills now appear to lack occupation. The sites appear to vary also in their frequency of occupation. Unlike the situation in the Late Palaeolithic, it is common to find Early Mesolithic sites with up to a meter of deposits and surface scatters of over 100 meters in diameter, containing thousands of artifacts. Other sites, by contrast, have small, thin deposits or scatters with only a handful of artifacts. The density of archaeological deposits across the landscape is much more differentiated than before.

Assemblages vary more in content among sites as well. Although most lithic collections are quite diverse, with a variety of retouched tool types and stages in reduction, the relative proportions of different artifact classes among sites are variable. Microliths, for example, range widely in importance among assemblages, suggesting considerable functional differentiation among the sites. Faunal assemblages vary as well, not only in the presence or absence of particular prey but also in the role of gross resource categories such as big game, small mammals, fish, and birds.

The heterogeneity of the sites seems to reflect the increasing environmental differentiation. As the landscape became less uniform, certain locations emerged as richer or more reliable and attracted repeated occupation, especially in the Neckar drainage, the Alb, and the larger lakes. The increasingly discrete distribution of different resources encouraged use of a greater variety of topographic locations, with each location exploited differently and thereby producing different assemblages of artifacts and food remains. The environmental variation, however, does not seem to have been sufficiently pronounced to have encouraged a strong logistic organization. Rather, it appears that much the same resources were available within the catchments of different locations, but that their local proportions and opportunities for capture varied.

It is difficult to determine whether these different components of settlement systems were articulated in a strong seasonal pattern. Perhaps the sites in the hills of the Neckar drainage and the edges of the Black Forest were primarily warm-weather camps tied to valley sites in fall, winter, and spring, but in these areas, only Rosi I and Rosi III provide any seasonal evidence, suggesting spring/summer/early fall occupations in these floodplain sites. The Alb caves and rockshelters indicate primarily fall and spring occupations on the basis of the presence of hazelnuts or eggshells and analyses of fish remains. Since hazelnuts may be stored, however, and tend to occur in the sites with greatest evidence for repeated reoccupation, the simple equation of their presence with fall occupations may be unjustified. Similarly at the Federsee, Taubried is considered to represent a fall camp on the basis of its hazelnuts, while Henauhof Nordwest Level 4 may be a warm-weather occupation on the evidence of unshed deer antler, the relative importance of fish and birds and the lack of hazelnuts despite excellent preservational conditions.

The evidence of stone raw material distributions suggests that the Federsee and the Alb may have been linked in one exploitation territory, but the patterns of movement may not have been as seasonally rigid as I originally suggested (Jochim, 1976). According to that model, groups would have spent summers on lakes such as the Federsee and then dispersed into the Alb valleys from fall through spring. Hunting would have been of greatest importance in fall and winter, and fishing and gathering (except nuts) in spring and summer. Actually, some degree of geographic patterning is present among the Early Mesolithic sites in these areas. Sites in the western and central Alb tend to have assemblages dominated by big game and microliths and tend to contain hazelnuts, whereas sites in the eastern Alb and Henauhof Nordwest on the Federsee have greater proportions of small game, fish, and birds in their assemblages, contain relatively fewer microliths, and less frequently have remains of hazelnuts. There may have been a general seasonal axis of mobility linking warm-weather residential occupations in the eastern Alb and Oberschwaben with cold-season camps higher along the Danube in the central and western Alb (Fig. 81). Transitional seasons might have been spent in either region, accounting for the widespread evidence of spring and fall seasonal indicators.

Despite the variations among sites, they generally share a number of characteristics. Lithic assemblages are diverse, with few clear examples of specialized toolkits that might represent logistic extraction camps. Only some of the sites, such as Jägerhaushöhle, and upland sites on the eastern flanks of the Black Forest, where microliths make up over 75% of all retouched tools, might represent more special-purpose camps. Kind (1996) has recently evaluated a number of the Early Mesolithic assemblages and suggested that they may, in fact, be separated into two functional types. Base camps are characterized by relatively low proportions of microliths among the retouched tools and by relatively high proportions of cores among the entire assemblage. Special-purpose (hunting) camps, by contrast, contain relatively many microliths and few cores. Most of the proposed hunting camps are caves and rockshelters in the Alb but

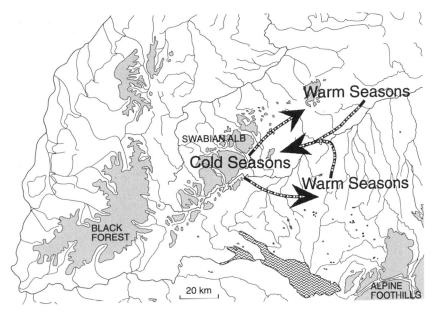

Figure 81. Possible seasonal movements during the Early Mesolithic.

also include the open-air site of Rosi III, Level III. Base camps are largely open-air (including the other Rosi sites and Henauhof Nordwest) but also the rock-shelters of Felsställe and Inzigkofen.

The distribution of activities, like that of sites, appears to be diffuse and variable across the landscape, with areas like the Neckar Valley floor serving as the location of both residential and hunting camps. Supporting this view is the diversity of most faunal assemblages as well, indicating that subsistence activities at these locations were generalized. Virtually all stone raw materials used were available within 10–20 kilometers of each site, suggesting that stone procurement and tool manufacture were ongoing and probably embedded in other activities. Most sites have abundant evidence of cores and manufacturing debris. No specialized procurement or anticipatory gearing up seems to have occurred. This expedient approach to tool-making suggests that resource predictability was still not high and that stone raw material was widespread. Although almost ubiquitous in local gravels, however, the stone nodules appear to have been small and of varying quality, which may account for one other feature common to most assemblages: the purposeful heating or tempering of stone to enhance its fracturing qualities. Early Mesolithic artifacts are often recognizable for the pink-to-red colors and high sheen that result from this process. Finally, the microliths that are the hallmark of this period appear to represent an extreme situation of tool maintainability. These small insets for composite tools could be quickly replaced in the field and may be an attempt to cope with unpredictable contexts of tool use and repair requirements.

14.3. SYNTHESIS

Subsistence during the Early Mesolithic does not appear to have been easy. Travel was difficult in the increasingly dense forests and game was scattered and diverse. The intensity of bone fracturing suggests that maximum use was made of mammalian prey. Fish and birds may have been abundant, but the diverse assemblages of fish and bird bones indicate that no one species was numerous and predictable. The regular inclusion into diets of small mammals, shellfish, and nuts supports the inference that big game hunting was a rather precarious food base. Mobility appears to have been high, but some sites were occupied long enough to accumulate separate trash areas and to warrant the investment in a variety of features. Technology emphasized expedience and easy repair of implements. If increasing vegetational diversity provided some measure of spatial predictability to resource distributions, its main impact seems to have been to encourage repeated use of certain locations.

The broadening diets that now regularly included qualitatively different sorts of foods—nuts, eggs, shellfish—may have encouraged a greater separation of sex roles in subsistence than previously. Arguing from ethnographic analogy, it is easy to envision women and children taking primary responsibility for these new resources. This distinction may, in turn, be one aspect of a growing demarcation of individual roles and identities, as witnessed by the increasing relative frequency of pendants, beads, and other ornaments in the archaeological record. Such social processes may have been encouraged by a growing population. The social landscape, like the natural landscape, was becoming more differentiated.

Residential groups were small and appear to have confined themselves largely to relatively limited regions of ca. 80–100 kilometers diameter, to judge from patterns of stone raw material distribution. Nevertheless, these groups were not isolated. Exchange connected most regions to areas to the north—the Steinheim and Mainz basins (fossil shells)—and possibly to areas to the east (banded chert, fossil shells) (Fig. 82). Such exchange may have functioned as insurance against subsistence failures.

A study of ornaments also suggests the existence of some type of social grouping centered on the upper Danube, which has been equated with ethnographically known hunter–gatherer bands (Newell, Kielman, Constandse-Westermann, Van der Sanden, and Van Gijn, 1990). This "Fish Tooth Band," in turn, forms part of a larger "tribal" grouping of ornaments extending to the

Figure 82. Early Mesolithic exchange patterns.

east, west, and south. Similarities in microlith styles reinforce this pattern, placing the study area within a larger "Beuron-Coincy" region that includes neighboring portions of France, Switzerland, and Austria (Kozlowski, 1973).

This nested hierarchy of spatial patterning suggests that social groups were not closed, but rather participated in networks of interaction across most of central and western Europe. Flexibility in association and movement may have been a useful mechanism for coping with both subsistence and social problems. As the physical environment became more differentiated, attachment to specific places may have emerged as more important than earlier, but strict territoriality seems not to have developed, given the widespread similarities in material culture across the entire region. The skull burials at Hohlenstein, if Early Mesolithic in age, may hint at the beginnings of territorial demarcation. Ritual and ideology may have begun to incorporate specific geographic knowledge that recognized the emergence of particular locations as exceptional in the economic landscape.

Chapter 15

The Late Mesolithic Landscape

15.1. RESOURCE EFFICIENCY, PRODUCTIVITY, AND RISK

The Early Atlantic was a period of higher temperatures and rainfall than the preceding Boreal. Immigration of a variety of deciduous trees and other plants proceeded during this time and a mosaic of vegetational communities continued to develop. The natural landscape became increasingly differentiated into various relatively stable patches in different topographic and edaphic contexts. Vegetational density was also generally increasing.

The effects of these gradual changes on hunter–gatherers living in the region would have been both positive and negative. Travel and long-range visibility would have been increasingly difficult, leading to greater overall subsistence costs. At the same time, the more structured natural environment would have imposed greater predictability upon resource locations and movements. Productive locations for particular plants and small game would have been easy to learn. The routine movements of larger game would have been easier to predict. Moreover, if big game hunting remained the economic mainstay, alternative backup resources may have increased as potential plant foods diversified. The effect would have been one of greater overall subsistence reliability.

Among the 12 sites with faunal remains, eight different species of big game are represented, with any 1 site having between three and six (38–75%) of these. The average number per site is 3.6, or 45%. Red deer and boar are found at all 12 sites, while roe deer occurs at 11. Ten different species of small game occur at these sites, with an average of 3.1 (31%) per site and a range of 0–7 (0–70%). Marten is now the most common (8 sites), followed by beaver (7 sites) and wildcat (5 sites). Fish occur at 10 sites (83%), birds at 8 (67%), shell-

209

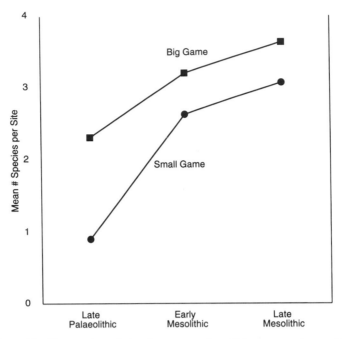

Figure 83. Changes through time in mean number of big game species per site.

fish at 3 to 5 (25–42%; the range is due to the difficulty of assigning finds to particular levels at some of the cave sites), and hazelnuts at 2 (17%).

In comparison to the Early Mesolithic, there is evidence of even greater diversification of the subsistence (Figs. 83, 84). Late Mesolithic sites have higher average numbers of both big and small mammals and more of these sites have additional, nonmammalian resources as well.

15.2. SETTLEMENT

As the vegetational communities became more varied across the landscape, it is likely that food resources became more disparate in their distributions, that it became more difficult to satisfy needs in single locales, and that a more logistic settlement organization developed, with residential camps placed in restricted areas of greatest resource diversity and special-purpose camps established elsewhere to provide access to other resources. The emerging "hot spots" of resource diversity are difficult to specify without knowing the details of resource distributions but are likely to have been in areas of great topographic and vegetational diversity.

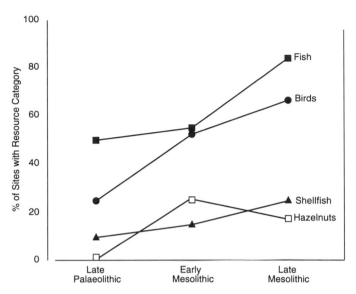

Figure 84. Changes through time in percentage of sites with nonmammalian food remains.

If such areas, providing the security of a diverse set of local resources, became increasingly restricted in number and distribution, then residential mobility may have decreased, while logistic mobility for hunting or other activities may have increased. The only evidence for a dwelling structure, however, is a bark floor at Henauhof Nord II, which may have been a short-term logistic camp. Other sites, like Henauhof Nordwest and a number of the upper Danube caves, do have thicker cultural layers, denser and more numerous artifact concentrations, and sometimes clear midden areas. Locations on valley floodplains, along narrow valleys, and on complex portions of lakeshores seem to have been favored as residential bases, all apparently providing a predictable diversity and abundance of resources. Other areas, such as the hills of the Neckar and the Alb, may have been used only for ephemeral visits with little archaeological visibility.

Fewer sites would have been created and greater contrasts among sites would have emerged, with many activities, including most tool manufacture, being largely confined to the residential camps. The narrower range of numbers of game species per site, particularly of big game species, however, suggests somewhat less variation among sites than was true in the Early Mesolithic, and less than expected for the complete settlement system. Perhaps the virtual abandonment of so many regions and the concentration of major settlements around areas of greatest diversity, productivity, and stability resulted in a greater uniformity of subsistence resources available to each site. If there existed more special-purpose, logistical camps, potentially differing greatly among themselves in subsistence activities, we seem to be largely lacking them in the archaeological record. Lautereck and possibly Henauhof Nord I may represent specialized fishing camps occupied from base camps elsewhere. Henauhof Nordwest 2 and Henauhof Nord II also appear to represent short-term logistic camps that contrast with the intensely occupied sites like Falkensteinhöhle and Henauhof Nordwest.

15.3. SYNTHESIS

In this context of more logistic organization, careful core preparation and blade manufacture may have increased in prominence as "gearing up" took place in the residential camps for logistical forays (Fisher, 1990). Henauhof Nord II appears to represent just such a logistic camp to which previously manufactured blades were carried. Tool reliability may have become more important in artifact design at the expense of maintainability if limited periods of animal movements were anticipated and targeted. This would have led to a decline in the use of arrows with multiple stone barbs (and fewer microliths) and the development of some larger, complex implements, carefully made with redundant parts, such as the barbed antler harpoons, which would have been difficult to repair.

As the Late Mesolithic developed, the increasing subsistence predictability created by the emergence of stable vegetational patches and reliable "hot spots" would have lessened the need for social alliances across long distances to provide economic insurance. The social world of each local group may have contracted somewhat, and the landscape become increasingly compartmentalized into social and economic units. Newell et al. (1990) document a contraction of the cluster of ornament styles at this time, with sharper boundaries and less overlap between clusters. They interpret these patterns as evidence of "increased levels of ethnicity and boundary maintenance" (p. 376).

As particular areas emerged as relatively richer and more reliably productive of foods, competition for such areas may have arisen, depending on their scarcity. Social and material boundaries would have become increasingly distinct in this more compartmentalized and competitive landscape. Territoriality may have become more clearly defined, perhaps marked by such features as the burials found at the site of Grosse Ofnet, just outside of the study area to the east. Here, the highly ritualized burial of 33 skulls of men, women, and children was found, dated to 7560 + 110 and 7360 + 80 b.p. (Schulte im Walde, Freundlich, Schwabedissen, and Taute, 1986). All skulls were placed in depressions facing west and many showed signs of blows to the head and decapitation.

If competition took the form of true conflict, as this evidence might also suggest, then social ties of a different sort may have ultimately developed, stimulated by the formation of mutual alliances. Because competitors would likely have been immediate neighbors, alliances might leapfrog to connect groups at some distance, and not necessarily groups with differing schedules of hardship. Exchange might link such groups and be archaeologically visible. It does seem that exchange networks expanded at this time, bringing in materials from greater distances, including the Mediterranean (Fig. 85). The site of Grosse Ofnet mentioned earlier contained over 4000 Mediterranean shells associated with the skulls.

Figure 85. Late Mesolithic exchange patterns.

Aggregations would have become more sustainable and regular in their occurrence, centering on the emerging areas of greater economic importance. It may well be that clearer patterns of seasonal fission and fusion developed, with aggregations of longer duration timed to coincide with ease of travel and food diversity and abundance in the warmer months.

Social relations within groups may have changed as well. Two possible developments—the increasing importance of plant foods and the greater use of specialized, logistical hunting camps—could have led to increasing segregation of men's and women's spheres of activity. This process may also have influenced their relative status. By virtue of their association with the traditional and always valued big game meat, men may have exerted more influence and control than women, who may have become increasingly involved with the collection of newer and less valued foods. Alternatively, women may have increased in status as they increasingly provided the more reliable dietary components, although this does not seem to be the case among modern hunter–gatherers. At the very least, men and women may have come to symbolize their identity and status in increasingly different terms and media. The Mediterranean shells and other ornaments at Grosse Ofnet were associated with the women's skulls, not with the men's.

With a more predictable and diverse food base, it is possible that households became economically more autonomous, with sharing the norm only for the larger game and used increasingly as a means of defining status. Skill may have become more important than luck in hunting and the best hunters may have more consistently brought home game and used meat to build obligations and acquire influence and possibly wives. Although individual status differences may still have been small in comparison to those in modern, complex hunter–gatherer societies, they may have exceeded those of the preceding periods.

In this increasingly populated and differentiated social landscape, interpersonal relations may have more often drawn the attention of ritual and ideology. Sorcery and witchcraft may have become more prominent, as might some particularly adept practitioners. At the same time, ritual relations with the more predictable natural world may have waned in importance, although the importance of ritual "mapping" of the more stable, rich resource locations may have increased.

Chapter 16

Southwest Germany in the West European Landscape

16.1. INTRODUCTION

Archaeological studies of hunter–gatherers usually emphasize adaptation to the immediate natural environment in explaining cultural behavior. Often neglected are two crucial elements in human ecological relationships: (1) the social environment, and (2) the preceding history of adaptations. People cope with problems in the natural environment as social beings, in a social context presenting its own problems, with cultural tools developed in past generations. Without consideration of these factors, cultural behavior cannot be fully intelligible.

The Stone Age of southwest Germany exemplifies the need for such a broad focus. From the late Upper Palaeolithic through the Mesolithic and into the Neolithic, this area underwent profound changes in both economy and natural environment. It is highly likely that the two sets of changes are related and that an ecological approach should hold promise for understanding the cultural changes. Yet the relationships are not deterministic, and the specific changes that occurred seem to have been determined as much by social relations and past history as they were by local changes in the natural environment. An examination of this region within the broader West European context may help illuminate these relationships.

16.2. ENVIRONMENTAL AND CULTURAL CHANGES

As discussed previously, southwest Germany witnessed dramatic environmental changes from the late Pleistocene through the early Holocene. At the last glacial maximum, ca. 18,000 b.p., this region was a virtual polar desert, characterized by high winds, long, cold winters, and scant vegetation. The sequence of changes over the ensuing millenia is well documented: significant warming, development of a rich herbaceous tundra gradually transformed into closed forests, and appearance of a rich tundra fauna that is supplanted by forest animal communities. By the beginning of the Neolithic, ca. 6500 b.p., dense mixed forests covered the area and formed a habitat for a variety of medium and small game.

The patterns of prehistoric occupation and economic activities show a number of changes during this period as well, and many of these changes make sense in terms of adaptations to the local ecological transformations. During the glacial maximum, when plant and animal biomass were low and living conditions severe, human occupation was either nonexistent or extremely sparse (Jochim, 1987). The development of the richer tundras of the late Pleistocene was accompanied by an influx of people who built an apparently successful and stable adaptation around migrating reindeer herds, supplemented by horse and a variety of other prey (Weniger, 1982). Periodic aggregations synchronized with the reindeer movements formed an important part of this adaptation and resulted in the creation of a number of sites impressive for their artifact density, variety of features, and abundance of artistic as well as utilitarian objects.

The Late Palaeolithic in some ways represents a significant change in behavior, with evidence for large group aggregations and most artistic activity now disappearing from the archaeological record. Artifact inventories of both stone and bone become relatively impoverished as well, and there appears to be some tendency for a shift in the focus of settlement more toward the open, rolling country of Oberschwaben and away from the narrow valleys in the limestone Alb. Many of these changes make sense in terms of the local ecology: the disappearance of predictable reindeer herds and the development of pine-birch forests with smaller, more scattered prey encouraged the development of greater human mobility and flexibility of settlement, and made difficult the regular aggregation of large groups.

The Early Mesolithic continues these trends in both natural environment and behavior. Mixed deciduous forests with scattered prey encouraged continued mobility, with the result that sites of this period are widespread in virtually all environmental and topographic locations. Most of these are small and suggest no regular pattern of seasonal aggregation. One major change, represented by the spectacular increase in microlithic stone technology, can be interpreted in terms of the advantages of easily repaired, composite arrows for stalking and encounter hunting in the increasingly dense forests.

With the Late Mesolithic appear a number of changes. Stone technology becomes characterized by an emphasis on the manufacture of regular blades and the appearance of trapezoidal microliths, both normally interpreted as increases in adaptive efficiency—of stone use and tool manufacture, and of killing prey. Sites become far less abundant than earlier, and concentrated in certain areas like the uppermost Danube and some lakes in Oberschwaben. These settlement shifts have variously been interpreted as indications of population decline, decreased site visibility, or a shift in settlement to areas of greatest resource abundance and diversity. These, in turn, are all related to increases in moisture and forest density, leading to both increased deposition to bury sites and greater difficulty in hunting due to prey scarcity and lower visibility.

The onset of the Neolithic appears to be an abrupt set of changes in technology, subsistence, and settlement patterns. Village sites with a full suite of domesticated plants and animals appear and represent a new adaptation to the European forests. The traditional interpretation of these changes is that they reflect an immigration of farming groups from the east and southeast, able to replace the indigenous hunter–gatherers who had low population densities and an increasingly difficult and marginal subsistence economy.

Thus, at one level the environmental and cultural changes of this period do appear to be intimately related. The changing costs and risks of food getting and movement encouraged changing configurations of human subsistence and settlement, as might be predicted by assumptions of optimal adaptations to local environmental circumstances.

16.3. THE IMPORTANCE OF ENVIRONMENTAL HISTORY

A broadening of focus, however, reveals that an interpretation of local adaptive change is not sufficient to explain the cultural patterns in southwest Germany. If it were, then many areas of western Europe should show a convergence toward similar adaptations during the Late Mesolithic, for example, because their mixed-oak forest habitats were quite similar. Instead, we see remarkable differences among regions. North Germany, Denmark, England, the Netherlands, Belgium, and Luxemburg provide an illustration of these differences (Cziesla, 1992; Myers, 1989; Price, 1985). In these northern regions the Late Mesolithic is characterized by an increase in site numbers as compared to the Early Mesolithic, by considerable evidence for larger sites and greater sedentism, and by hints of greater social complexity—all contrasting considerably from the south German patterns. In Switzerland, as well, the Late Mesolithic is represented by more sites than is the Early Mesolithic (Sakellaridis, 1979).

The keys to understanding these differences may lie, in part, in the differing environmental history of each area. Both regions witnessed a transition from tundra to closed forest, but in the south, this was a long, gradual process extending over more than 5000 years, whereas in the north, the reforestation was interrupted by the more pronounced climatic events of the Younger Dryas period, so that the last transition was compressed into a much shorter period. Moreover, climatic and environmental variability during this transition appear to have been greater in the north. Finally, the north experienced a significant loss of formerly inhabited land due to sea level rise during this period, while the south did not. This sea level rise cut Britain off from the rest of the continent shortly after 8000 b.p., providing for a unique experiment in cultural isolation during the Late Mesolithic. Consequently, the specific environmental history of each area was quite different and, as a result, so too was the history of cultural changes.

Because of the loss of old lands, the northern continental groups were subjected to population packing and greater relative population densities. Some of these problems would have been alleviated by the emergence of new areas due to glacial retreat and isostatic rebound. These changes, coupled with the more rapid environmental changes and the greater environmental variability, necessitated more dramatic alterations in behavior than was true in the south. These northern groups both broadened their diets and intensified their subsistence on certain resources. Mobility would have been restricted by both the greater population densities and the intensification of subsistence. The appearance of cemeteries and elements of social differentiation may be related to these changes in settlement and increasing control over intensified resources. Each step in this sequence of cultural changes set the stage for the next. By the time that farming groups appeared in neighboring areas, north Germany and Denmark were occupied by dense populations with successful, intensified hunting and gathering economies and, as a result, the appearance of agriculture into this area was delayed for several thousand years.

In England, on the other hand, the "ecological experiment" of relative isolation led to a different pattern. In this area Late Mesolithic sites tend to be smaller and are found in a greater variety of locations than earlier sites, suggesting a greater diversification of subsistence areas and less intensive use of only the more stable and productive locations. Specific models of Late Mesolithic hunting strategies in both England and Denmark have been developed, suggesting substantial differences in the risks and productivity of big game hunting between the two areas (Mithen, 1990; Myers, 1989). Such models, especially if expanded or supplemented by others to include other resources, could help us understand the decision mechanisms underlying these regional differences.

Southwest Germany showed a different environmental and cultural trajectory. The history of more gradual and less variable environmental changes and lack of population packing required less dramatic changes in behavior. This is reflected in numerous continuities through time in raw material use and scale of seasonal movements, as well as, in some periods, technology, site use, and general economic patterns (Eriksen, 1991; Jochim, 1993). A pattern of remarkable cultural inertia appears to characterize this region, with various changes occurring when necessary (in settlement patterns, technology, economy, or ritual behavior) against a background of strong cultural traditions. Even the transition to the Neolithic is now viewed by some as involving much greater continuity with the Late Mesolithic than was previously recognized (Keefer, 1993; Kind, 1991; Tillman, 1993), suggesting a rapid acculturation of local groups undergoing subsistence stress.

16.4. THE IMPORTANCE OF SOCIAL RELATIONS

If time depth needs to be added to local ecology in interpreting cultural changes, so too does the social environment. At all periods of the past, southwest German groups were embedded in a web of social relations, which had a profound effect on the problems they confronted and the means by which they solved them. Like the historical trajectories, the social networks require examination at different spatial scales for fuller understanding.

During the Upper Palaeolithic and Mesolithic, southwest Germany was part of different nested spatial hierarchies of material similarity, presumably mirroring social interaction and communication of various sorts. In the Magdalenian, it formed one region of a large zone of lithic and artistic similarities stretching from Spain to Moravia, Within this zone, south Germany and north Switzerland were set apart from adjacent regions such as the Middle Rhine and Central Germany by its economic focus (on reindeer, not horse), its dominant raw material for art objects (jet rather than stone or ivory), and by some minor art motifs (insects rather than mammoth or rhinoceros) (Weniger, 1989). In turn, this area was subdivided into smaller regions that seem to represent annual use-areas of more local groups with relatively distinct patterns of seasonal movements, of which the best studied is the upper Danube Valley.

During the Early Mesolithic, south Germany was the center of a larger region (the Beuronien) defined in terms of styles of microliths and dominant method of core platform preparation (Kozlowski, 1973; Tillman, 1993). This was one of a number of stylistic provinces in Europe, each of which averages about 200 kilometers in radius (Kozlowski, 1973). At a similar scale, projectile points with surface retouch in the Mesolithic of Belgium and adjacent areas are distributed over an area with a maximum radius of about 200 kilometers (Gendel, 1990). Both Early and Late Mesolithic sites in the upper Danube regularly contain small amounts of banded chert from the east or fossil shells from the northwest, both sources about 200 kilometers away. These distributions apparently document exchange and interaction among neighboring groups on a regular basis.

These regions were made up of smaller areas defined by raw material distributions, subsistence economy, and patterns of seasonal movement, which may reflect the primary areas of annual movement, the areas in which most subsistence activities occurred. These areas appear to extend to about 40–50 kilometers in radius. One of these areas is the upper Danube drainage, separate from Lake Constance, the Rhine Valley, and the Neckar Valley.

During the Late Mesolithic, some changes in this spatial patterning occurs. Gendel (1990) has found that stylistic patterning of stone tools becomes more distinct in Belgium and Holland at this time, perhaps reflecting both the greater stability of vegetational communities and growth in human populations in this area. He also cites research in Denmark that describes Late Mesolithic stylistic areas of only 25 kilometers radius. In fact, Price (1981) generalizes for the whole of the North European Plain that Late Mesolithic stylistic territories become smaller and more distinct.

In southwestern Germany, Newell et al. (1990) suggest a similar contraction and stronger delineation of stylistic provinces of ornaments. One feature that sets southwestern Germany apart from the rest of Mesolithic western Europe is the use of fish teeth as ornaments. Perforated fish teeth occur in sites of both the Early and Late Mesolithic in this area, but nowhere else in Europe. As mentioned earlier, over 4000 were found with the skulls at Ofnet Cave in Bavaria just to the east of the study area, associated solely with the skulls of females. Newell et al. have used this feature to characterize southwestern German Mesolithic groups as the "Fish Tooth Band," although there is no concrete evidence of the specific nature of social organization that warrants the use of the term "band."

In this postprocessual age, it would be tempting to develop an interpretation of the use of fish teeth as a major form of ornamentation, particularly in light of the importance of teeth of quite different animals as ornaments elsewhere in Mesolithic Europe. In southern Sweden, Denmark, and northern Germany, for example, important and characteristic ornaments included the teeth of lynx, bear, wolf, marten, moose, aurochs, red deer, wildcat, badger, seal, boar, fox, and roe deer. Given the widespread symbolic and mythological significance of animals among living hunter–gatherer societies, one might suppose that they occupied a similar position in prehistoric ideologies, and that these ornaments provide a clue to their interpretation.

Perhaps the connection between the fish teeth and female skulls derives from an association between women and fishing, suggesting a division of labor in which men hunted and women fished and gathered. Perhaps, too, the use of carnivore and large herbivore teeth in northern Europe indicates that hunting and fierceness were important mythologically and were sources of individual identity and status, presumably especially for men. By contrast, in southern Germany an important component of ideology, therefore, would have been fishing and, perhaps, the reliability it (and the women) provided to the subsistence economy, particularly given the increasing difficulty of large game hunting in the southern German forests during the course of the Mesolithic. One might further argue that women's status was higher in southern Germany than it was in the societies of northern Europe.

On the other hand, such speculations are quite unsupported by any evidence at hand. Moreover, several cautionary counterexamples are available in the ethnographic literature. Among many Athabaskan groups in northern Canada and Alaska, for example, a common ornamental motif was floral patterns created using porcupine quills sewn onto hides. It is difficult to find a prominent role for either flowers or porcupines in the mythology of these groups. Furthermore, many of the Basawra groups of the Kalahari used ostrich eggshell beads as decorative ornaments, yet the ostrich did not occupy an important position in either their economy or ideology. One might, I suppose, emphasize the additional role of ostrich eggshells as water containers and, in turn, relate this to the economic (and possibly ideological) importance of water in the arid Kalahari, but this logical leap appears unjustified. At this stage, unfortunately, we really cannot say much with confidence about Mesolithic ideology in southern Germany, however great our desire to "flesh out" the past.

In contrast to the apparent contraction of stylistic provinces, exchange networks in this area seem to have expanded in the Late Mesolithic. Shells from the Mediterranean, presumably from the French coast, now appear in south German sites across a distance of 600 kilometers, as do fossil shells from the middle Danube, about 400 or more kilometers away.

At the beginning of the Neolithic, south Germany lay on the periphery of the initial spread of the Bandkeramik from the east, as well as on the edge of the distribution or spread of the La Hoguette phenomenon from the west, which may represent acculturated hunter–gatherer groups who had adopted domesticated animals and ceramic technology (Fig. 86; Lüning, Kloos, and Albert, 1989). Throughout the rest of the Neolithic this region is on the periphery of influences from the west/southwest and the east, and often the boundaries of recognized culture groups cross through this area (Schlichtherle, 1990).

Consequently, if southwest Germany was a center of continuity, adapting to local environmental changes along its own historical trajectory, it was not doing so in isolation. It was a dynamic center, linked to other groups and regions and influenced by them. It may well be that some of the changes seen in southwest Germany reflect these social relations, and would not be predictable from local ecology at all. The most obvious examples of the effects of such social relations are the appearance of trapezoidal microliths and of agriculture.

Trapezoids were not developed in southwest Germany; their appearance there during the Late Mesolithic was part of an extensive expansion of their distribution across most of western Europe at this time. These new microlithic

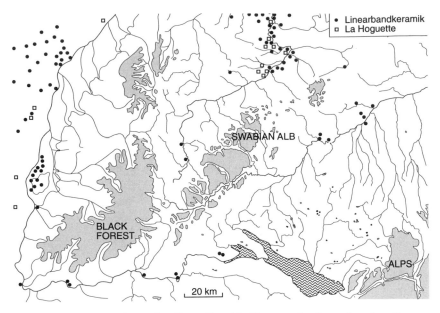

Figure 86. Distribution of Linearbandkeramik and La Hoguette sites in southwestern Germany.

forms might have been adopted by southwest German groups because of the superior cutting and wounding power of such projectiles, but their adoption might also be explicable in more social terms, related, for example, to solidifying partnerships or alliances by sharing common weaponry, or to competing more effectively in hunting or warfare with neighboring groups.

Similarly, whatever the role of local Mesolithic groups in the spread of the Bandkeramik, they did not invent agriculture to solve local environmental problems. The traditional view is that they were essentially pushed out of their territories by the agricultural immigrants, but this may be unlikely because the initial dispersal of agriculture appears to have followed the distribution of loess soils. This distribution happens to coincide with the area of lower densities of Late Mesolithic sites in this area.

The fate of the Mesolithic groups is unknown, but their rapid disappearance from the archaeological record suggests absorption into agricultural communities, adoption of fully agricultural economies through contact, or ultimately hostile displacement. Which of these occurred probably depended on more local social and ecological factors. In Belgium, for example, the early LBK villages are fortified, suggesting that the Late Mesolithic groups in this northern region were sufficiently dense and organized to pose a hostile threat (Keeley and Cahen, 1989). In the upper Danube, on the other hand, the withdrawal of Late Mesolithic groups to the upper valleys and lakes reduced the subsequent possibility for competition with incoming farmers, who sought the loess soils and broader alluvial habitats. Switzerland as a whole constituted a similar kind of Late Mesolithic refuge and thus was not settled by farming groups until later.

In the upper Danube, this habitat separation could have permitted the co-existence of two quite different ways of life, and there is some evidence for exchange or other sorts of contact between the two groups, such as the Neolithic grinding stones at Henauhof Nordwest and polished axes in some of the cave sites. Nevertheless, the Late Mesolithic refuge seems to have become a shrinking enclave, increasingly surrounded on the east, north, and west by LBK groups. The Late Mesolithic hunting and gathering economy, already under some stress, would have increasingly been denied the option of movement as an adaptive strategy. In this context the adoption of agricultural lifeways may have occurred rapidly. The hunter–gatherers may have begun imitating their neighbors in order to compete more effectively, or to make better use of their gradually shrinking enclaves, or to forge stronger economic and social relations. The preexisting networks of social relations and the specific intergroup processes of interaction were probably of paramount importance in accounting for the changes observed.

16.5. CONCLUSIONS

Too often, ecological approaches to the understanding of cultural changes concentrate on responses to changes in the local natural environment. This concentration not only ignores too many possibly significant causes of cultural change but also is not true to the meaning of ecology. Ecological relations involve both the natural and the social environments, and interaction with other groups can be just as important in shaping behavior as interaction with the natural realm. In addition, both humans and other animals react to environmental changes with a certain repertoire of known behaviors determined by past history; completely innovative solutions to environmental problems are rare. It is foolish to expect that behavior is so plastic and free of historical constraints that it can easily adjust to some new, optimum state of adaptation to new environmental situations. The cultural history of southwest Germany demonstrates these concepts well. Lying at the center of the continent, this region was a center with a strong pattern of continuity throughout a sequence of profound environmental changes. Each cultural change was influenced by the specific historical trajectory of this region. In addition, each change took place within a set of social relations linking this area ultimately to most of Europe. In order to understand this region's cultural history, it is essential to look beyond the local natural environment, to the past, and to the social realm, and to use various spatial scales to do so.

References

Albrecht, G., 1983, Das Spätpaläolithikum. In *Urgeschichte in Baden-Württemberg*, edited by II. Müller-Beck, pp. 354–362. Konrad Theiss Verlag, Stuttgart.

Albrecht, G., 1984, Der Spätpleistozäne und Altholozäne Fundplatz Malerfels I. In *Die Steinzeitliche Besiedlung des Eselburger Tales bei Heidenheim*, edited by J. Hahn, pp. 90–122. Konrad Theiss Verlag, Stuttgart.

Bamforth, D., 1991, Technological Efficiency and Tool Curation. *American Antiquity* 51:38–50.

Barker, G., 1985, *Prehistoric Farming in Europe*. Cambridge University Press, Cambridge.

Barkow, J., Cosmides, L., and Tooby, J., 1992, *The Adapted Mind: Evolutionary Psychology and the Generation of Culture*. Oxford University Press, Oxford.

Bell, G., 1992, Microwear Analysis Project: Site of Henauhof West, Southern Germany. Unpublished paper, University of California, Santa Barbara.

Belovsky, G., 1987, Hunter–Gatherer Foraging: A Linear Programming Approach. *Journal of Anthropological Archaeology* 6:29–76.

Belovsky, G., 1988, An Optimal Foraging-Based Model of Hunter–Gatherer Population Dynamics. *Journal of Anthropological Archaeology* 7:329–372.

Berndt, R., 1972, The Walmadjeri and Gugadja. In *Hunters and Gatherers Today,* edited by M. Bicchieri, pp. 177–216. Waveland Press, Prospect Heights, Illinois.

Bertrando, E., 1993, From Artifact to Cluster: The Interpretation of Two Autumn Lakeside Occupations during the Late Mesolithic of Southwest Germany. Unpublished MA thesis, University of California, Santa Barbara.

Bertsch, A., 1931, Paläobotanische Monographie des Federseerieds. *Bibliotheka Botanika* 103:1–127.

Bertsch, A., 1961, Untersuchungen zur Spätglazialen Vegetationsgeschichte Südwestdeutschlands. *Flora* 151:243–280.

Bettinger, R., 1980, Explanatory/Predictive Models of Hunter–Gatherer Adaptation. In *Advances in Archaeological Method and Theory*, edited by M. Schiffer, pp. 189–255. Academic Press, New York.

Bettinger, R. 1991, *Hunter–Gatherers: Archaeological and Evolutionary Theory*. Plenum, New York.

Billamboz, A. and Schlichtherle, H., 1982, Moor und Seeufersiedlungen. Die Sondagen 1981 des "Projekts Bodensee-Oberschwaben." *Archäologische Ausgrabungen in Baden-Württemberg 1981*, pp. 36–50.

225

Binford, L., 1976, Forty-Seven Trips: A Case Study in the Character of Some Formation Processes of the Archaeological Record. In *Contributions to Archaeology: The Interior Peoples of Northern Alaska,* edited by E. Hall, pp. 299–351. National Museum of Man Mercury Series 49, Ottawa.

Binford, L., 1978, *Nunamiut Ethnoarchaeology.* Academic Press, New York.

Binford, L., 1980, Willow Smoke and Dogs' Tails: Hunter–Gatherer Settlement Systems and Archaeological Site Formation. *American Antiquity* 43:330–361.

Binford, L., 1982, The Archaeology of Place. *Journal of Anthropological Archaeology* 1:5–31.

Bleed, P., 1986, The Optimal Design of Hunting Weapons: Maintainability or Reliability. *American Antiquity* 51:737–747.

Boessneck, J., 1978a, Die Tierknochenfunde aus den Mesolithischen Kulturschichten der Jägerhaushöhle, Markung Bronnen, im Oberen Donautal. In *Das Mesolithikum in Süddeutschland, Teil 2: Naturwissenschaftliche Untersuchungen,* edited by W. Taute, pp. 77–86. Tübinger Monographien zur Urgeschichte 5/2. Archaeologica Venatoria, Tübingen.

Boessneck, J., 1978b, Die Tierknochenfunde aus der Mesolithischen Kulturshicht der Falkensteinhöhle, Markung Thiergarten, im Oberen Donautal. In *Das Mesolithikum in Süddeutschland, Teil 2: Naturwissenschaftliche Untersuchungen,* edited by W. Taute, pp. 87–99. Tübinger Monographien zur Urgeschichte 5/2. Archaeologica Venatoria, Tübingen.

Boessneck, J., 1978c, Tierknochenfunde aus der Mesolithischen Kulturschicht unter dem Felsdach Inzigkofen im Oberen Donautal. In *Das Mesolithikum in Süddeutschland, Teil 2: Naturwissenschaftliche Untersuchungen,* edited by W. Taute, pp. 101–116. Tübinger Monographien zur Urgeschichte 5/2. Archaeologica Venatoria, Tübingen.

Boyd, R. and Richerson, P., 1985, *Culture and the Evolutionary Process.* University of Chicago Press, Chicago.

Campen, I., Kind, C. and C. Lauxmann, 1983, Ein Rotgefärbter Kalkstein aus dem Mesolithischen Horizont vom "Felsställe," Ehingen-Mühlen, Alb-Donau Kreis. *Archäologisches Korrespondenzblatt* 13:299–303.

Cashdan, E., 1990, *Risk and Uncertainty in Tribal and Peasant Economics.* Westview Press, Boulder, Colorado.

Champion, T., Gamble, C., Shennan, S. and Whittle, A., 1984, *Prehistoric Europe.* Academic Press, New York.

Clark, G., 1952, *Prehistoric Europe: The Economic Basis.* Methuen, London.

Clark, G. and Neeley, M., 1987, Social Differentiation in European Mesolithic Burial Data. In *Mesolithic Northwest Europe: Recent Trends,* edited by P. Rowley-Conwy, M. Zvelebil and H. Blankholm, pp. 121–127. Department of Archaeology and Prehistory, Sheffield, England.

Clark, J., Merkt, J., and Müller, H., 1989, Postglacial Fire, Vegetation, and Human History on the Northern Alpine Forelands, Southwestern Germany. *Journal of Ecology* 77:897–925.

Clarke, D., 1976, Mesolithic Europe: The Economic Basis. In *Problems in Economic and Social Archaeology,* edited by G. Sieveking, I. Longworth, and K. Wilson, pp. 449–481. Duckworth, London.

Conkey, M., 1991, Contexts of Action, Contexts for Power: Material Culture and Gender in the Magdalenian. In *Engendering Archaeology,* edited by J. Gero and M. Conkey, pp. 57–92. Blackwell, Cambridge, England.

Croes, D. and Hackenberger, S., 1988, Hoko River Archaeological Complex: Modelling Prehistoric Northwest Coast Economic Evolution. In *Prehistoric Economies of the Pacific Northwest Coast,* edited by B. Isaac, pp. 19–85. Research in Economic Anthropology, Supplement 3. JAI Press, Greenwich, Connecticut.

Cziesla, E., 1992, *Jäger und Sammler: Die Mittlere Steinzeit im Landkreis Pirmasens.* Lindensoft, Brühl.

Dämmler, H., Reim, H. and Taute, W., 1975, Probegrabungen in der Burghöhle von Dietfurt im Oberen Donautal. *Fundberichte aus Baden-Württemberg* 1:1–25.

Eberhardt, H., Keefer, E., Kind, C.-J., Rensch, H. and Ziegler, H., 1987, Jungpaläolithische und Mesolithische Fundstellen aus der Aichbühler Bucht. *Fundberichte aus Baden-Württemberg* 12:1–51.

Enghoff, I., 1986, Freshwater Fishing from a Sea-Coast Settlement. *Journal of Danish Archaeology* 5:62–76.

Eriksen, B., 1991, *Change and Continuity in a Prehistoric Hunter–Gatherer Society*. Archaeologica Venatoria 12. Archaeologica Venatoria, Tübingen.

Filzer, P., 1978, Pollenanalytische Untersuchungen in den Mesolithischen Kultur-schichten der Jägerhaus-Höhle an der Oberen Donau. In *Das Mesolithikum in Süddeutschland, Teil 2: Naturwissenschaftliche Untersuchungen*, edited by W. Taute, pp. 21–32. Tübinger Monographien zur Urgeschichte 5/2. Archaeologica Venatoria, Tübingen.

Finlayson, B., 1990, The Function of Microliths: Evidence from Smittons and Starr, SW Scotland. *Mesolithic Miscellany* 11:2–6.

Firbas, F., 1949, *Spät- und Nacheiszeitliche Waldgeschichte Mitteleuropas Nördlich der Alpen*. Gustav Fischer, Jena.

Fisher, L., 1990, Mobility and Technology: Variable Core Reduction Strategies in the Southwest German Magdalenian. Unpublished MA thesis, University of Michigan, Ann Arbor.

Frenzel, B., 1983, Die Vegetationsgeschichte Süddeutschlands im Eiszeitalter. In *Urgeschichte in Baden-Württemberg*, edited by H. Müller-Beck, pp. 91–165. Konrad Theiss Verlag, Stuttgart.

Gendel, P., 1990, The Analysis of Lithic Styles through Distributional Profiles of Variation: Examples from the Western European Mesolithic. In *The Mesolithic in Europe*, edited by C. Bonsall, pp. 40–47. University of Edinburgh Press, Edinburgh.

Gero, J. and Conkey, M., 1991, *Engendering Archaeology*. Blackwell, Cambridge, England.

Gersbach, E., 1951, Das Mittelbadische Mesolithikum. *Badische Fundberichte* 19:1–17.

Gersbach, E., 1968, Urgeschichte des Hochrheins. *Badische Fundberichte*, Sonderheft 11.

Goodale, J., 1971, *Tiwi Wives: A Study of the Women of Melville Island, North Australia*. University of Washington Press, Seattle.

Göttlich, K., 1965, Der Vorgeschichtliche Damm von Moosburg zum "Insele" im Seelenhofer Ried. *Jahresheft des Vereins Vaterländische Naturkunde in Württemberg* 120:216–221.

Gould, R., 1976, Ecology and Adaptive Response among the Tolowa Indians of Northwestern California. In *Native Californians: A Theoretical Retrospective*, edited by L. Bean and T. Blackburn, pp. 49–78. Ballena Press, Ramona, CA.

Gregg, S., 1986, *Foragers and Farmers: Population Interaction and Agricultural Expansion in Prehistoric Europe*. University of Chicago Press, Chicago.

Gregg, S., 1993, Henauhof-Nordwest: Die Keramik. In *Henauhof NW: Ein Mittelsteinzeitlicher Lagerplatz am Federsee*, edited by M. Jochim, pp. 122–123. Materialhefte zur Vor- und Frühgeschichte 19, Landesdenkmalamt Baden-Württemberg. Konrad Theiss Verlag, Stuttgart.

Greiser, S., 1985, Predictive Models of Hunter–Gatherer Subsistence and Settlement Strategies on the Central High Plains. *Plains Anthropologist* 30, No. 110, Pt. 2, Memoir 20.

Hahn, J., 1978, New Aspects of the Magdalenian in Central Europe. *Reviews in Anthropology* 5/3:313–331.

Hahn, J., 1983, Die Frühe Mittelsteinzeit. In *Urgeschichte in Baden-Württemberg*, edited by H. Müller-Beck, pp. 363–392. Konrad Theiss Verlag, Stuttgart.

Hahn, J., 1984, *Die Steinzeitliche Besiedlung des Eselburger Tales bei Heidenheim*. Konrad Theiss Verlag, Stuttgart.

Hahn, J. and Kind, C.-J., 1991, Neue Mesolithische Fundstellen in Rottenburg a. N., Kreis Tübingen. *Archäologische Ausgrabungen in Baden-Württemberg 1990*, pp. 26–29.

Hahn, J. and Kind, C.-J., 1992, Sondierungen im Bereich der Fundstelle Rottenburg Siebenlinden III, Kreis Tübingen. *Archäologische Ausgrabungen in Baden-Württemberg 1991*, pp. 38–40.

Hahn, J., Kind, C.-J., and Steppan, K., 1993, Mesolithische Rentierjäger in Südwestdeutschland? Der Mittelsteinzeitliche Freilandfundplatz Rottenburg "Siebenlinden I" (Vorbericht). *Fundberichte aus Baden-Württemberg* 18:29–52.

Hahn, J. and A. Scheer, 1983, Das Helga-Abri am Hohlenfelsen bei Schelklingen: Eine Mesolithische und Jungpaläolithische Schichtenfolge. *Archäologische Korrespondenzblatt* 13:19–28.

Halstead, P. and J. O'Shea, 1989, Introduction: Cultural Responses to Risk and Uncertainty. In *Bad Year Economics*, edited by P. Halstead and J. O'Shea, pp. 1–7. Cambridge University Press, Cambridge.

Hames, R. and Vickers, W., 1982, Optimal Foraging Theory as a Model to Explain Variability in Amazonian Hunting. *American Ethnologist* 9:358–378.

Handsman, R., 1991, Whose Art Was Found at Lepenski Vir? Gender Relations and Power in Archaeology. In *Engendering Archaeology*, edited by J. Gero and M. Conkey, pp. 329–365. Blackwell, Cambridge, England.

Hawkes, K., 1990, Why Do Men Hunt? Some Benefits for Risky Strategies. In *Risk and Uncertainty in Tribal and Peasant Economics*, edited by E. Cashdan, pp. 145–166. Westview Press, Boulder, Colorado.

Hayden, B., 1981, Research and Development in the Stone Age: Technological Transitions among Hunter–Gatherers. *Current Anthropology* 22:519–548.

Hayden, B., 1990, Nimrods, Piscators, Pluckers, and Planters: The Emergence of Food Production. *Journal of Anthropological Archaeology* 9:31–69.

Hill, K., Kaplan, H., Hawkes, K. and Hurtado, A., 1987, Foraging Decisions among Ache Hunter–Gatherers: New Data and Implications for Optimal Foraging Models. *Ethology and Sociobiology* 8:1–36.

Hodder, I., 1986, *Reading the Past: Current Approaches to Interpretation in Archaeology.* Cambridge University Press, Cambridge.

Hodder, I., 1990, *The Domestication of Europe.* Blackwell, Oxford.

Jochim, M., 1976, *Hunter–Gatherer Subsistence and Settlement: A Predictive Model.* Academic Press, New York.

Jochim, M., 1979, Catches and Caches: Ethnographic Alternatives and Prehistory. In *Ethnoarchaeology*, edited by C. Kramer, pp. 219–246. Columbia University Press, New York.

Jochim, M., 1981, *Strategies for Survival.* Academic Press, New York.

Jochim, M., 1983, Optimization Models in Context. In *Archaeological Hammers and Theories*, edited by J. Moore and A. Keene, pp. 157–170. Academic Press, New York.

Jochim, M., 1987, Late Pleistocene Refugia in Europe. In *The Pleistocene Old World: Regional Perspectives*, edited by O. Soffer, pp. 317–332. Plenum, New York.

Jochim, M., 1988, Optimal Foraging and the Division of Labor. *American Anthropologist* 90:130–136.

Jochim, M., 1989, Stone Tools and Optimization. In *Time, Energy and Stone Tools*, edited by R. Torrence, pp. 106–111. Cambridge University Press, Cambridge.

Jochim, M., 1990, The Late Mesolithic in Southwest Germany: Culture Change or Population Decline? In *Contributions to the Mesolithic in Europe*, edited by P. Vermeersch and P. Van Peer, pp. 183–192. Leuven University Press, Leuven.

Jochim, M., 1991, Archaeology as Long-Term Ethnography. *American Anthropologist* 93:308–321.

Jochim, M., 1993, *Henauhof NW: Ein Mittelsteinzeitlicher Lagerplatz am Federsee.* Materialhefte zur Vor- und Frühgeschichte 19, Landesdenkmalamt Baden-Württemberg. Konrad Theiss Verlag, Stuttgart.

Jochim, M., 1995, Two Late Palaeolithic Sites on the Federsee, South Germany. *Journal of Field Archaeology* 22:263–273.

Jochim, M., Glass, M., Fisher, L. and McCartney, P., in press, The South German Survey Project: An Interim Report. *Proceedings of the Mesolithic Conference*, edited by N. Conard. University of Tübingen.

Kaplan, H. and Hill, K., 1985, Food Sharing among Ache Foragers: Tests of Explanatory Hypotheses. *Current Anthropology* 26:223–245.

Kaplan, H., Hill, K., and Hurtado, A., 1990, Risk, Foraging, and Food Sharing. In *Risk and Uncertainty in the Food Supply*, edited by E. Cashdan, pp. 107–144. Westview Press, Boulder, Colorado.

Keefer, E., 1993, *Steinzeit*. Sammlungen des Württembergischen Landesmuseums, Stuttgart.

Keeley, L., 1988, Hunter–Gatherer Economic Complexity and "Population Pressure": A Cross-Cultural Analysis. *Journal of Anthropological Archaeology* 7:373–411.

Keeley, L. and Cahen, D., 1989, Early Neolithic Forts and Villages in NE Belgium: A Preliminary Report. *Journal of Field Archaeology* 16:157–176.

Keene, A., 1981, *Prehistoric Foraging in a Temperate Forest: A Linear Programming Model*. Academic Press, New York.

Kieselbach, P., 1996, Überlegungen zum ökonomieverhalten bei der Silexbearbeitung und zum Siedlungssystem im Mesolithikum. In *Spuren der Jagd—Die Jagd Nach Spuren*, edited by I. Campen, J. Hahn and M. Uerpmann, pp. 319–324. Tübinger Monographien zur Urgeschichte 11. Mo Vince Verlag, Tübingen.

Kieselbach, P. and Richter, D., 1992, Die Mesolithische Freilandstation Rottenburg- Siebenlinden II, Kreis Tübingen. *Archäologische Ausgrabungen in Baden-Württemberg 1991*, pp. 35–37.

Kind, C.-J., (ed.) 1987, *Das Felsställe: Eine Jungpalaolighisch-Frühmesolithische Abri-Station bei Ehingen-Mühlen, Alb-Donau-Kreis*. Forschungen und Berichte zur Vor- und Frühgeschichte in Baden-Württemberg 23. Konrad Theiss Verlag, Stuttgart.

Kind, C.-J., 1990, Die Spätmesolithischen Uferrandlagerplätze am Henauhof bei Bad Buchau am Federsee, Kreis Biberach. *Archäologische Ausgrabungen in Baden-Württemberg 1989*, pp. 30–35.

Kind, C.-J., 1991, Mesolithikum, In *Urgeschichte in Oberschwaben und der Mittleren Schwäbischen Alb*, edited by J. Hahn and C.-J. Kind, pp. 60–64. Archäologische Informationen aus Baden-Württemberg 17. Konrad Theiss Verlag, Stuttgart.

Kind, C.-J., 1992, Der Freilandfundplatz Henauhof Nord II am Federsee und die "Buchauer Gruppe" des Endmesolithikums. *Archäologisches Korrespondenzblatt* 22:341–353.

Kind, C.-J., 1995, Eine Weitere Frühmesolithische Feuerstelle in Rottenburg Siebenlinden III. *Archäologische Ausgrabungen in Baden-Württemberg 1994*, pp. 30–34.

Kind, C.-J., 1996, Bemerkungen zur Diversität des Südwestdeutschen Frühmesolithikums. In *Spuren der Jagd—Die Jagd Nach Spuren*, edited by I. Campen, J. Hahn, and M. Uerpmann, pp. 325–330. Tübinger Monographien zur Urgeschichte 11. Mo Vince Verlag, Tübingen.

Kintigh, K., 1984, Measuring Archaeological Diversity by Comparison with Simulated Assemblages. *American Antiquity* 49:44–54.

Kozlowski, S., 1973, Introduction to the History of Europe in Early Holocene. In *The Mesolithic in Europe*, edited by S. Kozlowski, pp. 331–366. Warsaw University Press, Warsaw.

Kroll, E. and Price, T., 1991, *The Interpretation of Archaeological Spatial Patterning*. Plenum, New York.

Kvamme, K. and Jochim, M., 1990, The Environmental Basis of Mesolithic Settlement. In *The Mesolithic in Europe*, edited by C. Bonsall, pp. 1–12. University of Edinburgh Press, Edinburgh.

Lais, R., 1929, Ein Werkplatz des Azilio-Tardenoisiens am Isteiner Klotz. *Badische Fundberichte* II:97–107.

Larsson, L., 1978, *Ageröd I:B—Ageröd I:D. A Study of Early Atlantic Settlement in Scania*. Acta Archaeologica Lundensia Series in 4, no. 12. CWK Gleerup, Lund.

Lepiksaar, J., 1978, Fischreste aus den Mesolithischen Kulturschichten der Falkensteinhöhle bei Thiergarten und des Felsdaches Inzigkofen im Oberen Donautal. In *Das Mesolithikum in Süddeutschland, Teil 2: Naturwissenschaftliche Untersuchungen*, edited by W. Taute, pp. 153–158. Tübinger Monographien zur Urgeschichte 5/2. Archaeologica Venatoria, Tübingen.

Liese-Kleiber, H., 1988, Zur zeitlichen Verknüpfung von Verlandungsverlauf und Siedlungsge-schichte des Federsees. In *Der Prähistorische Mensch und Seine Umwelt*, edited by H. Küster, pp. 163–176. Forschungen und Berichte zur Vor- und Frühgeschichte in Baden-Württemberg 31. Konrad Theiss Verlag, Stuttgart.

Lüning, J., Kloos, U. and Albert, S., 1989, Westliche Nachbarn der Bandkeramischen Kultur: Die Keramikgruppen "La Hoguette" und "Limburg." *Germania* 67:355- 420.

Mieg, M., 1904, Stations Prehistoriques de Kleinkems (Grand-duche de Bade). *Bulletin de la Societe des Sciences de Nancy*. Series III, Tome V:97–108.

Milisauskas, S., 1978, *European Prehistory*. Academic Press, New York.

Minc, L., 1986, Scarcity and Survival: The Role of Oral Tradition in Mediating Subsistence Crisis. *Journal of Anthropological Archaeology* 5:39–113.

Mithen, S., 1990, *Thoughtful Foragers*. Cambridge University Press, Cambridge.

Moore, J., 1981, The Effects of Information Networks in Hunter–Gatherer Societies. In *Hunter–Gatherer Foraging Strategies*, edited by B. Winterhalder and E. Smith, pp. 194–217. University of Chicago Press, Chicago.

Müller-Beck, H., 1983, Die Späte Mittelsteinzeit. In *Urgeschichte in Baden-Württemberg*, edited by H. Müller-Beck, pp. 393–404. Konrad Theiss Verlag, Stuttgart.

Myers, A., 1989, Reliable and Maintainable Technological Strategies in the Mesolithic of Mainland Britain. In *Time, Energy and Stone Tools*, edited by R. Torrence, pp. 78–91. Cambridge University Press, Cambridge.

Nelson, R., 1973, *Hunters of the Northern Forest: Designs for Survival among the Alaskan Kutchin*. University of Chicago Press, Chicago.

Newell, R., Kielman, D., Constandse-Westermann, T., Van der Sanden, W. and Van Gijn, A., 1990, *An Inquiry into the Ethnic Resolution of Mesolithic Regional Groups*. E. J. Brill, Leiden.

Oberg, K., 1973, *The Social Economy of the Tlingit Indians*. University of Washington Press, Seattle.

Orphal, J., 1994, A Comparison of Two Hunting Camps on the Federsee, Southwest Germany. Unpublished Senior Honors Thesis, Department of Anthropology, University of California, Santa Barbara.

Owen, L. and Pawlik, A., 1993, Funktionsinterpretationen Durch Merkmals- und Gebrauch-ssurenanalysen an Steinartefakten der Spätmesolithischen Fundstelle Henauhof-Nord II. *Archäologisches Korrespondenzblatt* 23:413- 426.

Paret, O., 1951, Die "Strassendämme" am Rand des Federseebeckens. *Germania* 29:1–5.

Parry, W. and Kelly, R., 1987, Expedient Core Technology and Sedentism. In *The Organization of Core Technology*, edited by J. Johnson and C. Morrow, pp. 285–304. Westview Press, Boulder, Colorado.

Pasda, C., 1994, Altensteig und Ettlingen: Mesolithische Fundplätze am Rand des Nordschwarzwaldes. *Fundberichte aus Baden-Württemberg* 19(1):99–174.

Penck, A. and Brückner, E., 1909, *Die Alpen im Eiszeitalter*. Tauchnitz, Leipzig.

Peters, E., 1935, Die Mesolithische Silex- und Knochenindustrie vom Rappenfels auf der Schwäbischen Alb. *Germania* 19:281–286.

Peters, E., 1941, Die Stuttgarter Gruppe der Mittelsteinzeitlichen Kulturen. *Veröffentlichungen der Archiv der Stadt Stuttgart* 7. Stuttgart.

Peters, E., 1946, *Meine Tätigkeit im Dienst der Vorgeschichte Südwestdeutschlands*. Privatdruck, Veringenstadt.

Piddocke, S., 1969 The Potlatch System of the Southern Kwakiutl: A New Perspective. In *Environment and Cultural Behavior*, edited by A. Vayda, pp. 130–156. Natural History Press, Garden City, NY.

Price, T., 1973, A Proposed Model for Procurement Systems in the Mesolithic of Northwest Europe. In *The Mesolithic in Europe*, edited by S. Kozlowski, pp. 455–476. Warsaw University Press, Warsaw.

Price, T., 1981, Regional approaches to Human Adaptation in the Mesolithic of the North European Plain. In *Mesolithikum in Europa*, edited by B. Gramsch, pp. 217–234. Veröffentlichungen des Meuseums für Ur- und Frühgeschichte Potsdam 14/15. VEB Deutscher Verlag der Wissenschaften, Berlin.

Price, T., 1985, Affluent Foragers of Mesolithic Southern Scandinavia. In *Prehistoric Hunter–Gatherers: The Emergence of Cultural Complexity*, edited by T. Price and J. Brown, pp. 341–364. Academic Press, New York.

Price, T. and Brown, J., 1985, *Prehistoric Hunter–Gatherers: The Emergence of Cultural Complexity*. Academic Press, New York.

Probst, E., 1993, *Deutschland in der Steinzeit*. Bertelsmann, Munich.

Radovanovic, I., 1996, *The Iron Gates Mesolithic*. International Monographs in Prehistory, Archaeological Series 11, Ann Arbor, Michigan.

Reidhead, V., 1980, The Economics of Subsistence Change: A Test of an Optimization Model. In *Modeling Change in Prehistoric Subsistence Economies*, edited by T. Earle and A. Christenson, pp. 141–186. Academic Press, New York.

Reinerth, H., 1929, *Das Federseemoor als Siedlungsland des Vorzeitmenschen*. Führer zur Urgeschichte 9, Augsburg.

Reinerth, H., 1953, Die Mittlere Steinzeit am Bodensee. *Vorzeit am Bodensee*, Heft 1, pp. 1–32.

Reinerth, H., 1956, Die Älteste Besiedlung des Allgäues. *Vorzeit am Bodensee*, Heft 1–4, pp. 1–35.

Richter, D., 1996, Die Mesolithische Freilandstation Rottenburg-Siebenlinden II. In *Spuren der Jagd—Die Jagd Nach Spuren*, edited by I. Campen, J. Hahn and M. Uerpmann, pp. 341–350. Tübinger Monographien zur Urgeschichte 11. Mo Vince Verlag, Tübingen.

Roehrig, E. and B. Ulrich, 1991, *Temperate Deciduous Forests*. Ecosystems of the World, 7. Elsevier, Amsterdam.

Sakellaridis, M., 1979, *The Economic Exploitation of the Swiss Area in the Mesolithic and Neolithic Periods*. British Archaeological Reports International Series 67. Oxford University Press, Oxford.

Schlichtherle, H., 1980, Sondierungen in Jungsteinzeitlichen Moorsiedlungen des Federsees. *Archäologische Ausgrabungen in Baden-Württemberg 1979*, pp. 3–34.

Schlichtherle, H., 1988, Henauhof-Nord, ein Mesolithischer Lagerplatz im Federseemoor, Stadt Bad Buchau, Kreis Biberach. *Archäologische Ausgrabungen in Baden-Württemberg 1987*, pp. 28–34.

Schlichtherle, H., 1990, Aspekte der Siedlungsarchäologischen Erforschung von Neolithikum und Bronzezeit im Südwestdeutschen Alpenvorland. *Siedlungsarchäologische Untersuchungen im Alpenvorland*, pp. 208–244. Bericht des Römisch-Germanischen Kommissions 71, Mainz.

Schlichtherle, H., 1994, Exotische Feuersteingeräte am Bodensee. *Plattform* 3:46–59.

Schlichtherle, H., 1996, Ein Holzspeer aus dem Taubried und die Frage Nach Steinzeitlichen Fischfangplätzen im Südlichen Federseemoor. In *Spuren der Jagd—Die Jagd Nach Spuren*, edited by I. Campen, J. Hahn and M. Uerpmann, pp. 351–358. Tübinger Monographien zur Urgeschichte 11. Mo Vince Verlag, Tübingen.

Schmid, E., 1962, Der Isteiner Klotz in Ur- und Frühgeschichtlicher Zeit. In *Istein und der Isteiner Klotz*, edited by F. Schülin and H. Schäfer, pp. 13–18. Rombach & Company, Freiburg.

Schmitt, K., 1984, Zwei Neue Karten zur Nacheiszeitlichen Besiedlungsgeschichte des Federseebeckens. In *Berichte zu Ufer- und Moorsiedlungen Süddeutschlands I*, pp. 101–115. Materialhefte zur Vor- und Frühgeschichte in Baden-Württemberg 4. Konrad Theiss Verlag, Stuttgart.

Schulte im Walde, T., Freundlich, J., Schwabedissen, H. and Taute, W., 1986, Köln Radiocarbon Dates III. *Radiocarbon* 28:134–140.

Schweingruber, F., 1978, Vegetationsgeschichtlich-archäologische Auswertung der Holzkohlenfunde Mesolithischer Höhlensedimente Süddeutschlands. In *Das Mesolithikum in Süddeut-*

schland, Teil 2: Naturwissenschaftliche Untersuchungen, edited by W. Taute, pp. 33–46. Tübinger Monographien zur Urgeschichte 5/2. Archaeologica Venatoria, Tübingen.

Smith, E., 1991, Inujjuamiut Foraging Strategies. Aldine de Gruyter, New York.

Smith, E. and Winterhalder, B., 1992, Evolutionary Ecology and Human Behavior. Aldine de Gruyter, New York.

Speth, J. and Spielmann, K., 1983, Energy Source, Protein Metabolism and Hunter–Gatherer Subsistence Strategies. Journal of Anthropological Archaeology 1:1–31.

Spielmann, K., 1986, Interdependence among Egalitarian Societies. Journal of Anthropological Archaeology 5:279–312.

Stephens, D. and E. Charnov, 1982, Optimal Foraging: Some Simple Stochastic Models. Behavioral Ecology and Sociobiology 10:251–263.

Stoll, H., 1932, Mesolithikum aus dem Ostschwarzwald. Germania 16:91–97.

Stoll, H., 1933, Urgeschichte des Oberen Gäues. Veröffentlichungen des Württembergischen Landesamts für Denkmalpflege, Stuttgart.

Taladay, L., Keller, D. and Munson, P., 1984, Hickory Nuts, Walnuts, Butternuts, and Hazelnuts: Observations and Experiments Relevant to Their Aboriginal Exploitation in Eastern North America. In Experiments and Observations on Aboriginal Wild Plant Food Utilization in Eastern North America, edited by P. Munson, pp. 349–362. Indiana Historical Society, Indianapolis.

Tanaka, J., 1980, The San: Hunter–Gatherers of the Kalahari. University of Tokyo Press, Tokyo.

Tanner, A., 1979, Bringing Home Animals: Religious Ideology and the Mode of Production of the Mistassini Cree Hunters. Social and Economic Studies 23. Institute of Social and Economic Research, Memorial University of Newfoundland. C. Hurst and Company, London.

Tauber, H., 1981, C-13 Evidence for Dietary Habits of Prehistoric Man in Denmark. Nature 292:332–333.

Taute, W., 1967a, Das Felsdach Lauereck, eine Mesolithisch-Neolithisch- Bronzezeitliche Stratigraphie an der Oberen Donau. Palaeohistoria XII:483–504.

Taute, W., 1967b, Grabungen zur Mittleren Steinzeit in Höhlen und unter Felsdächern der Schwäbischen Alb, 1961 bis 1965. Fundberichte aus Schwaben 18/I:14- 21.

Taute, W., 1972a, Funde aus der Steinzeit in der Jägerhaus-Höhle bei Bronnen. In Fridingen—Stadt on der Oberen Donau, pp. 21–26.

Taute, W., 1972b, Die Spätpaläolithisch-Frühmesolithische Schichtenfolge im Zigeunerfels bei Sigmaringen. Archäologische Information 1:29–40.

Taute, W., 1972/73, Neue Forschungen zur Chronologie von Spätpaläolithikum und Frühmesolithikum in Süddeutschland. Archäologische Informationen 2/3:60- 66.

Taute, W. (ed.), 1978, Das Mesolithikum in Süddeutschland, Teil 2: Naturwissenschaftliche Untersuchungen. Tübinger Monographien zur Urgeschichte 5/2. Archaeologica Venatoria, Tübingen.

Thomas, D., 1973, An Empirical Test for Steward's Model of Great Basin Settlement Patterns. American Antiquity 38:155–176.

Tilley, C. (ed.), 1990, Reading Material Culture. Blackwell, Oxford.

Tillmann, A., 1993, Kontinuität oder Diskontinuität? Zur Frage einer Bandkeramischen Landnahme im Südlichen Mitteleuropa. Archäologische Informationen 16(2):157–187.

Tonkinson, R., 1978, The Mardudjara Aborigines. Holt, Rinehart and Winston, New York.

Torke, W., 1981, Fischreste als Quellen der ökologie und ökonomie in der Steinzeit Südwestdeutschlands. Urgeschichtliche Materialhefte 4. Archäologica Venatoria, Tübingen.

Torke, W., 1993, Die Fischerei am Prähistorischen Federsee. Archäologisches Korrespondenzblatt 23:49–66.

Torrence, R., 1989, Retooling: Towards a Behavioral Theory of Stone Tools. In Time, Energy and Stone Tools, edited by R. Torrence, pp. 57–66. Cambridge University Press, Cambridge, England.

Tringham, R., 1991, Households with Faces: The Challenge of Gender in Prehistoric Architectural Remains. In *Engendering Archaeology*, edited by J. Gero and M. Conkey, pp. 93–131. Blackwell, Cambridge, England.

Vogelgesang, O., 1948, *Der Mittelsteinzeitliche Wohnplatz Bollschweil bei Freiburg i. Breisgau*. Freiburger Beiträge zur Urgeschichte, Band I.

Von Koenigswald, W., 1972, Der Faunenwandel an der Pleistozän-Holozän-Grenze im Zigeunerfels bei Sigmaringen. *Archäologische Information* 1:41–45.

Wagner, E., 1975, Neue Endpaläolithische und Mesolithische Funde vom Federsee. *Fundberichte aus Baden-Württemberg* 1:45–52.

Wagner, E., 1979, *Eiszeitjäger im Blaubeurener Tal*. Führer zu Archäologischen Denkmälern in Baden-Württemberg 6. Konrad Theiss Verlag, Stuttgart.

Walker, P. and B. Hewlett, 1990, Dental Health, Diet, and Social Status among Central African Foragers and Farmers. *American Anthropologist* 92:383–398.

Wall, E., 1961, Der Federsee von der Eiszeit bis zur Gegenwart. In *Der Federsee*, edited by W. Zimmermann, pp. 228–315. Schwäbischer Albverein, Stuttgart.

Weniger, G., 1982, *Wildbeuter und Ihre Umwelt*. Archaeologica Venatoria 5. Archaeologica Venatoria, Tübingen.

Weniger, G., 1989, The Magdalenian in Western Central Europe: Settlement Pattern and Regionality. *Journal of World Prehistory* 3:323–372.

Wiessner, P., 1982, Risk, Reciprocity and Social Influences on !Kung San Economics. In *Politics and History in Band Societies*, edited by E. Leacock and R. Lee, pp. 61–84. Cambridge University Press.

Winterhalder, B., 1981, Optimal Foraging Strategies and Hunter–Gatherer Research in Anthropology: Theory and Models. In *Hunter–Gatherer Foraging Strategies*, edited by B. Winterhalder and E. Smith, pp. 13–35. University of Chicago Press, Chicago.

Winterhalder, B., 1986, Diet Choice, Risk, and Food Sharing in a Stochastic Environment. *Journal of Anthropological Archaeology* 5:369–392.

Winterhalder, B., 1990, Open Field, Common Pot: Harvest Variability and Risk Avoidance in Agricultural and Foraging Societies. In *Risk and Uncertainty in Tribal and Peasant Economics*, edited by E. Cashdan. Westview Press, Boulder, Colorado.

Winterhalder, B. and Smith, E., 1981, *Hunter–Gatherer Foraging Strategies*. University of Chicago Press, Chicago.

Winters, H., 1969, *The Riverton Culture: A Second Millenium Occupation in the Central Wabash Valley*. Report of Investigations 13, Illinois State Museum, Springfield.

Yellen, J., 1977, *Archaeological Approaches to the Present*. Academic Press, New York.

Zimmermann, W., 1961, *Der Federsee*. Schwäbischer Albverein, Stuttgart.

Zvelebil, M., 1986, Postglacial Foraging in the Forests of Europe. *Scientific American* 254/5:104–115.

Zvelebil, M., 1994, Plant Use in the Mesolithic and Its Role in the Transition to Farming. *Proceedings of the Prehistoric Society* 60:35–74.

Index

Abraders, 65
Abri Klemmer, 78
Ache, 16, 17
Adzes, 87, 146f, 167
Aggregation size, 14, 15, 16, 17
Agriculture, 218
Aichbühler Bucht, 81, 98
Aichbühl Neolithic Culture, 110, 151
Aitrach Valley, 60t, 82, 84f, 85
Alaska, 23, 221
Alb: see Swabian Alb
Alleröd, 35, 43, 193
Alpine foothills
    description of, 33
    in Early Mesolithic, 59t, 69–70, 203
    in Late Mesolithic, 89t, 93
    in Late Palaeolithic, 45t, 52–53, 196,
        199
    spatial patterns in, 37, 38, 41, 42
Alpine glacier, 34, 35
Alps, 31
Amazonia, 16
Ambush hunting, 201–202
Ammonite, 116, 117, 198
Antler axes, 144, 146f, 151, 167
Antlers
    of Early Mesolithic, 75
    harpoons: see Barbed antler harpoons
    of Henauhof Nordwest, 136, 143–144,
        154, 188, 191

Antlers (cont.)
    of Late Mesolithic, 177, 179
    shed, 188
    unshed, 188, 189, 190, 204
    unworked, 134–135
    worked: see Worked antlers
Antler sleeves, 95
Apples, 67
Archaic, 4
Arctic hare, 36
Arrows, 69, 71, 87, 167, 212
Ash, 36, 75, 82, 137
Athabaskan groups, 23, 221
Atlantic, 148
    Early, 36, 137, 162, 165, 209
Aurochs, 36, 220
    of Early Mesolithic, 61t, 67, 68, 201
    of Henauhof Nordwest, 114, 117t, 121t, 130,
        131t, 140, 141t, 150t, 165
    of Henauhof Nordwest 2, 180t
    of Henauhof West, 173t
    of Late Mesolithic, 90t, 93, 95, 175, 179
    of Late Palaeolithic, 46t, 194, 195
Australia, 25, 26
Australian Aborigines, 1
Awls, 95, 164
Axes, 87, 223
    antler, 144, 146f, 151, 167
    stone, 94, 95
Azilian, 43

Backed blades
  of Early Mesolithic, 57, 65, 76
  of Federsee, 102*f*, 103
  of Henauhof Nordwest, 116*t*, 167
  of Henauhof West, 171*t*
  of Late Palaeolithic, 50, 54, 171
Backed points
  bilaterally, micro, 57
  of Henauhof Nordwest, 116*t*, 136
  of Henauhof West, 171*t*
  of Late Palaeolithic, 50, 53, 54, 55, 56, 171
Baden-Baden, 44, 45*t*, 51, 59*t*, 62*f*, 89*t*
Badgers, 220
  of Early Mesolithic, 61*t*, 77
  of Henauhof Nordwest, 130, 131*t*, 140, 141*t*, 166
  of Late Mesolithic, 90*t*
Badsee, 60*t*, 82, 83*f*
Banded chert
  of Early Mesolithic, 206, 219
  of Henauhof Nordwest, 114, 119, 127, 138, 149, 158–159
  of Late Mesolithic, 175, 178, 219
  of Late Palaeolithic, 56, 171, 198
Bandkeramik, 222
Barbed antler harpoons, 87, 94, 95, 96, 167, 212
Bärenfelsgrotte, 53, 78
Basawra groups, 221
Basel, 45*t*, 49, 51, 59*t*, 89*t*
Bavaria, 51, 56, 220
Bears, 46*t*, 61*t*, 90*t*, 95, 194, 220
Beavers, 36
  of Early Mesolithic, 61*t*, 67, 68, 202
  of Henauhof Nordwest, 140, 141*t*, 166
  of Henauhof Nordwest 2, 180*t*
  of Late Mesolithic, 90*t*, 179, 209
  of Late Palaeolithic, 46*t*, 194, 195
Beaver teeth, 75
Beech, 75
Belgium, 217, 219, 220, 222
Bernaufels Cave, 94
Beuron-Coincy region, 207
Beuronien, 7, 101, 219; *see also* Early Mesolithic
Beuronien A, 7, 57–58
  Bärenfelsgrotte in, 78
  Dietfurt Cave in, 74
  Fohlenhaus in, 77
  Geissenklösterle in, 77
  Henauhof Nordwest in, 81, 168

Jägerhaushöhle in, 70, 71, 72
  Malerfels in, 78
  Neckar drainage in, 68
  Schuntershöhle in, 76
  Siedlung Forschner in, 82
  Zigeunerfels in, 75
Beuronien B, 7, 57–58
  Bärenfelsgrotte in, 78
  Dietfurt Cave in, 74
  Fohlenhaus in, 77
  Helga-Abri in, 76
  Henauhof Nordwest in, 81, 126, 168, 189
  Jägerhaushöhle in, 70, 71, 72
  Neckar drainage in, 65, 67, 68
  Rappenfels in, 79
  Schuntershöhle in, 76
  Siedlung Forschner in, 82
  Site Fe-5s in, 107
  Site Fe-8 in, 103
  Zigeunerfels in, 75
Beuronien C, 7, 57–58
  Dietfurt Cave in, 74
  Felsställe in, 75
  Fohlenhaus in, 77
  Helga-Abri in, 76
  Henauhof Nordwest in, 81, 160, 167, 186, 189
  Jägerhaushöhle in, 70, 71, 72
  Neckar drainage in, 68
  Probstfels in, 73
  Rappenfels in, 79
  Schuntershöhle in, 76
Big game
  of Early Mesolithic, 72, 74, 202, 204, 206
  efficiency of hunting, 16, 17
  of Henauhof Nordwest, 130, 164–165, 168, 186, 188, 190
  of Late Mesolithic, 209, 210*f*, 211, 214, 218
  of Late Palaeolithic, 194, 195
  prestige and, 24
  reliability of hunting, 19
Bilaterally backed micropoints, 57
Bilateral points, 116*t*
Birch, 35, 117, 124, 137, 193; *see also* Pine-birch forests
Birds, 36
  of Early Mesolithic, 61*t*, 67, 68, 72, 73–74, 75, 78, 202, 204, 206
  of Henauhof Nordwest, 109, 117*t*, 121*t*, 123, 131–132, 141, 150, 156, 166, 168, 186–187, 188, 189–190

Birds (*cont.*)
 of Henauhof Nordwest 2, 180*t*
 of Henauhof West, 173*t*
 of Late Mesolithic, 90*t*, 95, 96, 175, 179, 209
 of Late Palaeolithic, 46*t*, 194, 195
Birkenkopf, 65, 203
Birsmatten Basisgrotte, 160
Bison, 165
Black Forest, 32, 117, 198
 description of, 33
 in Early Mesolithic, 59*t*, 69, 203, 204
 in Late Mesolithic, 89*t*, 91, 93, 94
 in Late Palaeolithic, 45*t*, 47, 50, 51, 195, 199
 spatial patterns in, 37, 38, 41, 42
 temporal patterns in, 34, 35
Black grouse, 187
Blades
 backed: *see* Backed blades
 broken, 116*t*, 128, 156, 171*t*, 179*t*
 core rejuvenation, 116*t*, 171*t*, 179*t*
 cortex, 116*t*, 179*t*
 of Early Mesolithic, 68
 of Henauhof Nordwest, 110, 116*t*, 136, 140,
  151, 153, 157, 160, 161*f*, 162–163,
  167
 of Henauhof Nordwest 2, 179*t*
 of Henauhof West, 171*t*
 of Late Mesolithic, 175, 212
 of Late Palaeolithic, 53, 199
 micro, 109
 notched, 47, 87, 139
 regular: *see* Regular blades
 retouched: *see* Retouched blades
 of Tannstock, 107
 unretouched, 47, 53, 58, 62
 utilized, 65, 136, 181
Blaubeuren Valley, 35
Boar, 36, 220
 of Bronze Age, 181
 of Early Mesolithic, 61*t*, 67, 68, 72, 73, 75,
  201
 of Henauhof Nordwest, 114, 117*t*, 121*t*,
  122–123, 130, 131*t*, 136, 140, 141,
  149, 150*t*, 152, 154, 165
 of Henauhof Nordwest 2, 180*t*
 of Henauhof West, 173*t*
 of Late Mesolithic, 90*t*, 93, 95, 96, 175, 179,
  209
 of Late Palaeolithic, 46*t*, 171, 194
 of Tannstock, 107
Boar's tusk: *see* Worked boar's tusk

Bone-fracturing, 173, 206
Bone pendants, 96
Bone points
 of Early Mesolithic, 75, 79, 82
 of Henauhof Nordwest, 123, 124*f*, 133–134,
  135, 143, 144–145, 150–151, 166,
  168, 187–188, 190
 of Late Mesolithic, 94, 96
 of Tannstock, 105
Bone tools, 74, 79
Bone weights
 in Henauhof Nordwest, 156, 157, 164–165,
  166
 in Henauhof Nordwest 2, 178–179
 in Henauhof West, 175
Bone-working: *see* Worked bone
Boreal, 36, 73, 209
 Helga-Abri in, 76
 Henauhof Nordwest in, 124, 125, 166, 190
Borers
 of Early Mesolithic, 58, 74, 75
 of Henauhof Nordwest, 116*t*
 of Henauhof West, 171*t*
 of Late Mesolithic, 178
 of Late Palaeolithic, 47, 50, 54, 55
Bovids, 109, 122–123, 149–150, 152, 165
Bream, 140, 141*t*
Brenz Valley, 35
Broken blades, 116*t*, 128, 156, 171*t*, 179*t*
Bronze Age, 6, 8, 181
Brown bears, 194
Brown chert, 197
Burials, 212; *see also* Cemeteries
Burins
 of Early Mesolithic, 58, 65, 67, 71, 73, 74,
  75, 77, 78, 83
 of Henauhof Nordwest, 110, 116*t*, 163–164,
  187
 of Henauhof Nordwest 2, 179*t*
 of Henauhof West, 171*t*
 of Late Mesolithic, 95, 175, 178
 of Late Palaeolithic, 47, 49, 50, 53, 54, 55
 micro, 67, 95, 116*t*
Burin-scrapers, 116*t*, 160, 164
Burin spalls, 55
Butchering, 19, 122, 185

Cabbage, 67
Canada, 26, 194, 221
Canoes, 201
Capercaillie, 187

Caribou, 194
Catfish, 190; see also Wels
Cattle, 152
Caves, 53, 204, 211
Cemeteries, 6, 218; see also Burials
Ceramics
    of Bronze Age, 181
    of Henauhof Nordwest, 110, 144, 148–149,
        154
    of Tannstock, 105
Cervids, 130, 180t
Chamois, 90t, 94
Charcoal studies, 36
    of Early Mesolithic, 71
    of Federsee, 102
    of Henauhof Nord I, 96, 97
    of Henauhof Nordwest, 111–112, 113, 117,
        125, 132–133, 137, 138, 142, 148
    of Henauhof Nordwest 2, 177–178
    of Oberschwaben, 82
    of Swabian Alb, 74, 75, 78
Chert
    banded: see Banded chert
    brown, 197
    of Early Mesolithic, 68, 75
    of Federsee, 102, 103
    gray, 119
    of Henauhof Nordwest, 114, 154, 158–159
    Jurassic: see Jurassic chert
    of Late Mesolithic, 92
    of Late Palaeolithic, 51, 56, 171, 197
    tan, 127
    white, 67, 68, 98, 107
Chunks, 116t, 157, 171t, 179t
Climatic stations, 39f
Complex groups, 24
Coots, 131, 140, 141t
Core rejuvenation blades, 116t, 171t, 179t
Core rejuvenation flakes, 116t, 171t, 179t
Cores
    of Early Mesolithic, 58, 62, 65, 67, 68, 72,
        73, 74, 76, 78, 205, 219
    of Henauhof Nordwest, 110, 116t, 128, 129–
        130, 136, 157, 159–160, 162–163
    of Henauhof Nordwest 2, 179t
    of Henauhof West, 171t
    of Late Mesolithic, 95, 97, 98, 175, 178, 181,
        212
    of Late Palaeolithic, 49, 50, 199
Cormorant, 131t, 132
Cortex blades, 116t, 179t

Cortexes, 159–160
Cortex flakes, 92, 116t, 162–163, 171t, 179t
Cree, 16, 26, 202
Cultural changes, 216–217
Culture areas, 2
Currencies of choice, 20–23

Dam-ways, 105, 107
Danube, 6, 8, 9, 10, 66, 70, 75
    in Early Mesolithic, 204
    in Late Mesolithic, 211, 217
    in Late Palaeolithic, 195, 196
    social relations by, 219, 220, 222–223
    spatial patterns in, 37
    temporal patterns in, 35
Decision goals, 14–20
Decision models, 14
Deer
    giant, 194
    red: see Red deer
    roe: see Roe deer
Deer teeth, 74, 94, 96, 116
Denmark, 5, 87, 217, 218, 220
Dietfurt Cave, 53
    description of, 54
    in Early Mesolithic, 74
    in Late Mesolithic, 95
    in Late Palaeolithic, 43, 200
Division of labor, 17, 19, 21
    in Early Mesolithic, 206
    in Late Mesolithic, 214
    in Late Palaeolithic, 198
    role reversal in, 25–26
Dogs, 68, 90t, 141t, 152

Early Atlantic, 36, 137, 162, 165, 209
Early Mesolithic, 43, 57–85, 87, 201–208; see
        also Beuronien
    activities in, 205
    Alpine foothills in, 59t, 69–70, 203
    Black Forest in, 59t, 69, 203, 204
    environmental and cultural changes in,
        216
    environmental history of, 217
    Henauhof Nordwest in, 161, 167, 189, 204,
        205
    Henauhof Nordwest 2 in, 181
    Lake Constance in, 60t, 83–85
    Neckar drainage in, 63–69, 203
    Oberschwaben in, 60t, 80–83, 201, 203,
        204

Early Mesolithic (*cont.*)
  resource productivity, efficiency, and risk in, 201–202
  Rhine lowlands in, 58–62, 91, 201
  Rhine Valley in, 59*t*, 62, 92
  settlement patterns in, 202–206
  sites of, 59–60*t*
  social relations in, 219
  Swabian Alb in, 59*t*, 70–80, 203, 204
Efficiency, 14–18, 20
  in Early Mesolithic, 201–202
  in Late Mesolithic, 209–210
  in Late Palaeolithic, 193–194
Eggs/eggshells, 46*t*, 61*t*, 77, 196, 204, 206
Elk, 36, 130–131, 140, 165, 166
Elm, 36, 137
Endscrapers, 107
Energy, 20–22
England, 217, 218
Environmental changes, 216–217
Environmental history, 217–219
Ermine, 46*t*
Eskimos, 23
Evolutionary ecology, 13–23
Excavation
  of Henauhof Nordwest, 111–113
  of Henauhof Nordwest 2, 178*f*
  of Henauhof West, 170*f*
Exchange, 20, 197–198, 213, 221

Falkensteinhöhle, 6, 184, 185, 186, 189, 190
  in Early Mesolithic, 73–74
  in Late Mesolithic, 94–95, 212
Fat, 20, 21
Fauna
  of Early Mesolithic, 61*t*, 72, 203
  of Henauhof Nordwest, 187
    Stratum 1, 152
    Stratum 3, 140–142
    Stratum 4, 130–132
    Stratum 5, 119–123
    Stratum 6, 114–116, 117*t*
    Stratum C, 149–150
    Stratum G, 136
    Stratum P, 152
  of Henauhof Nordwest 2, 180*t*
  of Henauhof West, 173*t*
  of Late Mesolithic, 90*t*, 173*t*, 175, 180*t*, 209
  of Late Palaeolithic, 46*t*, 173*t*
Feasts, 24, 25
Federmesser, 43

Federsee, 6, 7–8, 99–100
  comparison with other sites, 183–192
  in Early Mesolithic, 60*t*, 80–81, 201, 204
  in Late Mesolithic, 89*t*
  in Late Palaeolithic, 43, 55–56, 195, 196, 197
  Site Fe-3, 100–103
  Site Fe-5: *see* Henauhof Nordwest
  Site Fe-5s, 107–108
  Site Fe-8, 103–105
  Site Fe-18: *see* Tannstock
  temporal patterns in, 35
Felsställe, 75–76, 205
Fish, 5, 16, 36
  of Early Mesolithic, 61*t*, 72, 74, 75, 77, 78, 82, 202, 204, 206
  of Henauhof Nordwest, 110, 114, 116, 117*t*, 121*t*, 123, 130, 131, 134, 140–141, 143, 148, 149, 150, 156, 166, 168, 184, 185, 186
  of Henauhof Nordwest 2, 180*t*
  of Henauhof West, 173*t*
  of Late Mesolithic, 90*t*, 95, 96, 179, 209
  of Late Palaeolithic, 46*t*, 48, 49, 54, 194, 195, 199
Fishing
  in Early Mesolithic, 66, 201
  efficiency of, 17
  in Henauhof Nordwest, 127, 134, 135, 145, 166, 188, 190
  in Late Palaeolithic, 195–196
  women and, 220–221
Fishing camps, 212
Fish teeth, 74, 220–221
Fish Tooth Band, 206–207, 220
Flake cores, 151, 199
Flakes
  core rejuvenation, 116*t*, 171*t*, 179*t*
  cortex: *see* Cortex flakes
  of Early Mesolithic, 68, 76
  of Federsee, 102, 103, 104, 107
  of Henauhof Nordwest, 110, 116*t*, 140, 151, 153–154, 157
  of Henauhof Nordwest 2, 179*t*
  of Henauhof West, 171*t*
  of Late Mesolithic, 97, 98, 175, 178
  of Late Palaeolithic, 49, 50, 53, 199
  retouched, 151
  unretouched, 47, 58, 62
  utilized, 65, 181
Fohlenhaus, 53, 54, 77

Food nutrients, 20–21
Food proportions, 164–167
Foraging efficiency: *see* Efficiency
Forests, 216; *see also* Pine-birch forests
    of Early Mesolithic, 201
    of Henauhof Nordwest, 137
    of Late Palaeolithic, 193–194
    temporal patterns in, 35–36
Foxes, 36, 220
    of Early Mesolithic, 61*t*, 67, 68, 202
    of Henauhof Nordwest, 121*t*, 123, 130, 131,
        166
    of Late Mesolithic, 90*t*
    of Late Palaeolithic, 46*t*
Fox teeth, 96, 134, 145
France, 43
Freiburg, 41, 42
    in Early Mesolithic, 58, 59*t*, 63*f*
    in Late Mesolithic, 89*t*, 91
    in Late Palaeolithic, 45*t*, 47–48, 51
Freudenstadt, 38, 42
Frogs, 74
Frosts, 38, 39*f*, 40*f*, 41–42, 197
Füssen, 70

Geissenklösterle, 77
Giant deer, 194
Gifts, 24
Glacial maximum, 216
Glaciers, 4, 34, 35
Goats, 152, 194
Goldeneye, 131
Gooseander, 131*t*, 132
Grain, 166–167
Gray chert, 119
Gray heron, 140, 141*t*
Grease, 72, 122, 130, 140
Grinding stones, 145, 147*f*, 148, 166, 168, 191,
        223
Grosse Ofnet, 212, 213, 214
Grouse, 78, 187
G/Wi, 25

Hammerstones, 54, 65, 75, 94, 96
Hare, 17
    arctic, 36
    of Early Mesolithic, 61*t*, 202
    of Henauhof Nordwest, 121*t*, 166
    of Late Mesolithic, 90*t*
    of Late Palaeolithic, 46*t*, 194
Harpoons: *see* Barbed antler harpoons

Hazel, 71, 73, 117, 124–125, 137
Hazel hens, 187
Hazelnuts
    of Early Mesolithic, 67, 68, 72, 74, 76, 77,
        81, 202, 204
    of Henauhof Nordwest, 111–112, 125, 166,
        168, 189
    of Late Mesolithic, 95, 97, 98, 210
Hearths
    of Early Mesolithic, 67, 68, 75, 77, 82, 203
    of Henauhof Nordwest, 133, 138, 142, 143, 148
    of Late Mesolithic, 92, 97, 98, 177, 180
    of Late Palaeolithic, 52, 53, 55, 173, 199
    of Tannstock, 105
Helga-Abri, 43, 53, 76–77, 196, 203
    description of, 55
Henauhof Nord I, 96–97, 192, 212
Henauhof Nord II, 97–98, 192, 211, 212
Henauhof Nordwest, 81, 82, 96, 111–154,
        155–168, 180, 223
    activities in, 162–167
    assemblage formation in, 156–157
    behavioral variation in, 158–167
    comparison with other sites, 183–192
    in Early Mesolithic, 161, 167, 189, 204, 205
    excavation techniques used in, 111–113
    exchange in, 197–198
    fauna of: *see* Fauna
    food proportions in, 164–167
    in Late Mesolithic, 126, 160, 163, 167, 168,
        186, 189, 190, 211, 212
    in Late Palaeolithic, 43, 55, 108, 148, 160,
        161, 165–166, 167, 173, 196, 197–198
    lithics of: *see* Lithics
    overview of, 108–110
    preservation in, 155–156
    sample size in, 157–158
    seasonality at, 162, 188–191
    Stratum 1, 151–152
    Stratum 3: *see* Stratum 3, Henauhof Nord-
        west
    Stratum 4: *see* Stratum 4, Henauhof Nord-
        west
    Stratum 5: *see* Stratum 5, Henauhof Nord-
        west
    Stratum 6: *see* Stratum 6, Henauhof Nord-
        west
    Stratum B, 152–154
    Stratum C, 148–151, 163
    Stratum G, 135–136, 137*f*
    Stratum P, 151–152

Henauhof Nordwest 2, 96, 177–182, 192, 212
   in Bronze Age, 181
   in Early Mesolithic, 181
   fauna of, 180*t*
   in Late Mesolithic, 177–181
   lithics of, 179*t*
   in Palaeolithic, 181
Henauhof West, 96, 169–176, 180–181, 191,
   192
   fauna of, 173*t*
   in Late Mesolithic, 175–176
   in Late Palaeolithic, 55, 171–175, 196
   lithics of, 171*t*, 174*f*
Hide-fleshers, 144, 164, 181
Hide-working: *see* Worked hides
Hohlenstein Stadel, 77
Holland, 87, 220
Holocene, 165, 216
Horses, 36, 216
   of Early Mesolithic, 61*t*, 201
   of Henauhof Nordwest, 114, 117*t*, 121*t*,
      122–123, 130, 131*t*, 140, 141*t*,
      165
   of Late Mesolithic, 90*t*
   of Late Palaeolithic, 46*t*, 194, 195, 198
Human remains, 173*t*; *see also* Burials; Ceme-
      teries; Skulls
Hunting
   ambush, 201–202
   big game: *see* Big game
   in Early Mesolithic, 201–202, 204
   in Late Palaeolithic, 194
   small game: *see* Small game
   spatial patterns in, 38
Hunting camps, 196, 205, 214
Hunting tallies, 134, 135*f*
Hut depressions, 82, 105, 203

Ibex, 46*t*
Ice age, 4, 34
Iller, 196
Imperfect knowledge, 22
Information, 20, 22–23
Inzigkofen, 74, 95, 184, 185, 186, 187, 189,
   190, 205
Iron Age, 152–154
Iron Gates region, 6
Isosceles triangles, 57
Isteiner Klotz, 49, 62, 64*f*, 91–92
Ivory, 219

Jägerhaushöhle, 7, 184, 185, 186, 187, 189,
   190
   description of, 54
   in Early Mesolithic, 70–73, 204
   in Late Mesolithic, 93–94
   in Late Palaeolithic, 53, 54
Jays, 131*t*, 132
Jehlefels, 53
Jet, 219
Juniper, 35
Jurassic chert
   of Early Mesolithic, 65, 68, 69, 71, 82, 83, 85
   of Late Mesolithic, 93, 178
   of Late Palaeolithic, 51, 56, 197, 199

Kalahari, 9, 25, 221
Karlsruhe, 41
Kleine Scheuer, 53, 77
Konstanz, 41, 42
!Kung San, 1, 9

La Hoguette site, 222*f*
Lake Constance, 6, 7, 8, 31, 220
   description of, 33
   in Early Mesolithic, 60*t*, 83–85
   in Late Mesolithic, 98
   in Late Palaeolithic, 45*t*, 56, 196, 198
   spatial patterns in, 37, 41, 42
   temporal patterns in, 35, 36
Lanceolate points, 57
Late Mesolithic, 7, 87–98, 209–214
   Alpine foothills in, 89*t*, 93
   Black Forest in, 89*t*, 91, 93, 94
   environmental and cultural changes in, 217
   environmental history in, 217, 218, 219
   fauna of, 90*t*, 173*t*, 175, 180*t*, 209
   Henauhof Nordwest in, 126, 160, 163, 166,
      167, 168, 186, 189, 190, 211, 212
   Henauhof Nordwest 2 in, 177–181
   Henauhof West in, 175–176
   Lake Constance in, 98
   lithics of, 171*t*, 179*t*
   Neckar drainage in, 92–93
   Oberschwaben in, 81, 89*t*, 96–98, 217
   resource efficiency, productivity, and risk in,
      209–210
   Rhine lowlands in, 58, 62, 88–92
   Rhine Valley in, 89*t*, 92
   settlement patterns in, 210–212
   Site Fe-5s in, 107
   Site Fe-8 in, 103

Late Mesolithic (*cont.*)
  sites of, 89*t*
  social relations in, 219, 220, 221–223
  spatial patterns in, 38
  Swabian Alb in, 73, 89*t*, 93–96, 211
Late Palaeolithic, 43–56, 193–200, 202, 203
  Alpine foothills in, 45*t*, 52–53, 196, 199
  Black Forest in, 45*t*, 47, 50, 51, 195, 199
  environmental and cultural changes in, 216
  fauna of, 46*t*, 173*t*
  Henauhof Nordwest in, 43, 55, 108, 148, 160,
      161, 165–166, 167, 173, 196, 197–198
  Henauhof West in, 55, 171–175, 196
  hunting in, 38
  Lake Constance in, 45*t*, 56, 196, 198
  lithics of, 171*t*, 174*f*
  Neckar drainage in, 50, 65
  Oberschwaben in, 45*t*, 55–56, 81, 195, 196,
      197, 198, 200, 216
  resource productivity, efficiency, and risk in,
      193–194
  Rhine lowlands in, 44–49, 58, 62, 91, 145
  Rhine Valley in, 45*t*, 49–50, 51, 62, 197
  settlement patterns in, 195–198
  Site Fe-8 in, 103
  sites of, 45*t*
  Swabian Alb in, 43, 45*t*, 53–55, 195, 196
  Tannstock in, 105
Late Pleistocene, 162, 216
Lautereck Shelter, 96, 139, 186, 190, 212
LBK villages, 222–223
Least-cost solutions, 14
Lepenski Vir, 28
Lime, 36, 124, 137
Linearbandkeramik site, 222*f*
Linear programming economic models, 14, 16,
      20
Lithics
  of Early Mesolithic, 69, 78, 204
  of Henauhof Nordwest, 112, 116*t*, 158–161
    Stratum 1, 151
    Stratum 3, 137, 138–140, 160
    Stratum 4, 127–130, 160
    Stratum 5, 118, 119, 160
    Stratum 6, 114
    Stratum B, 153–154
    Stratum C, 149
    Stratum P, 151
  of Henauhof Nordwest 2, 179*t*
  of Henauhof West, 171*t*, 174*f*
  of Late Mesolithic, 171*t*, 179*t*

Lithics (*cont.*)
  of Late Palaeolithic, 171*t*, 174*f*
  of Tannstock, 105
Luxemburg, 217
Lynx, 46*t*, 61*t*, 220

Mace heads, 5
Macroliths, 93, 96, 171*t*
Magdalenian, 43, 44, 198, 199
  Henauhof Nordwest in, 161, 165
  Neckar drainage in, 65
  social relations in, 219
  Swabian Alb in, 53
Maintainability, 199
Mainz Basin, 74, 95, 206
Malerfels, 53, 78, 186
Mammoth, 36
Maple, 36
Mardudjara, 25–26
Marriage, 199–200
Marrow, 72, 122, 130, 140
Martens, 36, 46*t*, 61*t*, 68, 90*t*, 141*t*, 166, 209, 220
Matter, 20–22
Meat, 72, 122, 130, 140, 167
Mesolithic, *see also* Early Mesolithic; Late
      Mesolithic
  background on investigation of, 6–9
  Black Forest in, 51
  Henauhof Nordwest in, 108, 160, 161, 165,
      166
  overview of, 3–6
  Rhine Valley in, 50
  Tannstock in, 105
Metten, 42
Microblades, 109
Microburins, 67, 95, 116*t*
Microliths
  of Early Mesolithic, 58, 65, 67, 68, 69, 71,
      73, 74, 75, 76, 77, 78, 79, 83, 203,
      204, 205–206, 207, 216, 219
  of Federsee, 102*f*
  of Henauhof Nordwest, 110, 116*t*, 157, 160,
      167
  of Henauhof Nordwest 2, 179*t*
  of Late Mesolithic, 95, 96, 178
  of Late Palaeolithic, 49, 50
  trapezoidal: *see* Trapezoidal microliths (tra-
      pezes)
Micropoints, 57
Middens, 211
Moles, 121*t*, 130, 131*t*, 141*t*, 150*t*

Moosburg, 81
Moose, 16, 220
    of Early Mesolithic, 61*t*, 201
    of Henauhof Nordwest, 131*t*, 141*t*
    of Late Mesolithic, 90*t*
    of Late Palaeolithic, 46*t*, 194, 195
Munich, 38, 42
Mussels, 72, 74
Mute swans, 121*t*, 123

Nagold Valley, 51, 69, 70*f*
Natural landscape, 31–42
    area, 31–33
    spatial patterns, 37–42
    temporal patterns, 33–37
Neckar drainage
    description of, 33
    in Early Mesolithic, 63–69, 203
    in Late Mesolithic, 92–93
    in Late Palaeolithic, 50, 65
Neckar Valley, 7, 220
    in Early Mesolithic, 59*t*, 205
    in Late Mesolithic, 89*t*
    in Late Palaeolithic, 45*t*, 196
    spatial patterns in, 37, 38, 41
    temporal patterns in, 35
Needles, 144–145, 150, 164
Neolithic, 3, 6, 8
    environmental and cultural changes in, 216
    environmental history in, 219
    Henauhof Nordwest in, 108, 140, 148–149
    Neckar drainage in, 65
    Oberschwaben in, 81
    Site Fe-8 in, 103
    social relations in, 221
    Tannstock in, 105
Netherlands, 217
Nets, 81
Net weights, 98
Nonfood benefits, 14
Northern Europe, 5–6, 87
Northern European Plain, 4, 43
Northern Germany, 87, 217, 218, 220
Notched blades, 47, 87, 139
Notched pieces
    of Early Mesolithic, 58, 65, 67, 72, 74, 76
    of Henauhof Nordwest, 116*t*, 140
    of Henauhof West, 171*t*
    of Late Mesolithic, 95, 96
    of Late Palaeolithic, 50
Nürnberg, 42

Oak, 36
    of Early Mesolithic, 71, 73, 74, 75, 78
    of Henauhof Nordwest, 124, 137
    of Late Mesolithic, 93
Oberschwaben, 8, 10, 69
    description of, 33
    in Early Mesolithic, 60*t*, 80–83, 201, 203, 204
    in Late Mesolithic, 81, 89*t*, 96–98, 217
    in Late Palaeolithic, 45*t*, 55–56, 81, 195, 196, 197, 198, 200, 216
    spatial patterns in, 37, 41, 42
    temporal patterns in, 34, 35
Obersee, 60*t*, 82, 83*f*, 203
Oberstdorf, 38, 42, 70
Ofnet Cave, 220
Optimal foraging models, 14, 15, 16, 20, 25, 26
Ornaments, 220–221; *see also* specific types
    of Early Mesolithic, 74, 206–207
    of Late Mesolithic, 212
Ostrich eggshell beads, 221
Otter, 61*t*, 90*t*

Package size, 16–17, 36, 201
Paintings, 75
Palaeolithic, 3, 181
    Late: *see* Late Palaeolithic
    Upper, 7, 38, 219
Peat, 6, 99, 102, 103
    of Henauhof Nordwest, 117–118, 121, 122, 135–136, 137, 155–156
    of Henauhof Nordwest 2, 177
    of Henauhof West, 169, 176
    of Tannstock, 105, 107
Pigs, 154
Pike, 117*t*, 121*t*, 123, 131, 140, 141*t*, 150, 190
Pine, 35
    of Early Mesolithic, 71, 73, 74, 78
    of Henauhof Nordwest, 117, 124, 137
    of Late Mesolithic, 93
Pine-birch forests, 37, 38, 193, 216
Plant foods
    of Early Mesolithic, 202
    of Henauhof Nordwest, 166, 188, 189
    of Late Mesolithic, 214
Plant-gathering
    efficiency of, 16, 17
    men in, 25–26
Pochard, 140, 141*t*

Points, 53
  backed: *see* Backed points
  bilateral, 116*t*
  bone: *see* Bone points
  lanceolate, 57
  projectile, 140, 219
Pollen studies, 8, 34, 35, 36, 71, 93
Porcupine quills, 221
Potlatches, 25
Preboreal, 36, 117, 165
Precipitation, 32–33
Preservation, 155–156
Prestige, 24–25
Prey aggregation size: *see* Aggregation size
Prey costs, 15
  processing, 16
  pursuit, 16, 17
  search, 17
Prey density, 16, 17
Prey mobility, 14, 15
Prey size, 16–17
Prey weight, 14, 15
Probstfels, 73
Projectile points, 140, 219
Protein, 20, 21
Ptarmigan, 36
Pygmies, 1, 25

Quantitative models, 17
Quartzite, 107

Radiocarbon dating
  of Henauhof Nord I, 96
  of Henauhof Nordwest, 113, 117, 125, 137,
    148, 152
  of Henauhof Nordwest 2, 177–178
  of Neckar drainage, 67, 68
  of Oberschwaben, 81
  of Swabian Alb, 71, 74, 75, 76, 77, 78, 94,
    95
Radiolarite
  of Early Mesolithic, 69, 82, 83
  of Henauhof Nordwest, 114, 119, 127, 138,
    149, 154, 158–159
  of Late Mesolithic, 175, 177, 178
  of Late Palaeolithic, 171, 197
Rainfall, 32, 33, 37, 209
Randecker Maar, 79
Rappenfels, 78–80
Raspberry, 67
Raw materials, 21–22; *see also* specific types

Red deer, 36, 220
  of Bronze Age, 181
  of Early Mesolithic, 61*t*, 67, 68, 72, 73, 75,
    77, 78, 201, 202
  of Henauhof Nordwest, 110, 114, 116, 117*t*,
    121, 122, 130, 131*t*, 134, 135, 136,
    140, 141*t*, 143, 144, 145, 149, 150*t*,
    151, 152, 154, 165, 190, 191
  of Henauhof Nordwest 2, 180*t*
  of Henauhof West, 173*t*
  of Late Mesolithic, 90*t*, 93, 95, 96, 175, 179,
    180, 209
  of Late Palaeolithic, 46*t*, 171, 194, 195,
    199
  of Tannstock, 107
Red foxes, 67, 68, 121*t*, 131*t*
Red ochre, 75, 95, 116, 134, 173
Reductionism, 27
Reese River Valley, 9
Reforestation, 194, 218
Regular blades
  of Henauhof Nordwest, 139
  of Late Mesolithic, 87, 95, 96, 98, 178, 217
Reindeer, 36, 38, 216, 219
  of Early Mesolithic, 61*t*, 67
  of Late Palaeolithic, 194, 195, 198
Reliability, 18–20
Resource productivity
  in Early Mesolithic, 201–202
  in Late Mesolithic, 209–210
  in Late Palaeolithic, 193–194
Resource-sharing, 18
Retouched blades
  of Early Mesolithic, 58, 65, 72, 73, 74, 75,
    76, 77, 78, 79
  of Late Mesolithic, 93, 95, 96
  of Late Palaeolithic, 47, 49, 50, 53
Retouched flakes, 151
Retouched pieces, 67
Retouched projectile points, 140
Retouched tools
  of Early Mesolithic, 83, 204
  of Henauhof Nordwest, 157, 158, 187
  of Henauhof Nordwest 2, 179*t*
  of Late Palaeolithic, 171
Rhine lowlands
  description of, 32
  in Early Mesolithic, 58–62, 91, 201
  in Late Mesolithic, 58, 62, 88–92
  in Late Palaeolithic, 44–49, 58, 62, 91, 195
  spatial patterns in, 37, 38, 41, 42

Rhine Valley, 220
  description of, 32–33
  in Early Mesolithic, 59*t*, 62, 92
  in Late Mesolithic, 89*t*, 92
  in Late Palaeolithic, 45*t*, 49–50, 51, 62, 197
Rhinoceros, 36
Risk, 18–19, 20
  in Early Mesolithic, 201–202
  in Late Mesolithic, 209–210
  in Late Palaeolithic, 193–194
Riverton Culture, 9
Rockshelters, 53, 204, 205
Roe deer, 36, 220
  of Early Mesolithic, 61*t*, 67, 68, 72, 73, 75,
    78, 201, 202
  of Henauhof Nordwest, 121*t*, 122–123, 130,
    131*t*, 135, 140, 141, 143, 149, 150*t*,
    152, 154, 165, 166, 190
  of Henauhof Nordwest 2, 180*t*
  of Late Mesolithic, 90*t*, 93, 95, 96, 179, 209
  of Late Palaeolithic, 46*t*, 194
Rosi I, 67, 204
Rosi II, 68
Rosi III, 68, 92, 204, 205
Rottenburg-Siebenlinden, 67

Sackingen, 50*f*, 51, 62, 64*f*, 92, 195
Sacrifice, 77
Salmon, 48, 195, 196
Scalene triangles, 57
Schuntershöhle, 76, 96
Schussenquelle, 6
Schussen River, 6
Scrapers
  burin, 116*t*, 160, 164
  of Early Mesolithic, 58, 65, 67, 71, 73, 74,
    75, 76, 77, 78, 83
  end, 107
  of Federsee, 102*f*
  of Henauhof Nordwest, 110, 116*t*, 151, 153
  of Henauhof Nordwest 2, 179*t*
  of Henauhof West, 171*t*
  of Late Mesolithic, 93, 95, 96, 178
  of Late Palaeolithic, 47, 49, 50, 53, 54
Sea level, 218
Seals, 220
Seasonality, 31–32, 38
  in Early Mesolithic, 66–67
  at Henauhof Nordwest, 162, 188–191
  in Late Palaeolithic, 196–197
Seekirch, 81

Settlement patterns
  in Early Mesolithic, 202–206
  in Late Mesolithic, 210–212
  in Late Palaeolithic, 195–198
Shafts, 133–134, 136, 144, 150–151
Shed antlers, 188
Sheep, 152
Shellfish, 36
  of Early Mesolithic, 61*t*, 72, 202, 206
  of Late Mesolithic, 90*t*, 95, 96, 209–210
  of Late Palaeolithic, 46*t*, 49, 194, 195
Shells
  of Early Mesolithic, 74, 206, 219
  of Henauhof Nordwest, 116
  of Late Mesolithic, 94, 95, 213, 214, 219
Siedlung Forschner, 81–82
Simple groups, 24
Site Fe-3, 100–103
Site Fe-5: *see* Henauhof Nordwest
Site Fe-5s, 107–108
Site Fe-8, 103–105
Site Fe-18: *see* Tannstock
Skulls, 77, 208, 212–213, 214, 220–221
Small game
  of Early Mesolithic, 202, 204
  of Henauhof Nordwest, 190
  of Late Mesolithic, 209
  of Late Palaeolithic, 194, 199
Snow, 32, 37, 38
Social context, 23–26
Social relations, 219–223
Sorrel, 94
Southwest Germany, 215–224
  environmental and cultural changes in, 216–
    217
  environmental history in, 217–219
  overview of, 6–9
  social relations in, 219–223
Spatial patterns, 37–42
Spears, 81, 82
Spitalhöhle, 53, 78, 186, 203
Squirrels, 36, 67, 130, 131*t*, 154, 166
Stadel, 53
Steinheim Basin, 74, 75, 77, 94, 206
Stone axes, 5, 94, 95
Stone tools, 4, 162–163, 220
Stratigraphy
  of Henauhof Nordwest, 137*f*
  of Henauhof Nordwest 2, 177, 178*f*
  of Henauhof West, 169, 170*f*
Stratum 1, Henauhof Nordwest, 151–152

Stratum 3, Henauhof Nordwest, 137–148, 164, 165, 166, 168, 188
  assemblage formation in, 156–157
  lithics of, 137, 138–140, 160
  preservation in, 155–156
  sample size in, 158
  seasonality at, 190–191
Stratum 4, Henauhof Nordwest, 124–135, 163–164, 166, 187, 188
  assemblage formation in, 157
  fauna of, 130–132
  features of, 132–133
  lithics of, 127–130, 160
  preservation in, 156
  sample size in, 158
  seasonality at, 189–190
Stratum 5, Henauhof Nordwest, 117–123, 163, 165, 188
  assemblage formation in, 156–157
  fauna of, 119–123
  lithics of, 118, 119, 160
  preservation in, 155–156
  sample size in, 158
Stratum 6, Henauhof Nordwest, 113–117, 118, 163, 165, 166
  assemblage formation in, 157
  fauna of, 114–116, 117t
  lithics of, 114
  preservation in, 156
  sample size in, 158
Stratum B, Henauhof Nordwest, 152–154
Stratum C, Henauhof Nordwest, 148–151, 163
Stratum G, Henauhof Nordwest, 135–136, 137f
Stratum P, Henauhof Nordwest, 151–152
Stuttgart, 41, 65
Swabian Alb, 7, 51, 56, 68, 69
  comparison with Henauhof Nordwest, 186–187, 191
  description of, 33
  in Early Mesolithic, 59t, 70–80, 203, 204
  in Late Mesolithic, 73, 89t, 93–96, 211
  in Late Palaeolithic, 43, 45t, 53–55, 195, 196
  spatial patterns in, 37, 41, 42
  temporal patterns in, 35
Sweden, 5, 87, 220
Sweetness of taste, 20
Swiss Jura, 32
Switzerland, 217, 219, 223

Tan chert, 127
Tannstock, 7, 82, 105–107, 203
Taubried, 81, 191, 204
Teal, 131t, 132, 140, 141t, 150
Teeth, 95, 136f
  beaver, 75
  deer, 74, 94, 96, 116
  fish, 74, 220–221
  fox, 96, 134, 145
  wolf, 145
Temperatures, 32, 33, 34–35, 38–42, 209
Temporal patterns, 33–37
Teufelsloch Cave, 94
Theoretical landscape, 13–29
  evolutionary ecology of, 13–23
  social context in, 23–26
Tiwi, 26
Torfgrube, 79
Trackways, 105
Trapezoidal microliths (trapezes)
  of Henauhof Nordwest, 138–139, 140, 167
  of Late Mesolithic, 87, 95, 98, 217, 221–222
Truncation, 171t
Tufted ducks, 121t, 123, 131t, 132

Ulm, 38, 42
Unretouched blades, 47, 53, 58, 62
Unretouched flakes, 47, 58, 62
Unshed antlers, 188, 189, 190, 204
Unworked antlers, 134–135
Upper Palaeolithic, 7, 38, 219
Urach, 79
Utilized blades, 65, 136, 181
Utilized flakes, 65, 181

Vegetation, 36, 37, 210
Vitamins, 20, 21

Wabash River, 9
Warfare, 200
Waterfowl, 36
  of Early Mesolithic, 78
  of Henauhof Nordwest, 114, 116, 130, 131–132, 140, 149, 152, 156, 168, 186, 189–190
  of Late Mesolithic, 96
  of Late Palaeolithic, 195
Weasels, 61t, 90t
Weiden, 42
Wels, 131, 140, 141t
Wheat, 167

White chert, 67, 68, 98, 107
Wild boar: *see* Boar
Wildcats, 220
  of Early Mesolithic, 61*t*, 68, 202
  of Henauhof Nordwest, 121*t*, 123, 140, 141*t*,
    152, 166
  of Late Mesolithic, 90*t*, 209
Willow, 35, 37, 193
Wolf teeth, 145
Wolves, 220
  of Early Mesolithic, 61*t*
  of Henauhof Nordwest, 114, 117*t*, 140, 141*t*,
    166
  of Late Mesolithic, 90*t*
  of Late Palaeolithic, 46*t*
Women
  division of labor and: *see* Division of labor
  skulls of, 220–221
Wood, 111–112, 117, 133, 138, 142, 152,
    153

Woolly rhinoceros, 36
Worked antlers
  of Early Mesolithic, 74, 75
  of Henauhof Nordwest, 123, 133, 144, 148,
    163–164, 191
  of Late Mesolithic, 87, 94, 95, 96, 180
Worked beaver tooth, 75
Worked boar's tusk, 75, 94, 95, 96
Worked bones
  of Henauhof Nordwest, 123, 133, 163–164
  of Late Mesolithic, 95, 96
Worked hides, 145, 148, 164, 180, 185
Worked quartzite, 107
Worked stone, 180
Wurzburg, 42

Yellow ochre, 116
Younger Dryas, 34, 35, 43, 54, 113, 193, 218

Zigeunerfels, 43, 53, 54, 75

INTERDISCIPLINARY CONTRIBUTIONS TO ARCHAEOLOGY
Chronological Listing of Volumes

THE PLEISTOCENE OLD WORLD
Regional Perspectives
Edited by Olga Soffer

HOLOCENE HUMAN ECOLOGY IN NORTHEASTERN NORTH AMERICA
Edited by George P. Nicholas

ECOLOGY AND HUMAN ORGANIZATION ON THE GREAT PLAINS
Douglas B. Bamforth

THE INTERPRETATION OF ARCHAEOLOGICAL SPATIAL PATTERNING
Edited by Ellen M. Kroll and T. Douglas Price

HUNTER–GATHERERS
Archaeological and Evolutionary Theory
Robert L. Bettinger

RESOURCES, POWER, AND INTERREGIONAL INTERACTION
Edited by Edward M. Schortman and Patricia A. Urban

POTTERY FUNCTION
A Use-Alteration Perspective
James M. Skibo

SPACE, TIME, AND ARCHAEOLOGICAL LANDSCAPES
Edited by Jacqueline Rossignol and LuAnn Wandsnider

ETHNOHISTORY AND ARCHAEOLOGY
Approaches to Postcontact Change in the Americas
Edited by J. Daniel Rogers and Samuel M. Wilson

THE AMERICAN SOUTHWEST AND MESOAMERICA
Systems of Prehistoric Exchange
Edited by Jonathon E. Ericson and Timothy G. Baugh

FROM KOSTENKI TO CLOVIS
Upper Paleolithic–Paleo-Indian Adaptations
Edited by Olga Soffer and N. D. Praslov

EARLY HUNTER–GATHERERS OF THE CALIFORNIA COAST
Jon M. Erlandson

HOUSES AND HOUSEHOLDS
A Comparative Study
Richard E. Blanton

THE ARCHAEOLOGY OF GENDER
Separating the Spheres in Urban America
Diana diZerega Wall

ORIGINS OF ANATOMICALLY MODERN HUMANS
Edited by Matthew H. Nitecki and Doris V. Nitecki

PREHISTORIC EXCHANGE SYSTEMS IN NORTH AMERICA
Edited by Timothy G. Baugh and Jonathon E. Ericson

STYLE, SOCIETY, AND PERSON
Archaeological and Ethnological Perspectives
Edited by Christopher Carr and Jill E. Neitzel

REGIONAL APPROACHES TO MORTUARY ANALYSIS
Edited by Lane Anderson Beck

DIVERSITY AND COMPLEXITY IN PREHISTORIC MARITIME SOCIETIES
A Gulf of Maine Perspective
Bruce J. Bourque

CHESAPEAKE PREHISTORY
Old Traditions, New Directions
Richard J. Dent, Jr.

PREHISTORIC CULTURAL ECOLOGY AND EVOLUTION
Insights from Southern Jordan
Donald O. Henry

STONE TOOLS
Theoretical Insights into Human Prehistory
Edited by George H. Odell

THE ARCHAEOLOGY OF WEALTH
Consumer Behavior in English America
James G. Gibb

STATISTICS FOR ARCHAEOLOGISTS
A Commonsense Approach
Robert D. Drennan

DARWINIAN ARCHAEOLOGIES
Edited by Herbert Donald Graham Maschner

CASE STUDIES IN ENVIRONMENTAL ARCHAEOLOGY
Edited by Elizabeth J. Reitz, Lee A. Newsom, and Sylvia J. Scudder

HUMANS AT THE END OF THE ICE AGE
The Archaeology of the Pleistocene–Holocene Transition
Edited by Lawrence Guy Straus, Berit Valentin Eriksen, Jon M. Erlandson, and
David R. Yesner

VILLAGERS OF THE MAROS
A Portrait of an Early Bronze Age Society
John M. O'Shea

HUNTERS BETWEEN EAST AND WEST
The Paleolithic of Moravia
Jiří Svoboda, Vojen Ložek, and Emanuel Vlček

MISSISSIPPIAN POLITICAL ECONOMY
Jon Muller

PROJECTILE TECHNOLOGY
Edited by Heidi Knecht

A HUNTER–GATHERER LANDSCAPE
Southwest Germany in the Late Paleolithic and Mesolithic
Michael A. Jochim